HAUI

HAUNTED LIFE

Visual Culture and

Black Modernity

DAVID MARRIOTT

RUTGERS UNIVERSITY PRESS

New Brunswick, New Jersey, and London

Library of Congress Cataloging-in-Publication Data

Marriott, David.
Haunted life : visual culture and Black modernity / David Marriott.
     p.   cm.
Includes bibliographical references and index.
ISBN-13: 978–0-8135–4027–6 (hardcover : alk. paper)
ISBN-13: 978–0-8135–4028–3 (pbk. : alk. paper)
1. Blacks and mass media.   2. Blacks in literature.   3. Blacks in motion pictures.
4. Black race—Psychology.   5. Blacks—Race identity.   6. Visual sociology.
7. Racism.   I. Title.
P94.5.B55M37 2007
302.23089'96073—dc22

2006021870

A British Cataloging-in-Publication record for this book is available from the British Library.

Manufactured in the United States of America

for Ella, always . . .

"But the life of Spirit is not the life that shrinks from death and keeps itself untouched by devastation, but rather the life that endures it and maintains itself in it. It wins its truth only when, in utter dismemberment, it finds itself. . . . Spirit is this power only by looking the negative in the face, and tarrying with it."

G.W.F. Hegel, *Phenomenology of Spirit*

Contents

Preface

Power, in the postcolony, is carnivorous.

—Achille Mbembe, *On the Postcolony* (2001)

The following closed-circuit television (CCTV) footage shows a black boy running as he enters the frame of camera 5 (fig. 1). The child's race, gender, age, and the fact that he is running all single him out for surveillance by the CCTV operator. The camera follows him as he jumps across the stones of some civic sculpture—although recorded in real time the tape is soundless and somewhat random and arbitrary. For me, this is a boy at play in himself, and, perhaps with the image of himself, as he repossesses the civic space until it becomes the space of the imaginary. Let us see in this play not a refusal of the world but its repossession from the irreality in which it normally exists. The entire surface of the world now the realization of that imaginary as he appears and then disappears from the image on screen. But is this what the image shows? The CCTV operator sees a black boy running who, as such, becomes an immediate target of suspicion. Moreover, in CCTV there is no fundamental right to privacy. The date on the tape is Monday, 27 November 2000; the time is 15.43 P.M. It is at this point that the BBC news broadcast shifts to the videotape recorded by camera 13: the boy, running away now from the stones, can be seen crossing the grid of a deserted square in South London. It is 15.46 P.M. The next videotape shows him arriving; it shows him entering the lift of Peckham library with some other children, then it ends. The transposition of these soundless images recorded in real time to an edited TV news broadcast with voiceover radically alters their meaning—but let us not run too quickly.

Let us acknowledge that in CCTV there is a taped event which proceeds without pause, and almost without transition, from the time of the

Figure 1A Damilola in Peckham Square.

Figure 1B Damilola running away from the Square.

Figure 1C Damilola in the lift at Peckham Library.

event to the time of transmission.[1] Let us see in this movement not public existence but its sheer visibility in the process of realization; it is the randomness of worldly life which is being recorded on a multiplex video recorder. These moments are, in fact, fabulous moments: in them every event is absolute and every event is absolutely meaningless; every act is absolutely private and every act randomly public. What is more, what we are seeing here is only a fraction of the original video signal. Most multiplex CCTV systems opt to have only the primary monitor recorded in real time at twenty-five frames per second with the other cameras recorded at one frame per second on a single videotape. In themselves, then, these images of a black boy running do not tell a story; there is no story to be passed on. Yet, how does one connect these chance, randomly framed, and grainy images with what eventually makes them extraordinary, and unforeseeable? Less than fifteen minutes after he leaves the library, ten-year-old Damilola Taylor will be seen again; this time by a passerby who finds him slumped in a stairwell bleeding profusely from a stab wound to his left leg.

The death of the boy that weighs on this CCTV sequence, the death whose weight is crushing, continues to haunt the footage: where do we see it? At first sight it seems untraceable, impossible. The freedom to replay, freeze-frame, or enlarge the video image only realizes the following: these images are empty and inaccessible; they cannot act as witnessings to what we know (or imagine) as the death of this boy, a death which remains outside the time and processes of the televisual image. On this videotape his death has no aura; like a pure abstraction of the public sphere or an event without history, the CCTV image designates an excess of mimesis over that of narrative meaning. The third camera image has the word "lift" in the top left-hand corner; the word has a pure and simple resemblance to what we see appear in the image, but the word "lift" is also an image and, as such, it resembles nothing: one might say its appearance obliterates resemblance as such. The entire three sequences are haunted by this symbolic distance between what appears and what remains ungraspable as resemblance: the death of a boy that cannot be seen and which, because of that, appears everywhere in these images, but without which these images remain an empty sign of that event, a semblance in which his death has vanished. In this sense, the meaning of this sequence—its provocation and its passivity—goes infinitely beyond the indexical reality of CCTV, even though we must nonetheless read Damilola's death from within it. In order to register that death, we must destroy the image in its present form and create it in another form, transposing what it *shows* in order to make it *tell*. One result is the BBC news image which is itself the result of a juridical-televisual process of editing and simulation: it allows the death to be seen, touched, even read, but only via the infinite resources of the televisual. Let me be clear here: this is not an argument about wanting to see, nor a wish to make present what is missing from the CCTV image, but a question about the nonvision within CCTV itself behind which there are sociopolitical interests and in which categories of race, class, and gender repeatedly appear. What cannot be seen, in other words, are the discursive frameworks, political and commercial interests, that ensure that some social "targets" are rendered more visible by surveillance than others in the geopolitical space of urban cities. It is around that invisibility—of racial hegemony and capital—and the excessive visibility of the socially undesirable, that the political and commercial legitimacy of CCTV coheres.

Described by British Home Secretary Michael Howard "as a wonderful technological supplement to the police," the explosion of CCTV during the 1990s has also created the new mixed TV genre of "infotainment." What interests me here is the repeated use, by programmers, of footage from public CCTV systems, especially when they attest to the site of catastrophic public events such as the 1993 murder of the toddler James Bulger. Is there any connection between the anonymity of the public CCTV image and the affects called forth by these media spectacles? What is happening, for example, when such televised moments of loss, violence, and mourning, far from leaving us passive and unmoved and enclosed in a world of private fantasy, seem to surrender us profoundly to ourselves, literally shaken by our intimacy to documentary images? My question relates to the kinds of fascination being solicited by this looking—that is, what kind of gaze are we being asked to identify within the tranquil flows of CCTV; what kind of mourning or penalty is at work when the subject represented is either dead and/or raced?

It is hard not to be overwhelmed by these endlessly reproduced images of murdered children. Their unordered contingency denote more than just another form of documentary information, for what flies into focus and then out again is the absolute singularity of events passing across the field of vision. Incredulous, but nonetheless compelled, what are we waiting to see if not this dislocation within the emptiness of the image? The menace and postponement of what never arrives and is always about to come; the long arching journey of a life lost to time, yet to be seen; all the more so since it is the not-yet that simultaneously links the tracking backward of death's imminence and the anonymity of time's passing at the level of the image. The CCTV sequence showing Damilola's final journey disturbs because of what we know (but can never see) of his future. The sequence wounds because of its ruptural collision with that future-to-come, which it partially brings into focus, silently invokes, and is framed by. The sequence is divided and made aberrant by that irreparable cut, by that onrushing event shadowing Damilola's delves and swerves as we see him devising his own imaginary as he runs through the civic spaces of southeast London. And this composing movement and its differential affect—which is to say a certain fallen aura and out-of-timeness, is what defines our spectatorship of the news more generally and our exposure to the depressing emptiness of a nullity without horizon, received but never perceived by the nonmeaningful reproducibility of CCTV.

Nevertheless, TV does have a sort of sympathetic magic to it. Sit down and look. Rewind the tape back but not forward—see a black boy running against the cutting wind. The screen shows his documentary life as we strain to catch what he is seeing. Damilola's appearance reveals nothing except the lived tenor of things. And yet the image remains a disembodied fact—it's not the loss but the never-showing that is so unexpected and violent. For reasons that remain obvious, unbearably so, there is a sense of anticipation as he runs away from the stones; a sense of sequence and belatedness, and something else, a future memorialized, and yet unseen. The recordings may act as the medium of release for this delay, but they are also absorbed by something much larger—the fate of knowing all the time we are watching that these images are much too late for the boy running into the future. But why this fixation on the unforeseeable? Why this

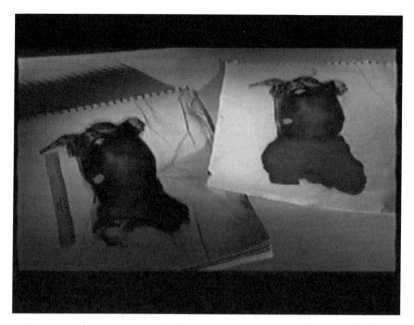

Figure 2 Adam. Courtesy of the London Metropolitan Police Authority.

wish to know and see the utterly ordinary ambiance of catastrophe? The chapters that follow are, in some respects, about what we expect to see, but also an attempt to write about the fragility of the visible as the future's never-arriving disjointure. As such, they are defined by what cannot appear, by what is missing. They are about what happens when fantasy, sexuality, and race combine as ways of seeing the unseeable that have less to do with the settling of differences than with difference itself. Intraracial desire on TV and film, the stain spreading out across the screen, corruptive and ruinous, the scotoma in each random glance.

Now, imagine a second death, a second example of "infotainment": on Friday, 21 September 2001, the torso of a boy is found floating in the waters of the Thames near the Globe Theatre (fig. 2). His head and limbs are missing. His dark glistening skin covered only by a pair of orange shorts. Discovered near the body are seven half-burned candles wrapped in a white sheet on which is written a name: Adekoye Jo Fola Adeoye. The name Fola Adeoye is also legible on one of the candles. These objects and inscriptions suggest an occult presence at the murder, indicating that the boy was perhaps trafficked or sold on to one of the group who killed him. In fact, he may have been sold on by members of his family. Kinship is one of the dark forces that will be central to the newsworthiness of the case and its all-too-familiar image of blackness as deadly and dangerous, but also primal, tyrannical, all-consuming. The media's lurid interest in the occult sacrifice (allied, here, with a story about hi-tech forensic work), combines a depressingly familiar "journey" into darkest Africa with a tale about enlightened Western reason and technology. But what makes the case exceptional is the chain linking black primal appetites and mystic currency to the forensic and televisual, at the end of which the story of the dismembered child effectively becomes some sort of primitivist melodrama.

Clearly affected by the state of the body and the singular violence enacted upon it, Commander Andre Baker of the Serious Crime Group announces to a crowd of reporters: "Until we can identify him and his family we will act as his family. And to remind everyone that he was a person we have given him a name. That name is Adam." "We will act as his family": here the work of detection emerges as a familial tie to the unidentified; as a wish to see "Adam" reunited with his past and family rather than a thing with no identity or name, a thing that is no longer a person; the creaturely work of unredeemed creation. It's a wish to humanize the cadaver and, in this way, to remind us of the resemblance between person and mortal remains; more strangely, it's also a wish to make the torso *resemble itself* as the image of a dead, but identifiable, person. To make the corpse reflect positive law rather than remain an inchoate thing that is *ante legum*. In these two acts of naming and kinship the torso disappears, only to reappear in the movement that allows the law to rename itself as Christian family, thereby reversing the murderousness of African kinship. Insofar as this torso was once a person he can be named; a dead child, identified as such, given a new name and family; a first name, first of the first, synonymous with fall, death, and creation, and one that immediately becomes global; reborn, via satellite, as a broadcast media image. Over the next few weeks and months, the power of the media will be pored over this body until it reforms it: from pathology lab to tribes and villages in Nigeria, strontium signatures to Muti ritual murder, DNA analysis to the horrors of people smuggling, this is a death that fascinates because of the essence of what remains—pollen in the stomach, strontium in the bones, masses of mitochondrial DNA, and, despite all, the unidentifiable torso of an unknown child, adrift in the margins of the history that produces it.[2]

Throughout all these curious rites of passage Adam remains unknown and unidentifiable, even his name begins in the void of what is missing from him: but what his ritualistic killing and dismemberment portrays is how the most bizarre, the most hidden occult economies are being driven by the international traffic in body parts; how the blood and tissue of the poor are being appropriated by the mostly invisible and abstract transnational forces of production and reproduction. Just as the expansion in the value of capital feeds on "living labor," these occult economies are driven to digest and extract the reproductive and spiritual wealth of the child as perishable commodity.[3] The magical "eating" of the world's disposable populations acting like a mirror to the digestive flows of global capital. The occult trade in body parts is, however, not just about displacement and negation: the recycling and consumption of viscera in potions for success in business and love—medicines in which the viscera of children is highly valued—suggests why fear of death-in-life is intimately bound both to capital accumulation and the production process. Consider the following story: Johannesburg, 29 April 1996. A thirty-eight-year-old man is arrested in a shopping mall after trying to sell a child's pair of blue eyes. The incident, according to the *Star* newspaper, "might be linked to the murder of street children for . . . traditional medicines"; medicines in which the viscera of white children fetch the highest prices. Here, what Marx called the "spectral objectivity" (*gespenstige Gegenständlichkeit*) of the commodity is reborn in images of African children consumed by the all-devouring eye of transglobal capital and media.[4] The bloody sacrifice and incorporation of children one more way of buying power and influence; the selling on of body parts one way of linking the invisibility of capital flows to the occult economies of Europe and Africa.

Adam only appears on TV as a forensic object, as the sacrificial object of ritual murder, and as the menacing nearness of African witchcraft in Europe—throughout all he is the image of what he resembles, and he is also nothing more. What he resembles is television's endless recycling of its ideological image of Africa. On the one hand, the single defining media image of Africa is one of a violently contagious body utterly consumed by war, murder, and the twin idolatries of riches and power. It's a recurring image in which state governance and the economy either eat people whole or leave them starving in the pursuit of Western capital/commodities.[5] On the other hand, the consumption of Adam—as spectacle, as commodity—reveals a connection here between a gaze that destroys and petrifies and a gaze that carries the wish to have what is seen enter into me as visceral capital.[6] There is a connection, in other words, between what we desire to see and the murderous exclusions attached to commodified desire and need. Adam's death not only reveals how the marketing of human flesh has become part of a global commodification of life per se, but how desire and economy are now firmly linked to a reenchantment of the public sphere: his death has the aura of sacred work; he was killed because of the value of human tissue in *muti* medicine, a murder which shows how intimate profit and the life of spirit have become. Such "enchanted, often unnervingly, visceral, modes of producing value," as the transnational media reminds us, is where the spectral life of the commodity endures and maintains itself in the magical eye of the camera.[7]

Television has always been the place—the screen—in which the convergence of consumer desire and the magic of capital has produced the most surprising sorts of transformation: TV's uncanny resemblance to commodification is a key element in this story.[8] Adam's dismemberment, the exchange of his viscera, adds a further aspect to that history, a history in which the circulation and production of the most virulent phantasms of race has always been part of the "question" that is the technological essence of the medium.[9] This is the "question" the two deaths of Damilola and Adam pose for me, the question that manifests itself in their reproduction as televisual images and their exchange value as commodities to be sold and consumed—that is, to be circulated and marketed as images of racial catastrophe and the endless vulnerability of children. In this sense, what is imparted by these televisual images is *absence,* the seeing and naming of absence; the *da* of the image bypassing both presence and the present in a truly negative, destructive act of separation and one that remains, in the end, spectral, haunted by the presences of what it is not.[10] This complicity itself refers to the fascination that the two cases hold for the news media: the meaning of the two deaths turns out to be "the lure of a referentiality perpetually deferred" (to borrow Stephen Heath's phrase), the reproduction of racial catastrophe as spectacle, the dissolution of life into TV.[11]

The death of two Nigerian boys in London becomes, in this instance, a metaphor for the central preoccupation of this book: the trauma of seeing an African past that keeps on happening. It's a history repeatedly shown on our TV screens, but via a code whose latent "ideological fantasy" goes repeatedly missing.[12] "That things 'just go on' *is* the catastrophe," according to Walter Benjamin, a point reminding us about ideology's invisible workings.[13] To which I would add: as long as documentary TV continues to show images of dead African children as the epitome of lawless violence, it remains haunted by its likeness to the hegemonic surveillance of CCTV; that is to say, showing everything, but revealing nothing, simply announcing—through its scopic regimes—the racialized exclusion of people as commodities to be disciplined by law, and, when caught, sold on to infotainment TV.

—————

The chapters that follow are all about spectrality and the visible and what links them: a failed mourning. *Haunted Life*'s main concern is with the repressed claims of that failure as both affect—remorse, guilt, blame, disavowal; the traces left by persons long dead—and spectacle; in particular, the occult presence of racial slavery, nowhere but nevertheless everywhere, a dead time which never arrives and does not stop arriving, as though by arriving it never happened until it happens again, then it never happened. This is a book, then, about what lives on from that happening, and about a projected future so dismal that it is impossible to remember why we should long for it to be fulfilled. The reflections to be developed here on life behind the veil do not begin with loss, but with the devastation of never having had. Here it is the power of exclusion that shapes black experience of political and ethical life and the awful feeling of one's visible invisibility. It is in the light of these reflections that I consider John Edgar Wideman's memoir, *The Island: Martinique*. In this book about history and disappearance, understood in the sense of what cannot be let go because never had, Wideman looks at the post-slavery world as one built on a heap of black corpses, but a catastrophe rarely seen or experienced as such. He compares this opacity to a kind of *seeing* that is both terminable and interminable, in which the dead keep on coming back. The footage keeps repeating and yet no one seems able to see it. The footage runs continuously but there is no acceptance of what is being shown. It is as if whites and blacks were watching different screens and the spectator's eye were geared to a differing set of frames and patterns. The internally contested meaning of what is seen and the power to make real the unseen is more a case of an unwitting blindness than conscious renunciation. The work of Frantz Fanon is central here for what he imparts to the closed circuit of power, race, and law in the image, both as a representation of black inner life and the racial logic of culture.

Fanon's phenomenological descriptions of that life and logic contrasts with Jean-Paul Sartre's neo-Hegelian notions of experience and overcoming. Without any assumptions of necessary advance or progression, Fanon's alternative descriptions of a dialectical "tension of opening" reopens the way to conceive of race as a kind of shareable darkness, as a sort of death plot in the mind—or ghosted unconsciousness—driving both intimacy and desire, shadowing what we see and know. Fanon's writing on the risks and failures of interracial desire becomes a model thereby for the book as a whole: how does one step in the void, each in the other, given the risks and deliria of racial mistrust and abuses? It's a question that is both boringly familiar and yet strikingly elusive. For me, the work of Richard Wright and Isaac Julien, though massively different, both ask how we racially see and know the unseen, both suggest that such positings seem to diminish us, as if the footage of race we replay in our minds and fantasies, seen belatedly, can now only mark a conceptual end, a failure to reimagine the other and so begin over.

For Alain Locke, too, because race seems so familiar, so intimate to the age and its people, it became his duty to teach others to admit the something hidden, disregarded, or unaccounted for imprinted in racial beliefs and imaginings. In turn-of-the century America, as Locke realized, racialism had led to a contraction of the private and public worlds; a separateness at the level of polity and affect neither recognized nor understood. "Race," an incantatory word, remains in that other world of phantoms: Locke renders it as a haunting illusion or fiction; a stultifying way of screening out the world of the seen by the unseen. Against the illusion of race as innate or natural, Locke will, over time, pursue the idea of race as a changing respite, as the last refuge of America. It is a balancing intention: to bring out into public life the spectral life of race; to show racism is the result of history and temperament; to expose the hysteria and violence behind America's ethnic character, a reaction brought on by crises of immigration and assimilation in the first decades of the century, crises which required the land and people of America to change. Locke's writing is defined by those crises, marked by their effects: just as his efforts to allay the taint of racialism remained, from the first, haunted by its spell. My chapter on Locke is an attempt to understand this haunted self; its symbolism and the balancing pragmatism of its image. It has taken me many years to understand the nature of this image—in particular, Locke's wish to avoid painful inner emptiness by bringing about the artistic labors of others and so derive something of the pleasure, the unconscious pleasure, of being the medium to a new imprinting by the images of others, in almost-becoming a mirror for the other's relief.

In contrast, my chapter on Sidney Poitier returns to the constrained promise of race on U.S. film, to the forces in the culture that could no longer imagine Poitier as the black man he was, substituting instead a game of white and black diagonals and verticals and the repressed mimesis of a strangely white blackness. Examining the radical disjunction between Poitier's status as a sixties racial icon for blacks and whites, this chapter turns to the disparity between Poitier's onscreen persona and his growing awareness of himself as the object of a cinematic gaze that judges, limits, but always eludes. This gaze that is blind and blinding—and this is an essential theme of the book—is the obverse of seeing and one that is ultimately blinding because it escapes the seeing subject. *Haunted Life* therefore ends where it begins, with myself in front of the TV watching the footage run continuously. The image is uncanny and morbid, but what is seen is a life blinded or veiled, a life that is nonetheless the object of unembarrassed fascination, even glee. But, of course, this is a distressed and weirdly detached form of happiness.

Acknowledgments

The essays collected here spring from a reading of race, psychoanalysis, and visuality begun in *On Black Men* (New York: Columbia University Press, 2000). Conceived and written as lectures, these texts bear the mark of those circumstances; a number of them have been published in earlier versions: chapter 1 in *The Journal of Visual Culture*, ed. Marquard Smith and Raiford Guins; chapter 2 in *Frantz Fanon, Black Skin, White Masks*, ed. Maxim Silverman (Manchester: University of Manchester Press, 2006); chapter 3 in *New Formations* (Spring 2001), ed. Vicky Lebeau, Christine Clegg, and Paul Myerscough, and *Where Id Was*, ed. Anthony Molino and Christine Ware (London: Continuum, 2001); chapter 6 in *Qui Parle*, ed. Jared Sexton and Huey Copeland (Spring/Summer 2003); and chapter 7 in *The Psychoanalysis of Race*, ed. Christopher Lane (New York: Columbia University Press, 1998). I wish to thank the editors for inviting me to publish and for permission to reuse the material. In all cases, the earlier versions have been revised and expanded.

I am also grateful to a large number of people in various universities for their support and encouragement. Let me mention in particular Teresa de Lauretis, Nicholas Royle, Martin Murray, Chris Connery, Maud Ellmann, Lynne Segal, Gail Herschatter, Carla Freccero, Tyrus Miller, David Hoy, Laura Marcus, Sally Alexander, Robert Bernasconi, Cora Kaplan, Alan Sinfield, Anne Janowitz, Jacqueline Rose, Cathy Sousloff, Christopher Lane, David Glover, James Clifford, Frank Wilderson, and Jared Sexton. This book is dedicated to Vicky Lebeau, whose friendship, support, and critique goes far beyond what I can acknowledge here.

I was the beneficiary of a Leverhulme Research Fellowship in 2002 and an Institute of Humanities Research Fellowship in 2004, both of which gave me time to complete my research. I would like to thank the staff at the Beinecke Rare Book and Manuscript Library, Yale University;

Moorland-Spingarn Research Center, Howard University; and the Schomburg Center for Research in Black Culture, New York Public Library, who were indispensable.

Finally, I'd like to thank my editor, Leslie Mitchner, for her patience and understanding.

HAUNTED LIFE

1 *Spooks*

WIDEMAN'S CATASTROPHE

> The ghost, always, is looking at me.
>
> —Jacques Derrida, *Specters of Marx* (1994)

This is a book about spooks—or at least the blackness that haunts. The anxious glance back over the shoulder when you realize the stranger behind you is black; the fear reducing you to child size when he comes near you, mobbing you like a legend or myth. In fact, the agonizingly frightful advance of the dark angel pounding toward you has, historically, been far more traumatic for blacks. At least you hope so. And how strange it is to see a thing like this, the unconscious revealed like a vast movie screen bearing the phantoms and fears of freedoms past. Such apparitions are the main concern of this book. In truth, my entire text is spooked by what remains but is nowhere to be seen; the deforming dark shadow melting away like a newly drenched witch. The spooky black.

But what is a spook? The word's many meanings conjure forth a host of images and unsettling shadowy echoes: the happy-go-lucky darky suddenly paralyzed, immobilized by fear ("de air am full of 'em," "I sho' does b'lieve in han'ts"); the assembled whites grinning, ridiculing this vague and innocent supernatural terror only to succumb themselves, pointing to the menacing nearness of the black bogeyman, stiff with fear. The spook speaks to us, and it speaks intimately to the terror within ourselves. But saying this is saying too little; the word *spook* reveals a connection between race and terror, magic and surveillance, idolatry and power; as a verb it makes visible the impenetrable unseen that our self-deceptions bid us master and so keep at a remove. In this way the spook fulfills one of its functions, which is to pacify, to humanize the unformed creatureliness floating toward us and whose existence reveals a residue of the human that cannot be incorporated.[1] In modernity, black life has always been the name for this scary thing, repeatedly projected onto the scrim, as it were, of white hatreds and terrors. Hence the history of "spooks" as a racial slur, a condescension passed on by popular media culture. In this blinded mediatized seeing, black life confirms our distance from the real and our ironic attachment to willed disbelief, but that life also acts as the dark remainder of the real's frightening opacity. This is the reason for the alleged spookiness of blacks: to submit to it is to suffer dissolution, even when our jouissance is summoning us to this deadly passability. Hence the dramatic visual effect achieved when blacks encounter the whitened-out obscurity of their own creaturely indetermination. What does it mean to stare at this eerie whiteness in the face, to be at its mercy, powerless before this presence become strangely mute and passive?

I have in mind here Frantz Fanon's 1952 account of the "lived experience of the black," where he talks about feelings of being naked, caught, afflicted (feelings which instantly shatter the ego). " 'Look, a Negro [nègre]!' . . . the corporeal schema crumbled, its place taken by a racial epidermal schema. . . . I took myself far off from my own presence, far indeed, and made myself an object. What else could it be for me but an amputation, an excision, a hemorrhage that spattered my whole body with black blood?"[2] We all know Fanon's account of his painful encounter with the phobic fear of a white child on the streets of Lyon. But this anecdote is, for me, not only about the sense of being breached by an intruding, ghostly imago ("Look, a nègre"); but about how the being of the black is rendered insubstantial by the white who sets his or her eyes upon it. I understand this as follows: in this form of looking, what haunts is not so much the imago spun through with myths, anecdotes, stories, but the shadow or stain that is sensed behind it and that disturbs well-being.

Something goes wrong—Fanon starts hemorrhaging; a little self-dramatizing maybe, but this metaphor of leakage and wounding points to a traumatizing extrusion taking place in or on the body. Instead of an intact "corporeal schema," what we see here is a body disembodied by image, language, thought; the word "nègre" acting like some kind of chemical dye converting epidermal surface into imago. Here's a funny thing, though: the body is a medium for what has been transferred on to Fanon, like a genetic flaw, and simultaneously what is penetrated and replaced by the ghostly incarnation that comes upon it, and whose effect gives Fanon vertigo. What cuts into the body rending it into a mutilated screen or mask is also what dissolves the boundaries between inside and outside, between, that is, a self possessed and a body dispossessed, desolidified by the imago. As a result, the body becomes both divided and aberrated: it has no body other than this heterogeneity that empties it of itself. More, as Fanon desperately tries to see himself from the point of view of the gaze enveloping him, erasing him as a subject, he feels himself becoming space: "I existed triply: I occupied space."[3] Crucially, this violence marking the body as phantasmagoric—as what cannot be subjectivized—comes to Fanon via the eyes. But it is what he fails to see, in the dark spaces of the visible, that dispossesses.

To take just one other example—of whites literally white with terror. In *Origins of Totalitarianism*, Hannah Arendt argues that the fear which greeted the ghostliness of the natives was at the origin of the first colonial massacres and enslavements. Because Africans appeared "unreal and ghostlike" "when European men massacred them they somehow were not aware that they had committed murder."[4] These were men who were contemptuous of what they saw as a *Dasein* without being in the world, a discovery whose "horror" led them to pass beyond civility to what Arendt calls the pleasures of "senseless massacre" (Arendt, *Origins*, 190, 192). The inhuman nature of Africans was seen as a maddening affront to Being itself, precisely because this "fright of something like oneself that still under no circumstances ought to be like oneself" introduced Europeans to the "full realization of their own phantom-like existence" as *white* men (190). If this *thing* is human, this thing that appears to be so alien and unreal before them, then what does this foretell about human nature, about us? What does its presence tell us about what came before?

Arendt's reading is certainly provocative. The fact that she seems to echo myths of the "Dark Continent" doesn't detract from her central insight; namely, that when Europeans first saw what stood before them in Africa, the sheer novelty of the data meant that it was impossible to separate spiritual fear from the sense of being haunted. But what is it that haunts: the phenomenal resemblance to an uncanny unlikeness, or the sudden dissemblance in the reflected image, as if one's own specular image had become ghosted in turn? What I think the word "ghostlike" attests to here is not simply the return of a repressed wish, but also the exposure—if that is the right word—of one's constancy and faith to an otherness that perturbs because of its failure to reflect back to Europeans a comprehensible self-image (this "fright of something like oneself that still under no circumstances ought to be like oneself").[5] This also means that the violence meted out to Africans was not only a defense against impenetrable mystery, but the foreclosure of the more disturbing possibility of the African as Double. As if blackness were a kind of ghost of whiteness to be hunted down or conjured away. And colonial violence, a kind of rescue service for a self-regard felt to be at the point of oblivion, which, because of that, wages an endless war against the disquieting phantomality of the black body. In Arendt's narrative, then, whiteness is under siege, enveloped by a black imago pressing in on the body with a spiritual violence that is uncanny, imperious, and deeply humiliating precisely because it comes from within. But what is also at stake, indissociably, is the spectacle of whites haunted by the image of Africans which they themselves have created as the ghost of ahuman naturality. It is a discourse of racial fetishism that is itself fetishistic and thus both blind and blinding.

Exactly the same narrative is reproduced, albeit inversely, and dialectically, by Fanon to describe the alienated black ego desperate to assert its independence from the white alter that it hates, envies, furiously resents, and yet wants to be recognized by. Its odd to hear this echoing so close to hand and from the mouth of blacks without fretting about the telepathic life of race (and maybe this is, after all, why a ghostly presence is an essential part of my reading), and its teleontology. In particular, I'm interested in why a drive to be black is so weak when faced with the alienating-possessing wish of whiteness. (I have my suspicions that whiteness also emerges here as a phantasm over which we have no control, erupting like a ghost of the real.) To examine this medium, the spirit of violence it entails, I therefore propose to begin with a genuinely haunted black text.

First published in 2003, John Edgar Wideman's memoir, *The Island: Martinique*, was originally commissioned by the National Geographic Society for its Literary Travel Series.[6] Far more than a travelogue, *The Island: Martinique* is a meditation on "revenants": of mourning, history, fiction, imagining, déjà vu, teletechnicity, Frantz Fanon, and documentary images. It is also the story of Martinique as "Le Pays des Revenants," the "country of comers-back": visitation is the book's central metaphor for the dilemmas of assimilation in black history and identity (and, a way of invoking the "haunted deadly past alive" in Martinican writing and cultural memory). But visitation is a metaphor, too, for the possibility and risk involved in being open to the Other, whose ghostly presence challenges the self's paranoid and repressed desire to be *"islanded,"* to be both the ground and origin of itself, virtually free from others (Wideman, *Island*, xix, xxviii).

In another sense, the book is a personal testimony to how Wideman himself is haunted and harassed by the island's colonial past that keeps on coming back. *The Island: Martinique* invokes that history through scenes of black death and suffering and of tourists strangely mesmerized by the spectacle "electronically magnified and projected on a portable stage in Ste. Anne" (34). The structure of this seeing is one of phantasm, of being haunted by the nothing there. Under the watchful eye of teletechnology, the terrors of colonial slavery remain unseen, lastingly virtual, ungraspable. In a grievance like this, the enslaved dead cannot be lamented because they have no witnesses. Wideman talks of a history that nobody remembers, but to whom everyone is subjected. An elsewhere that is also intimately lived. Martinique's slave past is "like a rerun of a familiar documentary I've never seen"; it haunts all vision and is the material remnant of all agency—even though people don't like to admit it (21). This need to see again recorded time beyond memory and time lost, to see life itself behind the phantasma of image and memory, is a wish to make visible that which remains inaccessible, the never had. Present but without presence: the island evidences what was not even there as having been, a phantasmatic history of a never happened that keeps on happening (blackness as the icon of this terrifying uncanniness—a fear that is also commodified and ideological). "How else account for stripped brown bodies celebrated, flaunted, flashing in your face everywhere," Wideman asks, "billboards, TV ads, labels and logos, dolls, souvenir calendars, posters—public proof of who owns the native body and can bare it with impunity" (37).

The Island: Martinique reads the affects of that seeing as strangely disembodied, is like the "keeping alive of what's never been alive" (34). "Whose sponsoring this ghost pageant in living color," Wideman asks (38). "Where in this spectacle am I supposed to find the pursuit of freedom, bloody resistance . . . [in this] gone-with-the-fucking-wind fantasy of the way things were" (38–39). On the island, Wideman finds himself brooding on the "risks" involved in allowing the self to be invaded by the island's otherness (the ghostly "creolization" of "who I am, who I might become"); but he also finds himself, unexpectedly, ambiguously, intrigued by the political power that comes with being able to compel the Other to become the perfect equivalent of my will (he is particularly interested in the power of the gaze as it goes from white to black, woman to man, tourist to native; in the self emptied and laid bare by the look that cannot be seen, only imagined) (xxvi). In this closed circuit of gaze and power, mastery is the fantasy of seeing without being seen, and subjugation the impossibility of not being seen, an impossibility that turns black visibility, viewed as the essence of the imperfectible and malign, into a question of law, surveillance, and judgment.

As a polemic aimed at such mediatization and spectralization, The Island: Martinique is a composed close-up on media technology and the racial slavery that haunts it: "all communication between descendants of masters and descendents of slaves remains haunted, stigmatized by the terms of the primal bargain that brought them together—the marketing of human flesh" (43). The metaphor of the unborn pervading the book is crucial here. If our anxiety about the dead is always ghosted by what they leave behind, the hope is that we can bear witness to such complicities rather than exclude them from the political demands of both the present and the future. This is not only because the specter of racial slavery continues to define the geopolitical world, but also because it remains deeply inscribed in the visual media as fetish, as the mask for a postracial right to representation that fails to appear and so can only be conjured and invoked as an invisibility whose visibility is this disavowal. It is as if the ghost, that is the occasion of all racial ontology, can only be seen insofar as one blinds oneself to it, and blindness is all the security and comfort that the whiteness of the eye needs.

Of course, Wideman is less interested in Martinican history than in the ongoing politics of racial disavowal that makes the island exemplary. This is why he is so transfixed by Fanon whose *Black Skin, White Masks* took a long dexterous swipe at the symbolics of disavowal in Martinique and whose precise psychoanalyses undid the racial dialectic at its disavowed core. Fanon haunts *The Island: Martinique*, or at least his writings feature prominently because they evoke the politics and ethics of *"what could have been"* (xxix). In truth, Wideman draws on the wistful, elegiac elements of Fanon's work to disclose that subjunctive possibility opposed to the ever-renewed image of Martinique as the virginal, edenic paradise waiting to be remade and rediscovered by world tourism. Again, what Fanon's writings make visible is the political vicissitudes of that illusion; the catastrophe that reduces historic violence to a logic of virtuality (but a virtuality still defined by neocolonial alignments of race and nation, global capital and exotic culture). Indeed, Fanon remains the most articulate representative of racial disavowal precisely because he too remains disavowed, his forgotten legacy part of the confidence trick Martinique continues to play on itself, suspicious of anyone or thing that challenges its reclaimed nationalism or its cross-dressing wish to unify purity of black culture with an impeccable Frenchness (or faux cosmopolitanism).

And so for this very reason, chapter 3 on "Fanon" opens with the following mystery. "We did not recognize the face stenciled with black spray paint on a greenish-gray metal shed," Wideman writes, we did not recognize the face even though it was "somehow familiar" (121). To add to the mystery there was "partly effaced writing beneath it—Arabic script, I guessed, so the words incomprehensible to us even if intact—the face a small detail during the two weeks we spent in Martinique over a Christmas holiday" (121). A small detail, but also an enigma whose uncanny affect refuses to go away. "And once it had registered, the face, like the island's beguiling complicity, never entirely disappeared" (122). Stranger still, "we seemed to be the only ones who saw it." Everyone asked about the face claimed to be "unaware" of its existence. Indelible, then, but also somehow missed or absent: "Could the face be there and not be there," Wideman wonders; is what is seen any testimony to its existence? (122). This is "a face nobody sees," he concludes (123). Unseen but always there, seen but nonsymbolizable; like the incomprehensible, partly legible script beneath it, this is an image that addresses us with a code about which there is nothing to decipher, or say—a face condemned to an indelible illegibility, a face almost eluding representation and memory.

"Fanon didn't claim" his face, Wideman writes, "until I recalled that he'd been born there [in Martinique]" (123). It's a recollection which frees other memories—Fanon's "face in a photo snapped during the first *Présence Africaine* conference in Paris in the 1950s, his face on the back cover of *The Wretched of the Earth*, a color shot of him illustrating a magazine review of *Black Skin, White Masks*" (123). From enigma, then, to memory; from the chance discovery of a shared hallucination to the evidentiary presence of the photograph: it is no surprise that Wideman asks himself: "Why had it taken me so long to recognize him" (123).[7] Wideman is not concerned with interrogating the question of resemblance between photograph and spray-painted image, but with the connection between loss and memory: "Losing what's come before," he writes, "as more stuff, instantly lost, disappears before it even has the chance to sink in, stir up the mix and be properly remembered or forgotten" (123). This is no simple memory. It's a concern with the impermeability of registration maybe, but also with the kinds of marks left behind by effigy and history as revealed by the painting-photograph and the words of Fanon's texts. If what occurs is lost before it even registers then there never was something "before" to be remembered in the first place. Which also means that loss already precedes and anticipates what can be properly remembered and forgotten. Faced with Fanon's image and photographs, Wideman encounters a catastrophe that is not yet memory but still haunting the present, *"a catastrophe which has already occurred"* (to borrow a phrase by Barthes), unsettling categories of time and history.[8]

Fanon's face speaks then of the return of what is not properly remembered or forgotten, but also of something lost or dead. Perhaps this is why Wideman refers to himself as a "ghostwriter" and writing as akin to a "séance" during which we summon our "invented second selves" (xxv). Perhaps this is why Wideman moves from the memory of how "Fanon's face had intruded" to another traumatic memory of an image. Returning to the actual time of writing down these memories in his Lower East Side apartment, Wideman states: "Then I noticed an enormous plume of dark smoke billowing above the skyline" and, from the "stunned, disbelieving comments" of fellow tenants, he learns that the Twin Towers in the distance have been hit by planes. "Fanon defined the *Third World* as a *colossal mass* facing Europe," he writes, its task to resolve problems to which Europe has found no solutions. "Now [with] a churning black cloud of smoke, [and giant] skyscrapers on fire . . . Somebody had launched their version of problem-solving" (124).[9]

The association of these two images—a face painted or photographic, a catastrophe almost wholly televisual—confirms a link between them: but what is it that connects the disturbance of memory in Martinique, its revival in the photographed face, to the stunned disbelief of spectators in the United States? Is it the persistence in memory of the nonsymbolizable or unassimilable? Is it the colossal, unquestionably Black, effigy of the Third World described here as Fanon's testimony and legacy, and one that emerges via an Arabic script barely legible through plumes of smoke? These questions are difficult to answer, even more so as Wideman often reminds us that he wrote *The Island: Martinique* to address the "visceral, visual presence of loss and waste": "who I am, who I might become" (xxviii; xxvi). Might become? *The Island: Martinique* is, I think, a nuanced account of how racial catastrophe continues to haunt both our intimacies and loss, and how America, having borne witness to the unfinished burden of improper loss—that is, of slavery—will never, ever be able to it throw off. As such, the public fascination with the TV footage of 9/11 recorded in real time (the fascination of seeing the past never stop happening in a repeated image caught on camera), is the symptom of a more general failure to grieve, and precisely because of the truer-to-life realness of this footage, its shock and fascination. For these reasons Wideman cannot, post-9/11, "relax and enjoy the show on TV," the "newsy entertainment" of a war "designed to keep the public tuned in, uninformed, distracted, convinced a real war is taking place."[10] But what is the "real" here and how does one attest to it? How does one bear witness to the real-time effect of the televisual and the spectral logic of modern technological war? I will have to defer discussion of these issues until later on, but I will say that Wideman seems to be implying that there is nothing but simulacrum and delusion. But this forgets his other insight into how virtuality itself now marks programmed events and the time and space of the televisual image.

At stake, for Wideman, is the affect on the living of a history that refuses to be simply past, that cannot be entirely possessed, a history that has happened and is always yet to happen insofar as it never stops happening. Perhaps this is why he describes his own confused proximity to catastrophe as "like a rerun of a familiar documentary I've never seen"— his future haunted by its transmission (21). On the colonial island, in

contrast, it is the unseen that re-exerts its ghostly grip on lives lost to a fate
a good deal worse than the televisual—bare lives endlessly repackaged for
those on holiday. So instead of an escape from metropolitan alienation in
the hope of finding a new ontology of self and place, Wideman encounters tourists who remain unmoved by the remnants of slavery defining the
alienation of New World blacks. As visitants they are lost, "lost in the
ether, the virtual"; it's a loss which arises when "the breathless, unending
narrative of desire is trivialized and reduced to buying what's offered for
sale on the island" (9). This complaint is not simply against the lure of
commodity fetishism, but about how we are enslaved, as consumers and
spectators, by the terrible existential tyranny of the virtual: "On the one
hand mesmerizing choice, on the other hand a closed circle—a lonely,
stark dependence on the owner and programmer of the apparatus, the
technology producing the spectacle/carnival of choices" (86–87). The confusion between "prime-time hours of awareness" and a "globalized, virtual, administered" world has, he argues, resulted in "a lonely stark
dependence" on the "technology producing the spectacle"; the "mesmerizing [but ultimately illusory] choice" of infinite channels that we use to
distract ourselves from the ever mournful and miserable routines of the
packaged holiday—the endless tours, the traipsing around of ruins, the
exclusive beach resorts in which the only valued relationship is one's ability to pay, and where the natives, very simply and precisely, are only there
to serve (86–87).[11]

But is Wideman not himself a tourist, one who also happens to have a
French blonde (Katrine) in tow? Admittedly, the task he undertakes, to
explore the island as a supposedly personal moment of self-implication, as
an acknowledgment of complicity and guilt, and thus a question of ethics
and politics, suits the development of his themes. But because he styles
himself as an exile from the island while on the island, he too easily falls
into a rhetoric of outrage and independence as if his identity, as a relatively
rich African American tourist, was any less compromised than that of
the French bourgeoisie. This is why the metaphor of a closed circle is

ambiguous: is Wideman writing from within or outside it? If inside, then is not his critique also a symptom of fetishistic disavowal? If outside, what could it possibly mean for him to transcend the bewildering currency and spectrality of the virtual? And, on the island, what could it possibly mean to say that blacks and whites are mesmerized (enslaved?) by globalization *in the same ways?*

For Wideman, virtual choice is a commodified illusion whose flip side is the political violence of nativism and racism; the wish to be rooted in the self-same rather than assume the risks involved in leaving one's homeland behind for an unknown place, an encounter with otherness, a destination not one's own. But is our dependence on the virtual "package deal—on choice preempted"—really a form of slavery (87)? Although Wideman writes "wouldn't it be silly, maybe even perverse to push the similarities [between commodified life and slavery] very far," his thinking is structured by this analogy between the effects of capital (the consumption of people as things) and racial reification (where the conversion of people into fetishistic stereotypes is part of a generalized experience of the virtual) (94). It's a point of view that sees commodity fetishism as the virtual enchantment of the modern world and the ontological slavery of persons as its perpetual unveiling. That said, it remains unclear why slavery appears to be one moment in the history of capital *and* the ongoing persistence of the racial ontology of the virtual. If the language (and image?) of the commodity is, as Marx tells us, haunted by the unreal, illusory character of value, it is not clear to me whether Wideman views racial disavowal as a specific example of such commodification or its fetishized remainder? But if, again recalling Marx, capitalist illusion is never simply an illusion veiling an underlying reality but a fiction which people have forgotten as such, doesn't this complicate Wideman's oppositions between bare life and virtuality, capital and ontology?

As it turns out, just as the slave's "vision of freedom" perpetuates slavery, we too are dispossessed by the mesmerizing media power of race (94). For it is the way we visualize freedom as self-sovereignty and self-possession that blinds our course. For Wideman, black autonomy is inevitably influenced by this blind of racism that is its starting point and which it is condemned to repeat again and again. It appears, then, that our very freedom to see is experienced as just another form of blind domination or domination by blindness; and black clairvoyance is both a gift and a curse. This leads to the emphasis throughout *The Island: Martinique* on spectatorship as a kind of fantasmatic blindness; an emphasis that is blindly tendentious and haunted at the same time. Since the specter of race represents the return of the past that persists unabated, the teleontology of race is a reactivation and reenactment of a prior and much more fundamental dialectic between the gaze we imagine and the gaze we are dispossessed by, a dialectic which has not disappeared but rather has been (unwillingly and inevitably) interiorized by white and black subjects. In this spectral vision, the spectator acts as a kind of Photomat, hemorrhaging images—think of all those Spirit photographs in which the medium's body pours forth white ectoplasmic images. Then think of the medium's body as black: a body altered, disfigured by the white gunk oozing from mouth and eyes; the spew of spirit. What is of interest here is the self's assimilation to race as spectral media; a haunted way of seeing the world where consciousness is collected and reproduced like the movement of film through a camera's body.

The problem with the above critique, which evokes a politics of freedom as adversarial to the politics of the simulacrum, is the equally problematic wish to be rid of the specter from the life made vulnerable by race and commodity value. Further, the emphasis on the media-state apparatus as the lure of the virtual implies that colonial history is now nothing more than simulacrum and delusion. Recall Wideman's earlier comments on the "newsy entertainment" of a war "designed to keep the public tuned in, uninformed, distracted, convinced a real war is taking place." Not only does this lose sight of the neocolonial process of selection and criteria still used to broadcast media events in the developing world, it also loses sight of the death and suffering caused by the ongoing consequences of that history and so reduces political acts of resistance solely to an adversarial relation to media representations of those events. These tensions, in my view, pervade Wideman's extraordinary reading of the emotional and political culture of post-9/11 as a state of emergency. This reading will be, later on, one of my references and points of departure for why blackness remains the veiled, spectral life of white America.

Let us recall that *The Island: Martinique* sets out to address the politics of racial disavowal. Wideman wants to bear witness to the catastrophe this represents—he wants the victims to appear, shadowing commuters to exotic locations. He wants to point a dramatic finger at the boneyard on which each exclusive resort is built. Unsurprisingly, he finds this reenvisioning of the dead in Martinique's creole culture. In creolization French hegemony gives way to the language of the other, which returns as an echo of the dead other, the other who is summoned because lost. It is this vision of language as spectral archive that leads Wideman to propose *métissage*—the merging and blurring of genres, texts, and identities; the political and cultural praxis of the enslaved—as a political ideal of fusion and hybridity (as a creative, spontaneously adaptive mimetic ideal that escapes the simulacra of the commodity). Such, in any event, is the ideal of creole as what exceeds the phantasms and phantoms of racial virtuality. In the refuge that is creole Wideman sees blacks reinventing themselves despite being condemned to live outside French language and culture; it's a form of resistance in which freedom is reinvented as a choice, or clear vision, when our so-called enslavement to media technology is precisely what precludes such clarity by haunting it. It's this vision of *métissage*, as a form of mimesis that disturbs rather than subtends colonial authority, that leads Wideman to hail creole culture as a refusal of the European demand that blacks learn to resemble their mediatized image. If the imitation of French colonial culture can only ever amount to a degraded copy, or play of appearances, the "wannabe replica of an original that doesn't exist," the island's creole culture "stimulates an alternative vision that rescues the viewer from the usual unexamined scenery dutifully absorbed" (41, 58).

Insisting on this disjunction between a vision of democratic movement (creole) and a vision reproducing the delusions and disavowals of colonial simulacra (the televisual), Wideman says why only the former gives difference actual coherence and liberated identity:

> Consider the chaos of a news broadcast on the television screen: an announcer's face and voice-over, sidebars, inset videos, the crawl of factoids, ticker-tape bulletins flashing, intermittent displays of logos, ads, call letters, etc. Now imagine integrating all that mess into what seems like a single coherent message while at the same time preserving the reams of info on the screen so that each message reaches a targeted segment of the audience without excessively distracting or disturbing other viewers. That's something like the art creolization strives to master. Preserving choice. Focus on one without sacrificing the many. And vice versa. Multiple presences, many possibilities available with minimal static and interference. (50)

Wideman's emphasis on creolization as an inclusive art suggests that, whereas TV is an example of a medium that sacrifices audience participation to the simulation of manyness, and so eradicates choice, creolization transforms the televisual into liberated communication without excessive disturbance or distraction. The ritual of this screening turns the message into one that can be individually appropriated by many different subjects. Creole here testifies to a unity of multiple presences rather than the obligatory being-together of community, race, or nationhood. It appears, then, that certain forms of programming can resist the mythology and temptations of televisual ideology, but only insofar as they don't excessively disturb or distract the viewer's attention. (At this point, creolization becomes a choice between a distressed but ultimately distracted form of attention and a form of fascination that never suffers to lose itself to the mimetic power of TV. That is, a choice between the imaginary solidarity of the many-as-one identity and the many-as-the-shared disidentity of multiple presences.) This could mean that the risk and responsibility of creole art can be better enjoyed because the self's sacrifice, exposed to the darkness of the other, to its own ensnaring deceptions, is never made. I say "never made" because if one is never at home in language, then essentially one speaks from an elsewhere that makes even the language of exile and deprivation uninhabitable. Non-arrival is, then, what beckons us to language; and dispossession is the way in which language possesses us, whether as integral message or simulacrum. Yet, in his story of creole, Wideman presumes a newly recovered way of being at home for the formerly alienated, a rediscovered self properly self-possessed, autonomous. But why, if the only way to include multiple presences is to protect the self from the other's alterity, to lower that interference to one single coherent message, is this encounter, or response, more open to the heterogeneity of the many than the televisual? Why is this art of refusal not also haunted by TV's spectral simulation of otherness conceiving, as it does, multiple presences within the logic of identity, the either/or that the dialectic of deception and sacrifice merely repeats?

At such moments, Wideman's reading seems to repeat the fetishistic structure he's writing against. Since the specters haunting the real traumatize precisely because of what is missing from the real, one can no longer account for what is missing within the language of representation and actuality. Wideman knows that racism is not simply to be overcome by identifying the imago that reproduces it: he knows that the power and authority of race is implicated in a drama of misrecognition that represents without ever presenting itself. Even when blacks are up there on screen, what is rarely noticed is how race assigns a ghostliness to their desires and disowns the black spiritual life it conjures. (One has only to think of those many listless, black screen figures in U.S. cinema to get the point: torpid, blank, directionless faces only animated when spooked by ghosts. Nothing funnier, then, than a spook spooked, especially when rolling eyes become rigid and frenzied and listlessness gives way to anxiety and fear.) But what is it that coerces and mortifies: the extruding ghost or its mediatizing apparatus? More, is the fact that we continue to gawp with unembarrassed fascination the true catastrophe, or that we remain blindly indifferent to what we see? But what does it mean to see blackness? It could well be argued that to get too close to the catastrophe that is blackness is already to *resemble* blindness. In this instance, the spook testifies to the necessity of an *evacuated life*—a life embedded so completely in tourism and use value it can only measure the distance between person and commodity/thing , hence its value as haunted life.

Such are the questions raised by Wideman's various polemics against the spectacle of black lives consumed painlessly, virtually, teletechnologically. Once again, the focus is on what is implicated in the commodity value of black death-in-life. In fact, Wideman's argument that a politics of the virtual has come to the fore during the recent state of emergency post-9/11 seeks to link colonial forms of state terror to new global forms of teletechnology and state sovereignty. The picture he builds up (connecting his life in the United States to his time on the island) is one in which blackness is the state of exception that defines the emerging melodramas of the New World; it is the excluded interiority that organizes and frames U.S. cinema and TV, as well as the bare life that founds the martial architecture of law and state. Recall that, for him, mass media spectatorship is essentially passive, endlessly distracted and enslaved by the real time presences and fictions of the televisual, which, he argues, amounts to "the modern imprisonment of all of us in somebody else's self-serving story, each lonely, distinct one of us trapped, enraptured, a performer in a globalized, virtual, administered show"; or "when slaves believe they are powerless, they become complicit in their servitude" (48, 77). Such statements on our complicity with "freedom usurped" turns spectatorship into a form of bad faith, the willed forfeiture of freedom and resistance; as such, Wideman forgets the specters haunting both image and technology, representation and the real; he also loses sight of the singularity of slavery (which is infinitely more complex than vision or simulacra, or visual "techniques" of domination or resistance) (96). Consequently, he fails to deconstruct the relation between the selective criteria informing the televised actuality of events and the differing ways in which people bear witness—interpretively, unconsciously, fantasmatically, etc.—to such actuality at the level of image, discourse, affect. (I am thinking here of those ghostly CCTV sequences of murdered children like Damilola Taylor, discussed in the preface. Here the unforeseeability of the event that shadows, but fails to appear in, the image is conditioned neither by the institutional surveillance that produces the image nor by the singularity of the child whose death is already dead *to* the image. Yet the image still acts like a veil whose unveiled promise is of a terror without end—as we shall see.)

———

The designation terrorist is produced by the one-way gaze of power. . . . To label an enemy a terrorist confers the same invisibility a colonist's gaze confers upon the native. Dismissing the possibility that the native can look back at you just as you are looking at him is a first step toward blinding him and ultimately rendering him or her invisible. (Wideman, "The Color of Terror," 36)

"Revenants," the second of two allegories bringing the chapter on "Fanon" to a close, was first published as a conclusion to Wideman's keynote address on "The American Dilemma Revisited: Psychoanalysis, Social Policy, and the Socio-Cultural Meaning of Race," held at New York University in 2002.[12] The epigraph—"Today I believe in the possibility of love"— firmly anchors the text in a reading of Fanon's chapter on "The Man of Color and the White Woman" from *Black Skin, White Masks*. Bringing together the deaths of Fanon and Marilyn Monroe, "Revenants" opens with a steady trickle of cops and hospital personnel taking turns to peer at Monroe's naked corpse on display. The narrative then switches to Washington, D.C., as curious doctors, nurses, interns, troop in and out to observe Fanon, this "fiery, white-hating revolutionary, prophet of terror," now helpless, dazed, unable to speak, dying of leukemia, his skin turning blacker and blacker because of the overload of leukocytes in the blood (Wideman, *Island*, 144).

Echoing the first part of the book, the focus is once again on our disturbing (as well as reassuring) mass-mediated voyeuristic pleasures, and something much more difficult to comprehend: the source of our unembarrassed fascination with the pain and suffering of others, a form of reverence mesmerized by its own mesmeric representation of lives never lived. "Revenants" is all about the abject and intruding violence of such viewing. Pairing Fanon and Monroe's tragic deaths as media spectacle, and as morbid counterparts to Wideman and Katrine's visit to Martinique, the allegory reimagines them as a couple chained together in the hold of a slave ship, naked, shitting, pissing, throwing up on each other, as the vessel is tossed by stormy seas while bound for America: everything that they once were is lost, everything that they now are is a nightmarish record of memory. Exhausted, bloody, and enchained, the two are hauled on deck to dance before a group of drunken sailors. It is during this sadistic spectacle—of seeing their misery and pain figured forth as enjoyment?— that they address each other: "How can they keep staring at us without going blind?" asks Marilyn. "Perhaps they are blind," Franz replies. "Perhaps we are, too." His notion goes unheard. "Why are they doing this. Why can't they take their eyes off us. What do they expect to see," she asks (145).

What is revealed here are signs of a bond that, looked at yet barely visible, is too strong to be broken. In this "ground-zero" moment the white woman and black man are both stripped and "emptied of meaning" by the "void" of "eyes fixing me in a stare" (59). This is not because what the sailors expect to see is missing, or belongs to no one here; rather, racist illusion is blinding because, being already blind, it has no fear of what it cannot see. Blind, and so shameless. What we are dealing with here is an eye that only sees what it sees on the condition of not seeing itself seeing the other as subject. This "one-way gaze of power" terrorizes the other, rendering him or her invisible. It is a spectacle, on the other hand, that would render both Marilyn and Franz visible, knowable, identifiable according to a vision that is iconic, media-attuned but also deeply affected by the media surveillance of race. "Slippery like a daydream," this illusory seeing not only infiltrates wish and ego but also cancels "the difference between what is and what we wish," the difference between imago and reality (60).

"Revenants" thus brings us back to *The Island: Martinique* as a whole: that is, the sadistic gaze of a kind of virtual tourism, the wish to escape from the eternal workfulness of metropolitan living but without encountering the bare life that is the measure of one's authentic sojourn. Yet, this wish to be landed is terrifying because what is revealed is the reduction of the world and its peoples to a kind of televisual virtuality—literally, a state of permanent exception—the violence concealed by the illusory freedom of capital. What is also concealed is how the native must endlessly suffer and endure this emblematizing vision of him or herself as a ghostly thing within creation and yet faceless, inessential, given over to reflecting back to the tourist an image of natural authenticity. It is the deepest kind of disavowal—one that establishes itself in the intimate lives of blacks whose diaspora remains the ultimate example of this emergency. This is why I think "Revenants" concludes both "Fanon" and "The American Dilemma Revisited"; it is about what happens when the history inside people's heads coerces them to vandalize their eyeballs so as to ensure that they don't see the intimacies of interracial contact.

Accordingly, blackness is "the bottom-line shared interest of Americans who think of themselves as white and must continue to think of themselves as white," writes Wideman (Wideman, "Dilemma," 40).[13] "Whiteness," he adds, "is desired racelessness that desires race"; it is also a dream work: "the fantasy or dream that the enunciator of the racial theory possesses no race"; a fantasy or dream that is also real—a virtual presence in and a pressure on the real; part of a persecutory history of looking at blacks as if they were spooky automata (41). Or: it's the power to make reality itself disappear, made and unmade by the fantasy of race, as argued in the following reading of Freud's theory of dreams:

Latent unconscious content of the dream—the dark, instinctual urges of the Id—becomes through the mechanism of dreaming, manifest content of whiteness: pure, supreme, unassailable. This whiteness grants the narcissistic wish of the ego to remain unchallenged by the presence of the other. The waking dream of whiteness induces its own kind of enabling medium, not sleep, more like narcotized trance. The sleeper is seduced, doesn't desire to awaken even though at times certain versions of the wish fulfilling fantasy are quite disturbing. Black sex, black power, black success, black beauty infiltrate the dreaming. Appear as fragments, distortions, disguises, contradictions that are experienced as frighteningly unwelcome and de-stabilizing even while they may simultaneously evoke pleasure. (41)

Who is the subject of the dream here? The subject is one mesmerized and constrained by all sorts of prohibitions and displacements of which it is simultaneously the expression and simulation. This is a dream life reduced to mirroring the narcissistic hatreds of the social. Accordingly, the dream is haunted by the imaginary fixations of whiteness in which the ego is abandoned to the mercy of inner terror and outer violence. In the "dream of white supremacy," Wideman tells us, an elision appears which enables the dreamer to prolong his or her sleep, to avoid awakening into reality. It is an elision, a displacement, barely detached from its subterranean surroundings in the Id, and which, in its manifest and superegoic content, "grants the narcissistic wish of the ego" (42). And it is true, the dreamer's wish to escape the terrifying reality of desire and drive impregnating the dream: "black sex, power, success, and beauty" is here reflected in paranoic solidarity with the ego. Reflection of a reflection, phantasm of a phantasm: the fantasy of whiteness is what obscures-disguises that desire: the first dupe is the ego, and at the very moment the wishful fantasy becomes it (via a kind of dispossessing self-possession). Does this mean that disguise is the work of the fantasy even though whiteness also acts as the censor that binds as well as blinds all those frighteningly unwelcome black part objects?

Listen to Wideman again: "borrowing Freud's classic terminology for dream analysis, whiteness can be construed as a fantasy constructed by the ego to disguise or make tolerable a profoundly unsettling fear of being contaminated or ruled by deep instinctual processes" (41). In other words, whiteness fulfills—displaces—a repressed wish; its disguise is the work of a repression. The transformational work of the dream seems to be operating regressively here, but via a fantasy that preserves the intelligibility of racial difference, even as the phobic terror of blackness is attached to a kind of terrifying illusion. Wideman says he borrows this idea from Freud, but he appears to be extending Freud's view of the dream as a disguised wish, to include the culturalization of the dreamwork by mass media news images. Accordingly, racism is not just a form of dreaming, or hallucinatory wish fantasy in the processes of the dreamwork, but a dreaming in which culture is already there agitating inside the dreamwork; a kind of "dreaming possessed not, or not only, by the subject's own wishful-shameful fantasies but by the real; or, more precisely, by the fantasies which make up the real"—what Fanon calls "real fantasies" (*phantasmes réels*) (41).[14] Wideman's understanding of these mandated images—they guard and protect the white supremacist imagination; they shroud the black ego by disrupting its imaginary integrity while allowing the white ego the fantasy of mastery—represents a fundamental insight into why whites remain blind to the misrecognitions of race even though, as a consequence, their psyches remain in a permanent state of exception.[15]

These reflections are continued in "Whose War? The Color of Terror," an essay first published in *Harper's* magazine in 2002.[16] In this text, Wideman pictures a post-9/11 America always watchful, but also anxious, hateful, paralyzed by its own phobias and fears. "Like a child pinned to its bed," he writes, "not moving a muscle for fear it will arouse" the image silhouetted in the dark, "we're immobilized, paralyzed by terror" (it perhaps goes without saying that the child who is stricken here is white, which means that what spooks is the return of what has been symbolically abolished from the fantasy and symbols of whiteness) (Wideman, "Whose War," 38). That anxiety, that sees manifestations of terror everywhere, is phobic anxiety in which repressed fears reappear as if from without, displaced onto the dramas and drives of cultural life. It's a view equating the televisual with the affect of a code which cannot be seen; and terror on TV with the materialization of a hallucinatory blindness (one that recalls the disavowal of slavery saw and heard in Martinique). More precisely, to produce, like the phobic child, the image of what one fears in order to disavow what one fears—America's War on Terror is, Wideman argues, an attempt to bind the trauma unleashed by 9/11 to a politics of race and fantasy set apart from the fragility of American cultural life. If America cannot not stop looking, that is because race has become a sort of camera, bodying forth the wild-eyed claim that America itself is a privileged witness to the unseen. Once again, it is the visual presence of race that binds catastrophe to memory, history to a moment of rupture between looking and misrecognition. In the movement, the relay, between the two, the experience of TV echoes that of a subject caught between enchantment and contamination; a subject produced when vision fails or when fear verges on paranoia. Further, race performs this role because it is the common fantasy of America, grounding all mastery, pleasure, desire and fear ("the racialized vision of ourselves and our future") (89).

"Is it too far fetched to see [Willie] Horton's face in the face of Osama Bin Laden," he asks, "faces [that have been] endlessly recycled, circulating, like O.J.'s face, that got blacker on the cover of *Time Magazine*?" (Wideman, "Dilemma," 40). Such superimpositions reveal why Wideman wants a less insipid and credulous belief in what is broadcast, in what is presented as real-time coverage of events, and why he wants to save the ghostly effect of memory, language, and image from the delusory living-presence of the televisual—the perverse virtualization of experience and the past as defined by commodified desire and need. A postracial future is one way of answering the threat to the future posed by life reduced to the simulacra of images, television, and the global and accelerated flow of digital communication. Although Wideman believes in specters, in revenants, he still wants to purify history of the virtual with respect to politics, justice, and freedom. He wants to indicate the conditions in which living experience, living production, effaces every trace of virtuality that reduces black existence to bare life or pure labor. This future is not one where a black purity of presence is to be unveiled once the corrupting use-values and fetishistic denials of whiteness are no longer; but a postracial messianism that presumes the being of the black is always corrupted, always ghostly. This is a future in which race constitutes the exception to the human. In this instance, Wideman shows himself to be as an acute reader of racial spectrality and specularity as Fanon, to whom *The Island: Martinique* is dedicated. This wish to be at home in a postracial singularity sees Wideman turn to the past (the slave past) in ways which reproduce the delusion and denegation of the phantomality of the media, as we have seen. It also sees him reproduce the metaphor of woman as the veil that conceals the veiled life of race (the seductions and compulsions of interracial heterosexual desire never really questioned beyond the experience of being overwhelmed, or awed, by the racist gaze "fixing me in a stare," as the masculine self is laid bare) (59). Consequently, *The Island: Martinique* can only reveal, judge, the hauntology of race through recourse to the very misrecognitions that constitutes it.

———

To recall, the chapter on "Fanon" includes two allegories about blindness and vision: "Revenants" and a second story about a doomed love affair between Chantal, a blond French woman, and Paul, an African American. It is the second that concerns me here, a fiction which turns on how the desire to see leads to the desire to possess, and about the boundless and imprudent force of that impulse in sexual intimacy. That said, both allegories reveal how racial fetishism casts its veil over being and appearance; how the feeling of being screened off, fixed inside somebody else's fantasy, is both what allows us to see, that saves us from the blind of racism, but also an inevitable consequence of that blind seeing. As when, after trying hard to uncover the gaze that condemns me, that punishes me without seeing me, what saves me from loss of sight is my own double consciousness when others, unaware of life behind the veil, are blinded by phantasm, obsession, pathology. Wanting to see and be seen, no matter what the cost—or, at any rate, to take on that warring struggle—is what allows me to distinguish the false clarities of what is given to be seen from what is unseen, the gaze looking on with contempt and pity. For the blinding glare that sears the eye, that unveils, is also a defense against the black abyss that darkens vision, that veils. In other words, both allegories reveal how forbidden sexual desires are veiled and sustained by the scopic law of race. As such, both allegories are about why a desperate wish to see is equally a desperate wish not to be seen, and about how concealed sexuality becomes visible racially. The allegory that concerns me here is also about what happens when the spectator's relation to the image is disturbed by a racial scopophilic gaze, and the eye is shorn of its pleasures and potency and the security of the seeing subject collapses. It is this moment, the point at which the violence of the gaze intrudes, that this allegory begins; that is when the gaze escapes the scopic field but continues to haunt vision, and all that is left of the seer is naked fear.

"They should not be here. She's known this all along in the deep place where things you don't want to know are known. Where the knowledge of things that can hurt you or kill you, and probably will or should if they don't, never sleeps" (117). So begins the story of Chantal and Paul; a "virtual couple" to the real couple of John and Katrine of the "Journal" (xxviii). Chantal is recollecting the time when she and her white lover, Antoine, found themselves lost and fearful in an all-black part of Martinique. "She was telling the story to free them [Chantal and Paul]. Trusting him. Trusting their love," but Paul does not see it, or rather, he does not want to know, would like not to know—that is to say, not to see—the imago or phantasm haunting her words (118). The gaze that Chantal thinks she sees, "One glimpse out of the corner of my eye enough. Could have been a shadow, could have been nothing, but it was enough," a mirror to Paul's refusal (118). In contrast, our first glimpse of Paul sees him watching a film showing the chopping up of Patrice Lumumba and the burning of his body parts in an oil drum. Here not only is the screen marked by negrophobic violence, it is also the point where inner and outer violence and psychic and cultural fantasy meet. As Paul looks up at the screen, he hears "my white friends giggling inside my skull" (119). In brief, he too is haunted by what he knows but doesn't want to know, he too is disturbed by the stain erupting in his wish to see what is missing from the image, blinded by its blindness.

But is Chantal's belief in trust not also blinded, that is, self-deceived: this wish to be free from the specular disturbance of the gaze is itself blind to the risk of blindness and so exposes a difference in viewpoint, which is to say, the story of her blindness, or how she came to see, cannot see what this vision also makes visible. That is, what is also shared and exchanged is a racial visibility that is itself blinding. Here, as the white eye of the tourist finds itself traversed and disturbed, observed by its own perilous fascination as the other follows and pursues it, the story can neither free them from the misrecognitions of race nor persuade Paul that Chantal is not concealing something. Indeed, the story serves to underlie the fact that there is something beyond them that is also intimately present, inside them, making them both feel culpable and guilty. This something is not a ghost but a deeply politicized crisis of self-identity, in which race is once again the source of what is exposed and precarious in the veiling of vision. Standing in the dark of night what does Chantal see if not the aura of race mixed in with her own fears and desires? It is the fantasy—the spectacle—of watching herself humiliated and terrified in the eyes of the (black) other. And, of course, what disturbs Paul is the fact that he sees her seeing; its the affect of her fascination that seizes and monopolizes him, leaving him exposed, without reprieve; for what he sees is a gaze that does not see him but is nonetheless blinding in the way it marks him as a black man. Instead of trust all he sees is her racial anxiety, and what he sees replays what he has known since he was a child; the trouble is that what he knows also mirrors his own unseeing.

Paul describes the "education" of his childhood: of being pursued "ruthlessly, systematically, [and] with malice" by media images and stories; images and stories that reappeared on the faces of white neighbors, friends, and schoolmates (120). In brief, Paul answers her story with a story about the disfiguration of seeing, an unforgettable moment of seeing, of bearing witness when all of a sudden one is disfigured by a gaze that one does not see, but which sees us, according to the law of its unseeing. In contrast, Chantal narrates her sexual and political "education" during the 1960s from her Algerian lover, Kamal: "To grow, I needed to hear those stories, . . . From Kamal I learned things about my country, myself, I'd never dreamed. I became ashamed of France. So much hate. So deep and ugly. An education preparing me for your country, Paul" (131).

Education, fascination, image: as the story oscillates between them, so "education" and "shame" become signifiers for how whites and blacks are differently founded in the realm of the visible (once again, the eyes are the source of guilt and are thus related to fears of shame or punishment; but what is also brought to light is how the eyes are also the source of memory, anxiety, and mourning). On the one hand, Paul recollects being forced to see himself in the dereliction his imago unleashes, while Chantal, hoping somehow to escape that ruination, ends up confirming her conformity to it (her refusal of white privilege something *more* than shame but something *less* than dereliction). For Chantal, the experience of seeing herself as white occasions shame because she now looks at herself through the eyes of Kamal, an Algerian. (Is shame here a consequence of the eye's reincorporealization or an exposure of its fantasized limits?) For Paul, in contrast, the act of seeing himself seen is shaming because of the abrupt reminder that he is that alien body for his friends and neighbors, the corporealized representative of shame as such. But in the end it is the feeling of being seen without actually seeing himself that opens up the gap between gaze and ego and that veils the curious loss of himself that occurs when the body is covered over by racist imago. In both instances, what emerges is the totalizing effect of the gaze on one's innermost desires; it matters little whether one is agent or victim, enraged or degraded. What is shameful is the self's intolerable discovery of itself as raced, as precisely the impossibility of fleeing the totality of race as what lays bare and hides one's entire being. Here, the racialization of agency presupposes how one is implicated in the stakes of reason and power, fantasy and political representation. Perhaps this is why Wideman connects the question of "education" to that of the "imagination," desire to the sadistic structure of the gaze. But why should Paul, in response to Chantal's story of black menace/white fear, ask her: "I want to know what you imagined. . . . What do you imagine you're doing here on this island with me?" (143).

And what proof is he looking for here if not the disclosure of her whiteness as now more dark and threatening than it was ever before? That her eyes reveal what her political identification conceals, a feeling that leads him to make his final reproach to her: "Proving to yourself you could still be white, if you chose" (135). Revealing, in the process, his own frustrations and difficulties with how he imagines he now looks to her. Both failures prove to be ruinous, their particular significance one of disavowal: what is inside, completely unknown to the subject, will come back to haunt it, piercing both eyeballs and what lies behind them. What pierces the eye is not the visible, but what haunts the phenomenality or essence of the visible, the shadows or emanations secreted onto the visible and that produce blindness, and whose inappearance is not unrelated to what Lacan calls the "real," the invisible remainder of vision itself that can be neither thought nor reflected and is thus blinded at the point where one sees. For Chantal, of course, there is no way out. To renounce the problematical relationship between whiteness and privilege smacks of a renunciation that, despite all appearances to the contrary, remains bound to delusion, the delusion of whiteness as the negation of racism's specular pleasures and fears rather than the cause of their exorbitant reproduction. The allegory shows that all such renunciation, the wish to vanquish the self, to sacrifice even desire itself, final proof that the disfiguring ghost (of whiteness) has finally taken over self-identity.

It has to be said, however, that if whiteness is the veil that veils itself, this is a veil interwoven with illusion, a veil of enigmatic possibilities, blinding with promise, deceit, theft, and seduction. This is not so much life behind the veil, as a life whose essence is to appear veiled. For my own part, the paranoia revealed suggests something discordant in the exchanged glances; something misrecognised, repugnant, tangled in a knot of desire and mistrust. The allegory illuminates, from the outset, Paul's suspicion that Chantal is keeping something hidden from him. That said, we are never sure whether this is clairvoyance on Paul's part or voyeurism: is he seeing something hidden or what he imagines to be hidden by her whiteness? The allegory thus turns on two forms of fetishistic disavowal and unveiling: across sexual difference and racial subjection there is superimposed the phantasmatic scene of the gaze as castration and the heterosexist binary of a racial politics of representation; it is in the complex, even contradictory, relation between the two—that is, the historical ways in which sexual relations between black men and white women have traditionally been seen, as well as their political desire to be seen differently—that the story (and *The Island: Martinique* more generally) plots the dynamics of the gaze, the real, and fantasy.

On a secluded beach in Martinique Paul admits that "I couldn't keep my eyes off you"; grateful for being allowed "to see you in ways I never have before," grateful for the intimacy that appears with Chantal's nakedness now that her desire to show herself is at one with his desire to see (an affirmation that will later change into her wish to be seen differently and his wish to see what she cannot reveal) (127). The relation between consent, intimacy, and the underlying deception—or deceitfulness—of how we see, or fail to see, ourselves forms the center of the story. Spectacle, too, as the starting point for a conflict over image as self-identity, a conflict that occurs over who endures being looked-at and who is nothing but this property of being-looked-at by eyes that are never his, or her, *own*, a conflict that reveals how a politics of representation haunts our experiences as desiring subjects. A white Frenchman soon appears and settles down near them. He, too, "can't take his eyes off you, but that's okay too, you decide, no need to conceal what he can't see"; "you can turn his gaze away, even if his eyes were as close to you as mine" (128).

If there is no need to conceal what cannot be seen, is it because there's nothing more to see beyond Chantal's nakedness, or is it because the white Frenchman can only see her nakedness as an exhibition, implicating him as witness? How does one read the distinction here between a woman who exhibits herself knowing she is seen and a woman who refuses to exhibit herself precisely because of that knowledge? To make the woman's exposure here a question of consent but also a powerful ability to realize herself as spectacle identifies the contest of gazes as one of possession and dispossession: "what could or couldn't be stolen from us, what couldn't be owned or possessed" (68). And yet, the ruse of the word "us" immediately opens up the question of who or what is being possessed and stolen here? Paul says: there is no need to conceal the intimacy between us since intimacy is already an open concealment as the gaze passes from him to the stranger—the stranger thinks he is seeing Chantal's body laid bare, but what she conceals has no significance in the passage from inner imagining to outside world and the eyes of the other. But let us not be mistaken here: it is Paul who must be convinced. There is more than a hint that he suspects Chantal, more than a hint that he distrusts her whiteness: in this extraordinary game of hide-and-seek in which Paul feels resentment, her femininity comes into play as the power that conceals and that conceals itself; a concealment that fascinates even as it threatens, that seduces even as it mocks. But only because he presumes a relationship between the woman-as-spectacle and the narcissistic pleasures of the male gaze. Paul is perturbed, not because Chantal exposes herself, but because he is unable to see her sexuality as anything more than a show for him, a spectacle to be owned or possessed.

The story ends with Chantal's "submission" to Paul's violence: "shaking her till she submits, her head flopping side to side as he looms over her, shaking, shaking, shaking whiteness out and blackness in or blackness in and whiteness out" (144). It's a scene of sacrifice and punishment, but also debt and repayment, as the love squandered equals the future lost. But let us not forget, it is this freedom to be *in* submission which really angers Paul, because what he sees everywhere in Martinique are blacks denied the same self-legislative freedoms of the white subject. Perhaps this is why Wideman adds the following interlude: In a moment of early morning

intimacy, submersed in recollections of Paul's anger and rage, Chantal
"remembers his unfocused stare"—"would Paul be jealous," she wonders,
"if she told him she found the hurt of his beautiful smile hovering in
Osama Bin Laden's eyes" (136). Once again it is the uncanniness of the relation between intimacy and violence and racial catastrophe that forms this
image of Paul and his likeness. It is a doubling in which the historic violence haunting black men merges with that of 9/11, the violence of Paul
with the enigmatic terror of Osama Bin Laden, the media image that continues to mask racial "hurt" under the moral law of whiteness as the place
of universal catastrophe.

In the allegory of Paul and Chantal, what we witness and what profoundly depresses us is the affect of racism on sexual desire. The allegory
was written, Wideman tells us, not so much as a protest as a kind of "negative talisman to ward off my ancient fear of losing what's most precious"
(xxviii). In the allegory this fear results, perhaps inevitably, from the uncertainty of what can be borne to be seen and what cannot even be looked on,
as if the eye and mind were driven by a wish not to be seen through
another's eyes, suddenly free, independent of all enchantment. It's an
uncertainty that directly connects Paul and Chantal to Wideman's reading
of Fanon in *The Island: Martinique*—the exemplary exceptionality of a life
ghosted by its own invisibility and whose singularity is to be envisioned
as such.

(This sense of the black body as ghosted is crucial to an understanding
of Fanon's account of negrophobic fantasy, without which one fails to
understand the "spookiness" of blacks. In brief, if for Fanon race is not just
phantasm and simulacra but also a deeply symptomatic way of screening
out the real, how would he have responded to Wideman's view of him?
How would he have responded to Wideman's use of his work to explore
the political and visual cultures of racial paranoia in the United States?)

One of the catastrophes of black life for W.E.B. Du Bois was cease-
lessly having to be, and see oneself, as a spectacle in the eyes of others,
eyes that looked on in "amused contempt and pity."[17] And yet as those eyes

looked on what they saw was deepened and thus lent a more uncanny reality by the images of blacks seen and heard in image and sound media, so that recognition of life behind the veil was, over and over again, made visible as a haunted technological medium. It seemed as if the awful, ghostly appearance of blacks was immanent to the technology and so infinitely more frightening and real, but the pity that engulfed them was, in effect, self-pity, and the contempt not simply an amusement at the spectacle, but an amused response to the life reduced to a kind of clairvoyant immateriality. For Wideman, it is white belief in the mediumistic spectacle that has ensured the permanence of this uncanny vision and its cultural catastrophe. By taking refuge in blackness as unnatural appearance, whites have remained blind, not so much to a supposed black truth beyond appearance, but to the illusion of race. Having deliberately closed their eyes to themselves as blinded (and therefore mediatized and spectral), the apparitions of race have, consequently, become unconscious. It is this will to illusion, legitimated as cultural right and privilege, that continues to veil racism's historical catastrophe and, in a context where watching becomes doing, continues to perform political violence as a just response to the imagined "spookiness" of blacks.

2   *That Within*

*All the world is a stage not only surrounding us
but even more so within.*

—Fritz Wittels, "Unconscious Phantoms in
Neurotics" (1939)

Frantz Fanon appears to have had a mania for white women. Not only is *Black Skin, White Masks* formed around a study of her; it is through her that he engages with the obsessive neuroses—the uncanny, weightless states of nonbeing; the feelings of being forever belated—plaguing the Martinican men of his text and his own authorship. What I mean is, at a certain point it becomes impossible to read this text without fielding her on-the-pitch prominence. She is not only the privileged representative of Fanon's psychoanalyses of Negrophobia but also the most tabloid, typed commonplace of the dreams and desires of his black male patients. In brief, her iconic stature has very much to do with being the most hateful and the most desired; her ambivalence is very much a mirror to the black man's own. Secondly, what she means to Fanon can only be properly understood, I fear, by attending to a highly condensed and opaque reference to *Hamlet*. To anticipate, briefly. Here the returning ghost does not require the black son to submit to paternal law. No, the son's deep sadness turns on being abandoned by any law as such. Indeed, the spectral here represents nothing more than the ruins of separation. Under the gaze of the ghost, the son reveals himself to be empty; that is, like Hamlet, he is already too full of the death living within him. That is why he is impelled toward the whiteness of the white woman—she is proof of the absence, the black death that rends him, mirror to his nonbeing.

There's more. In *Black Skin, White Masks* the white woman is inspiriting: loving her is to realize an unavoidably painful experience of loss. She conveys the promise of mastery to the black man, but only insofar as he negates himself as black. It's a self-institution achieved through an obliteration of being in which the self takes pleasure in the annihilation driving the self to expend itself. She is the fantasy supporting this aphanisis of the subject.[1] The black man's reward is a kind of morbid sovereignty. The servility he formerly resembled now transformed into mastery over his own symbolic death. This is her gift to him—a reemergent mastery achieved through her mediation and iconic recognition. She unveils the phantom buried deep within, whose loss the ego carries as its mask. Consider, for example, the opening sentences of "The Man of Color and the White Woman":

> Out of the blackest part of my soul, across the zebra striping of my mind, surges this desire to be suddenly *white*. I wish to be acknowledged not as *Black* but as *White*. Now—and this is a form of recognition that Hegel had not envisaged [*décrite*]—who but a white woman can do this for me? By loving me she proves that I am worthy of white love. I am loved like a white man. I am a white man. Her loves takes me onto the royal road that leads to total realization. (63)[2]

In this scenario Fanon reveals an anxious desire to be loved, to be sexed, but also a desire to have the white woman's sex not only reunite drive with the demands of culture but turn lust (impulse, wish, revenge, longing) into recognition: "I marry white culture, white beauty, white whiteness. When my restless hands caress those white breasts, they grasp white civilization and dignity and make them mine." "I am loved like a white man. I am a white man" (63). By loving me, in other words, the white woman embraces me with the whiteness of her love. That whiteness dazzles me with its promise, the conjuration of the white man buried within. In other words, by possessing her I possess my wished-for self. She is the answer to my unconscious wish, the means by which I can rectify the fault of my race, the means by which I can punish and revenge, via expiation, this expiation of my inner self. Through her I can transcend all that is inborn in me by redeeming the whiteness hidden within. Her love betokens what I was *meant* to be, not what I *am*. Such love is indeed a very discriminate gift and one that, in its necessity, I regard as an initiation and a rite. After having recently spoken with several Antilleans, Fanon calls it "this ritual of initiation into 'authentic' manhood" (72).

Authentic manhood: isn't this an embarrassing expression? Aside from Fanon's scare quotes, what impresses here is an authenticity that exceeds Hegelian recognition and sovereignty, not through trial or the anguish of death, but because it makes *visible* the meaning and work of whiteness as the repressed truth of black desire and sexual being. If this is "authentic" manhood, then it designates a sovereignty inscribed by a masochistic renunciation that exceeds dialectics, the intimate unfolding of "a wish to be white" that is also a "lust for revenge" (16). But what else is buried here? Why is this call to authenticity dumbfounded by its own wish for a reprieve while in fact desiring to have the Other's desire name its own? And why, in this dawning of a "total realization," does the black appear to be summoned by a mysterious, unignorable call when, in fact, it is his own repressed desire that sets in motion this search for love and recognition?

"But I have that within which passeth show;
These but the trappings and the suits of woe"
Hamlet, Act 1, Scene 2

In his chapter on "The Man of Color and the White Woman," Fanon does a remarkable reading of René Maran's 1947 semiautobiographical novel, *Un homme pareil aux autres*. Fanon turns to Jean Veneuse, the protagonist of Maran's novel, to address the following: "Jean Veneuse is not a Negro and does not wish to be a Negro. And yet, without his knowledge, a gulf has been created. There is something indefinable, irreversible, there is indeed *that within* of Harold Rosenberg" (Fanon, *Black Skin*, 71). And why precisely is Veneuse so troubled by the wish not to be a Negro, a wish that appears here via words—left in English—taken from Rosenberg's reading of *Hamlet*? And why does he suffer and endure this absence that masters him, this void that remains incomprehensible but whose heaviness and gravity nevertheless encloses him? And why is this indefinable, irreversible gulf inhabited by a white woman as its disavowed core?

Let us first begin with Harold Rosenberg. In 1947, Rosenberg published "The Stages: A Geography of Human Action" in the first issue of *Possibilities*.[3] A year later, the essay reappeared in French in *Les Temps Modernes* under the title "Du jeu au je: Esquisse d'une géographie de l'action"—a play on the many meanings of drama, game, the game of identity in the theatre of the world.[4] Translated by René Guyonnet and edited by Jean-Paul Sartre, this is the version Fanon uses in *Black Skin, White Masks*. For Rosenberg, *Hamlet* brings into focus the anguish of a man "who attempted in vain to seize his life as particular to him"—a man caught between the two worlds, or stages, of the dead and the living (Rosenberg, "Stages," 65). "Why is the graveyard so crowded?" Rosenberg wonders, reflecting on "the longing of the dead" who "have no place to go"—it is a void, an abyss, an emptiness—producing "a new ontological anxiety" (for those still clinging onto life's "single visible stage"): "the anxiety to get into the act. And to decide whether the part assigned is really one's own part" (47, 48). Suspended between these two stages, Hamlet is caught up in the difficulty of their relation, one complicated still further by his "tortured conscience" (to borrow Ernest Jones's phrase), his inability to transcend the contradiction between being and acting, "is and seems" (65).[5] At stake for Rosenberg are the connections between being and seeming—the wish "to denote oneself truly" as against "playing one's part" (50). To play a part or to act, this is Hamlet's anxiety, his situation haunted, according to Rosenberg, by something "hiddenly particular to him," something beyond "the visible platform of action"—"that within" (50).

Despite never mentioning the Shoah, Rosenberg's 1947 reflections on the auratic persistence of a gap or fault in identity, of being haunted by the no longer there, are clearly shaped by that traumatic history. "That within" is at once the return of what does not come back and what "fulfills the necessity of the past" (64).[6] It is a question of assuming liability for the past when one knows that past is absolutely lost, and not only accepting it but freely giving oneself up to it—as the source of all authenticity. Certainly, for Rosenberg, Hamlet learns his situation from the vision of the dead father, the phantom who summons and to whom "that within" calls: it is an inner mournful history imagined in the form of something intimate, unwilled—and, once again, part of what links Hamlet to "the dark off-stage" (49, 50). Hamlet behaves ethically toward the dead by abandoning himself to the negative worklessness of "that within." By obeying it he too begins his awakening, moving toward the extreme uncertainty of his situation. From the ghost—who arrives as the shadow of a murderous event—Hamlet learns to overcome the "fatal rupture of being from action," to become "the situation in which he is acting" (57, 60).[7] This is why Rosenberg reads *Hamlet* as a dialectical drama of *abandonment*: "On the one hand, to abandon himself to direction from without; on the other, to anticipate his own spontaneity and accurately to judge the quality of his deed" (54). Hamlet must not simply abandon himself to the resentments of "that within," for such abandonment returns him to the depth of impotence; no, he must claim and consecrate it as the image of an unavowable but testimonial absence freed of revenge and resentment. Only then will his self-imposed exile and mourning be able to reconcile that which must be done to his situation. Hamlet's "that within," then, this condition that is his risk, arises from the fact that who we are amounts to more than playing an actor's role or part, more than following orders. Through him Claudius's philosophy of man as actor is condemned and judged historically; for Hamlet belongs to the dead, "from whom no history is free," the dead who act, in Marx's words, as "a nightmare on the brain of the living" (52, 53).

For Rosenberg, then, "that within" speaks to both the uncertainty of existence and the ethics of authenticity where the self, no longer a morbid spectator to life, establishes itself in impossibility by testifying to a form of obligation neither projected nor disowned. Hamlet must externalize his resentment if "that within" is to become more than a memory of offense, more than a lingering wound or negative passion. But to unify deed and remembrance is an infinitely difficult task due to his "blindness of will" (52). Hamlet "must become passive for the sake of action, mystified for the sake of precision, a 'dull and muddy-mettled rascal' to play his role of hero" (54). And in this "negative movement" his tragedy lies (63). For, to submit to the enigmatic summoning of "that within" is to remain internally alienated and subjected; but to perform it is also a difficult, almost impossible, task leaving behind unconscious residues in the ego which, in its abandoning, remains the disembodied resemblance of the father's departing ghost. "The plot has won against the man," Rosenberg concludes, "which is to say that the dead have won by way of the hero transformed to them in their will to bring their action to its end" (64).

Perhaps this is why "The Stages" so appealed to Fanon and Sartre. Rosenberg's study of a gap in being that is both inexpressible and yet deeply haunting not only inhabits Sartre's reading of *Hamlet* and Fanon's reading of *Un homme pareil aux autres,* but also confirms their postwar views on the politics of guilt and racial authenticity. In their different ways, all three men struggle with an image of psychic life as one possessed, as one, in effect, forced to act out an unassignable command that both precedes and produces the self. An acting out understood as a blind, affective tie to an otherness of the other already inside the self, an otherness that also comes from without, outside the self, in the hallucinations and phantasms of the social world. What they each call "that within" testifies, then, to an overwhelming feeling of existential loss or abandonment: an enigmatic relation to otherness that speaks to the cadaverous presence of the indwelling dead; the value of this signification idealized as the task of ethics and politics. Here the void that returns signifies an internalized legacy of self-mistrust. Needless to say, in *Un homme pareil aux autres,* this encounter is profoundly raced.

To repeat: "Jean Veneuse is not a Negro and does not wish to be a Negro. And yet, without his knowledge, a gulf has been created. There is something indefinable, irreversible, there is indeed *that within* of Harold Rosenberg." These sentences are enigmatic. On the one hand, what is being described is a moment of denial that is the unconscious affect of a hiatus: in the *nègre* who is *not* there is a disarticulation and derangement that remains fundamentally opaque. On the other hand, Fanon finds himself up against something that is both indefinable and untranslatable; the words "that within"—words appearing here in English—register a gap, or hiatus, in the capacity of French to name this gulf in black identity which is not *nègre*. (As if there were a "that within" within Maran's representation of race and nationality in *Un homme pareil aux autres*, a sign of a certain distancing between his wish to be assimilated as a French *évolué* and his fear of being abandoned to *les nègres*, an ambivalence that can only be represented by a suspense *in* representation, by an unconscious *décalage*? Here it is well to remember that these words are Fanon's and not Maran's, even though they do touch on a key dialectic to be discussed throughout this chapter. That is, a being that is a fear of being; a desire that subsists by not being in the place of desire, sheltered from the desire of the other as such.)

Further, Fanon turns to René Guyonnet's translation to signal this disadjustment; to disinter this nothingness consuming the being of the black. (In Guyonnet's "Du jeu au je"—for reasons which remain unclear—whenever "that within" appears it is left untranslated and italicized, a move which exceeds the scene of translation because it does not occur in either of the originals that ostensibly produce it—neither Gide's 1946 translation nor Rosenberg's commentary.[8] In "The Stages" the phrase appears in scare quotes only once and is left in roman type throughout.) That disparity or dislocation, is, to be sure, also a haunting: "that within" as a figure of, and for, a kind of unconscious schism breaking forth into the being of the black, and the black as a kind of spectral repository for the aggressions and phobias of culture. But phobia, too, as the black's way of "replac[ing] the (love-hate) object which is missing, absent"; phobia as part of a defense against the psychotic gaps opened up in the subject when "that within" takes on "the terrifying form of not-being-there."[9] As we will see, Fanon turns to the work of the Swiss analyst Germaine Guex to consider the pre-Oedipal meaning of that "absence," the ambivalence it evinces, and the psychic vicissitudes with which it is composed.

In other words, behind the opening sentences of Fanon's reading of *Un homme pareil aux autres* can be glimpsed an already quite complex relationship to the text. Here what returns—as influence or echo—is also what allows us a glimpse into *Black Skin, White Masks* as itself a kind of spectral archive. The death that returns in this text is, I believe, intimately linked not only to the enigma of interracial sexuality but also to a colonial family romance in which fantasized loss, symbolic loss, is conjoined with the willed foreclosure of historical memory, having as its backdrop French colonial Africa. Consequently, in the Fanonian encounter between black man and white woman can be discerned two contrasted movements of love to revenge, but also of loss to recognition in which love of the other is the negative unworking of a self no longer transcendent but laid bare and condemned.

Maran's *Un homme pareil aux autres* is loosely based on his time spent as an administrator in the French Central African colony of Ubangi-Shari. In a letter to René Violaines, sent on 1 November 1947, he describes the novel as an untimely text:

> Unfortunately, I think I have committed an error in publishing *Un homme pareil aux autres* much too late. Perhaps I have also committed an error in living on the edge of my time [*en marge de mon temps*]. The problem that I have raised in all impartial good faith is nonetheless one that is extremely harrowing. People will realise one day that by raising it I have fulfilled my social duty as a writer.[10]

Here are two errors of belatedness: one out of time and one much too late. The time for reading the novel *Un homme pareil aux autres* has, it seems, come and passed but, in another sense, it has, like its author, never arrived, its future is still to come. When people realize their true value, both text and author will come back as if for the first time. They will be recognized as the fulfillment of a social duty, an ethical witness to *"angoissant au possible."* This is a question of repetition, perhaps, but one which begins by coming back.[11] In short, Maran is an author who will return from the margins of his times; like a ghost, or revenant, his time is not yet. Is this why readers, interpreters, and scholars have had such difficulty deciding between the history of the novel and the time of its writing, between the act of narration and the historical anachronism—time future—of the author?[12] As we shall see, it is a decision with which Fanon will struggle in his attempt to answer whether Maran is *a man like any other*, or whether his anxieties and fears are inseparable from his identity as a *black* man (in question, too, is Sartre's 1946 definition of racial "inauthenticity," which Fanon borrows from *Réflexions sur la Question Juive*). It is a struggle that sees Fanon constantly switch between fiction and anecdote, history and personal reminiscence as he tries to find a way to speak to what is particularly unique (hidden within) the neuroses of black men: in other words, why black men appear to themselves such uneasy, anxious, negatively enigmatic objects on the margins of history and of time and why, no doubt for the same reason, they seem to produce such haunted texts.

Un homme pareil aux autres tells the story of Jean Veneuse, a black bourgeois in love with Andrée Marielle, who is white. "What are the terms of this problem?" asks Fanon. Veneuse is black, therefore a *"nègre"*; but he is also European. "There is the conflict," Fanon tells us (Fanon, *Black Skin*, 64). The drama begins on a November day at the Bordeaux docks. Veneuse, heartbroken, is about to set sail for French Equatorial Africa to a post in colonial administration. To his old friend, Coulanges, he explains why he cannot declare his love for Andrée: "In the colonial world Jean Veneuse is a 'dirty nigger' [*sale nègre*], and a 'dirty nigger,' especially if he is in the colonial service, must avoid like the plague marrying a European, if he really loves that European and is loved by her."[13] When all is said and done what does this mean? That one should marry only if one doesn't love and is unloved? Or, as Fanon puts it: "let us not be misled: Jean Veneuse is the man who has to be convinced" (66). That is, it is he who is the obstacle.

He who does not want to be convinced. For, in the fantasy he has of himself, it is he who occupies the place of the phobic signifier, the "sale nègre." Here jouissance emerges as a defense against desiring. Veneuse's love is a love precisely designed to prevent desire from coming to term as a defense against the dark void within, as though the choice between desire and annihilation could only be sustained in relation to the desire of the white other, as though the proof of being desired were tied to the suspense of desiring.

Having "devoured" French colonial culture in the hope of being accepted as *"un homme pareil aux autres, un homme comme les autres,"* Veneuse discovers, instead, a troubling paradox: "the white race would not accept him as one of its own and the black virtually repudiated him." (67). Veneuse is a man, then, who, like Hamlet, is troubled by what he *knows*: unable to be white, no longer black, he finds himself affected by a disjunction, a rupture, that can be neither avowed nor disavowed. This discovery leads to a type of Adlerian *"ressentiment"* and *"agressivité,"* Fanon decides, enjoined to Veneuse's feelings of ambivalence and inferiority— and, once again, part of that "constellation of delirium" defining interracial desire and love (60). Let's say that Jean Veneuse—although he does not know it—is aware of a "that within," which means that he has been exposed to what Fanon calls the affective life of "negrophobogenesis"—or again, the "racial drama" [*drame racial*] played out in the existence of the black where what is revealed is an unconscious desire for whiteness (100, 150).

One could say that Fanon's entire work is taken up with this drama, a drama that confuses-disguises the wishes of the ego with a gulf that is real and profound, but ungraspable. In many ways, Fanon's image of that drama is one that embodies not so much existential anxiety as something like the feeling of being out of joint, "completely dislocated" [*désorienté*] by the phantasm rising between the ego and its others (112). An inner impoverishment that is felt to be both outside the self and inside the self while, simultaneously, a symbol of something foreclosed, forever lost, a loss that goes beyond being or acting. In other words, one of the major impacts of racism is the sense of coming across an intruding double in whose ghostly, enigmatic, and hallucinatory movement the ego undergoes "an amputation, an excision" [*un décollement, un arrachement*] (112). This disarticulation of self by its specular double takes place not only as a corrosive intrusion—Fanon's metaphors are exact here—but, more significantly, as the crumbling away of the self's phenomenological boundaries. The person who experiences this hemorrhaging maybe black, but the "I" acting as witness to the scar is, unexpectedly and bizarrely, white. In moments such as these, the "I" becomes aware that it is an indeterminate presence within the self, a dissemblance that repels blackness as self-image. This decisive separation, which is more visible, and shielded, than that between ego and other, is perhaps why the black is always out of place, unable to recognize himself as a being with *depth*. If to be black is to reenact an impeachment that is self-obliterating, how does one exhume a loss that erases the self as a cadaverous resemblance, and, because of that renunciation, is nothing more? In this sense, nothing appears to be the essence of blackness, nothing defines its drama and role. More, it is only through the presence of such spectral resentment that the black can resemble anything at all.

"The personality of the author does not emerge quite so easily as one might wish," acknowledges Fanon, opening his account of *Un homme pareil aux autres* (64). That wish, to read and interpret *Un homme pareil aux autres* as autobiography, is one endlessly repeated by Maran's critics. Aside from trying to isolate what properly belongs to Maran and his text—Fanon says he wants to put Maran back "into his place, his proper place," the place of a disjointed future and past—such readings tend to address the literature through the lens of Maran's childhood, or, more precisely, the drama of a self haunted by a childhood past (79). According to an anonymous 1923 profile published in *Opportunity*, Maran's fictions were haunted by loss and by memories of loss that were never transcended: "Then his father and an elder brother died and, as a consummation of misfortune, came an unhappy love-affair with a (white) girl who was estranged from him by her family. Maran cannot forget her and he makes her the heroine of many of his books."[14] Hence, what cannot be forgotten is both the loss and the trauma that it represents. Further, it is a scene of mourning, of "Nachträglichkeit," for whatever that gets lost along with the girl: her whiteness, perhaps, but also having to abandon that wished-for part of himself, that demand for recognition which, Fanon argues, forges the connection between black men and white women. What is more, the lost girl becomes a sign or symbol for what Maran is lacking. It is as though in the very heart of his destitution, she returns to him as loss, as something loved insofar as she is loss, allowing him to mourn the being of a whiteness-that-is-lacking. Never lost because never once possessed, she is the lack that defines Maran's solitude and the death that encloses him. It is a double loss, which may partly explain Maran's obsessive, fascinated self-loathing, his sense of being on the margins of his present time. We are left with the impression that Maran's fictions are, to borrow a phrase from Lacan, works of "an inexpiable debt," forever suspended in a time of mourning—a "that within" projected onto the child who suffers by the man who mourns.[15] More accurately, the hour of Maran's drama never arrives—he is always too late—which is why he refuses to act. He is like Hamlet, a man whose will has atrophied because of what he knows. In other words, Maran's fictions result from an obsession with loss and call forth mourning; the fictions are finally unable to fill up the sense of loss that drives them, hence the need to restage the same story of loss again and again. Between memory and loss, fiction emerges, then, as a repeated failure to bind the shattering impact of loss on narcissism and memory. What we are left with is an absence, a gap, making it difficult for readers to assign Maran to his proper place and time. This is a gap that, in the words of Rosenberg, makes Maran's fictions the effect of a "that within" binding them to loss, to what allows loss to be symbolized as a failure of symbolization.

Certainly, what *Un homme pareil aux autres* passes on to its readers is the forlorn image of a black man driven by anguish and loss, an anguish expressed by his desire to both speak his love and his guilty refusal to bring it about (the scene recalls *Hamlet*). Suspended between that refusal and desire, the story inevitably falls prey to lack and absence, one complicated still further by the many diversions, delays, obstacles, and postponements that Maran puts in the way of his lovers' consummation. To emphasize the point, we may say that unfulfillment supports the story's defense against the presence and predictability of loss aroused by the loss of Andrée. In fact, what remains, I believe, most striking about this story of loss and delay is the way in which it turns Veneuse's love for Andrée into an anguish of separation, and one which refigures her loss as a desire for love sustained by its impossibility. To put this another way—and to anticipate Fanon's argument—*Un homme pareil aux autres* tells the story of a man who longs to be redeemed by a whiteness whose threat cannot be borne, a man in love who finds it impossible to be loved, a man terrorized by the pre-Oedipal loss of blackness, yet a man disgusted by black women. *That* man (the remnant of a pre-Oedipal breakdown or *décalage*) can only love the white woman insofar as she embodies the lack-that-remains, the lack that keeps at bay that libidinal lack-in-being represented by blackness.[16] In loving him, she gives him what he does not have, what he lacks in relation to what is lacking in her. Andrée's whiteness allows Veneuse to memorialize feelings of maternal loss by instituting a form of mastery (over himself, over other blacks) that seeks its own undoing in the wish for whiteness. She is the force allowing him to propel the drive away from what is black toward the objects and signs that acknowledge him in his whiteness. At the same time, she also plays the role of absent auditor in Maran's text who, through the exchange of letters, will help to secure a representation of perversity that is inseparable from the experience of writing, and one that sustains the image of a white woman seduced and fascinated (maddened?) by the dramas and drives inhabiting a black man's words.

The striking thing about Fanon's chapter on Maran is that though he recasts Veneuse's neuroses as the syndrome of black abandonment, he also displaces them both psychically and politically. It is the weirdest kind of expulsion that derives from a shared confession of passive morbidity and impotence. "The Man of Color and the White Woman" *doubles* the displacements of *Un homme pareil aux autres*. In both texts, sexual desires for white women are linked to a kind of pathological self-delusion acting out a separation wholly illusory in character. More, as Fanon struggles to work this out via a reading of Maran, he begins to reveal a "that within" similar to Maran's, one that substantially identifies French colonialism with a disavowed interracial family romance in Martinique. In brief, it is through the figure of abandonment that Fanon reflects Maran and is unwittingly shadowed by him.

In "Les conditions intellectuelles et affectives de l'œdipe," first published in 1949, Germaine Guex describes the neuroses of abandonment as "powerful obstacles to the Oedipus [l'œdipe]" (265). Insecure, dominated by the need to be assured of love, the abandonic is, she says, "ever ready to regress to a primitive form of love" in his search for "unity and fusion" (266, 267). The abandonic is a "frustrated Oedipus" [œdipe fruste] whose ego is unable to establish a "positive rivalry" with the "semblable" or "other" (267, 269). These remarks lead Fanon to present Veneuse's neurotic delay in ways differing from the classic Freud-Jones reading of Hamlet's infamous patient impatience. Hamlet's torment, observes Freud in an 1897 letter to Wilhelm Fleiss, is "roused in him by the obscure memory that he himself had meditated the same deed against his father because of passion for his mother."[17] In contrast, Guex's abandonic does not enter onto the stage of such oedipal compromises; he can only express himself as a frustrated Oedipus, as an Oedipus that is lacking.[18] If we look at Fanon's reading of Maran in the light of this, and his writings on Martinique more generally, we see the failure of black sovereignty in Martinique linked to a community of disavowal, and one that reveals an incomplete oedipal resentment or rivalry with French society; we see a black collective psyche *occupied* by a colonial power whose authority has been so internalized that there has been a collective failure to symbolize it—the end result of which is a cultural dependency and an hallucinatory state of being in which blacks fantasize themselves as white, loved insofar as they are white, flushed with the more intense beauty of French values like a reflector capturing the sun.[19]

By analogy, *Un homme pareil aux autres* is in some sense ghosted by what it knows and does not want to know. Once again, it is the white woman who connects the spectacle of this appearing to its withholding. In loving her, Veneuse confirms the blackness he cannot escape and which, because of that, makes her love into an ideal that obliterates (*aufhebung*) the disgrace of the nègre that is his point of departure. Only by disappearing from his position as a desiring subject can he maintain the imaginary possibility of her white love. In common with his wish to protect Andrée from the inevitable scandal that marriage to the *sale nègre* brings, Veneuse's letters to her reveal a debate with himself concerning the meaning of this aporia. Is his love a lust for revenge or a wish for whiteness? In choosing her, is he really any different from those black men driven "to the extreme of denying both their countries and their mothers" (Maran, cited in Fanon, *Black Skin*, 69)? Struggling with the idea of interracial love as a symptom of a more extreme separation from the mother-motherland, Veneuse presents an image of the white woman as an active participant in the black man's anxious relation to separation and loss. There is, it seems, no trace here of Veneuse's sense of Andrée's love as a "gift"—"the gift of yourself you are making to me"—nor any doubt that his sadistic wishes for "the satisfaction of being the master [*dominer*] of a European woman" were his alone, part of a failed attempt to bind the anxiety unleashed by the phobic demands of cultural life (Maran, *Un homme*, 95). In fact, embedded in Veneuse's doubts is the image of the white woman as the privileged source of those demands, as the one driven to revenge herself on the imago of the *sale nègre* by asking for this extreme separation between desire and drive, jouissance and cultural life (141). "At the extreme," Fanon observes, "but it is exactly to the extreme that we have to go" [*A l'extrême . . . mais justement il s'agit d'y aller*] (Fanon, *Black Skin*, 65).

At that extreme we find versions of love and desire in which a white woman is an ambivalent object of fantasy. Veneuse's love for Andrée is a love that dare not avow itself except through the mediation of a prohibition. Fanon glosses this neurotic predicament as follows: "I do not wish to be loved and I will flee from love-objects"—that is, I do not want to be desired and I do not want to desire myself desiring (75). This double movement implies a fear of aphanisis or disappearance of desire that also speaks to the white woman as the symbolization of this cut or loss. But Veneuse's décalage also speaks to how interracial prohibition produces an enigma of desire that is inextricably linked to questions of sovereignty and loss. This is why Maran, in the essay "Manière de Blanc" presents interracial love as "the only pacificator, the only coloniser, the only civilising entity" and the "sole motherland."[20] That is, love and politics not only exchange places and pass for one another in Martinique, but their doubling also confirms a black sacrificial narcissism: desire me not as black, but love me for the whiteness I submit to, that I have lost; the loss whose interment I am.

It is a repressed illusion, Fanon argues, that is the result of a pre-Oedipal inhibition in which action and desire have become impossible. And so Fanon dismisses Veneuse with the phrase: "What a struggle to free himself of a subjective conflict" (70). It would be a mistake, I think, to miss the irony or ambiguity underlying Fanon's dismissal. This response is striking, however, because it appears to ignore the political strangeness of Veneuse's fear that his love for Andrée entails a rejection of his country *and* his mother. It's an occlusion which makes the mother ever more primary for an understanding of Veneuse's "I do not wish to be loved and I will flee from love-objects."

In fact, the figure of an abandoning mother also makes a telling appearance in *Black Skin, White Masks*: "When I am at home, my mother sings me French love songs in which there is never a word about Negroes. When I disobey, when I make too much noise, I am told to 'stop acting like a nigger' [*faire le nègre*]" (191). Here the mother's voice sings in an imaginary French tongue. Hers is a voice that evidently prohibits the young Fanon from acting or speaking nègre. As such, the scenario confirms what Fanon describes elsewhere as the black child's "sacrificial dedication" (*oblativité chargée*) to white racist culture which Martinican family life both demands and performs (147). What does it mean to see myself seen from without, such as I am under the tyrannical presence of what imposes its vision upon me? The affect, in any case, is an encounter with oneself in the mirror of colonial culture in which the being of black is reflected back as symbolically deprived, in which a dark hole in the real is provoked by what is missing from his image, a missing signifier that he cannot pay for except by sacrificing his black flesh and blood. For what first originates from the outside now returns as the repressed fantasy of "that within" which he can only master by submitting to it. And what matters here is that this captivating, alienating, seducing recognition comes from the mother. She is both the source and repository of that loss, the proof of what cannot be articulated at the level of the other, the ghost haunting him, the enigmatic *fantome* that he hears in her voice and in which her desire becomes manifest. She is the punishing source of the recognition that, in so far as he is a nègre, he is an undesired child.

Hence, as a black child threatened with the loss of love, a threat lived out in relation to the mother's voice, Fanon knows why a wish to be avenged poses itself in opposition to her. She is the symbolic mirror, Fanon suggests, in whom he sees his real image signified, with which he identifies himself; it is she who solicits this relationship in which he finds himself caught, and which sees him splintered by the desired whiteness of his castrated being. Or, as Maran writes, imagining Veneuse's imaginary address to a white child: "I love in you the child that I would have wished to have . . . I snatched myself from the gentleness of life that I should not know, because I was forbidden by my ugly black face [*vilain visage noir*], completely black, and because he who, knowingly prepares for himself the useless bitterness of future regrets, is to blame" (Maran, *Un homme*, 84–85). This is a perilous and humiliating wish, a wish both to be and to have a white child insofar as one is not it and can never be it, and one that finds the mother to be the source and memory of the failure to transcend the persecutory blackness that forbids it.[21]

Here it is the mother, and not the father, who returns as the ghost haunting the pre-Oedipal insecurities of her child. Or, what Fanon discovers, finally, is the mournful affect of her separation: hers is a loss unable to be borne, a narcissistic loss that, in turn, shadows the gaps or faults posed by the loving-hateful demands of French colonial culture. The lesson she passes on, in other words, is that the unseen is always returned and that its enigmatic form is a "that within" irreconcilable to the self. What brings the "that within" into focus, what makes it visible as a remnant, is the black child's wish to play his part so as to secure his mother's love. This is the servitude of his mastery. Here, the little black boy's first experiences of mastery are undone by the mother acting as the representative of that other mother, la Mère-Patrie.

Let us note the drama of this moment in Maran's narrative. It may be said that the entire narrative of Un homme pareil aux autres, like Hamlet, comes in response to a question to the mother, to the memory of her loss. Addressing himself to what he calls, following Guex, Veneuse's "affective self-rejection," Fanon is sensitive to this image of an adult self in mourning for the condensed-displaced figure of the child to be found there. But what is it, precisely, that Veneuse is lacking? A failed object relation to the mother, Fanon maintains. He argues that Veneuse's angry, mournful separation from Andrée is the acting out of earlier childhood scenarios, and these repetitions—the fantasies and impulses they express—echo Veneuse's melancholy attempts to find some kind of restitution for his mother's desertion. On this reading, then, her specter haunts "the whole symptomatology of this neurosis" (Maran, cited in Fanon, Black Skin, 73). Guex argues that that traumatic separation "paralyzes [the abandonic's] enthusiasm for living" and opens up a gap or "secret zone, which he cultivates and defends against every intrusion" (Guex, "Les conditions," 276). Fanon restates that view in the course of his discussion of Veneuse's compromise fantasy: "I do not wish to be loved and I will flee from love-objects," which he regards as an attempt to ward off the suffering that accompanies the fantasy of abandonment (Fanon, Black Skin, 75).

In other words, racialized oedipal aggression is a belated reaction to "that within" for Fanon and for Maran. And yet Fanon writes: "I contend that Jean Veneuse represents not an example of black-white relations,

but a certain mode of behavior in a neurotic who by coincidence is black"
(78). "Where does this analysis lead us?" he asks. "To nothing short of
proving to Jean Veneuse that in fact he is not like the rest [*il n'est pas pareil
aux autres*]," that he is, in short, (not) like me (79, 78). We are left with the
impression that Veneuse's morbid state of mind remains a symptom of a
pre-Oedipal crisis, provoked by Andrée, who is an echo, of someone or
something, which dies away through the pages of *Un homme pareil aux
autres* to become the problem, or puzzle, of the book. Accordingly, *Un
homme pareil aux autres* is merely the echo of maternal loss and abandonment, an echo that Fanon summons through the image of his own abandoning, an echo that leads him to see Veneuse's wish not to be seen as a
nègre as a restaging of his own pre-Oedipal loss. That reading presents
Veneuse's relation to loss (the loss of a fantasized whiteness) as the symptom of a prior catastrophe and Maran's fiction as a defense against the pre-
Oedipal mother experienced as missing or absent.

But if, as Fanon also suggests here, racism is a "coincidence" to
Veneuse's neuroses, why does the novel insist that race and loss are closely
bound to the way in which he, Veneuse, associates "that within" with the
insecure being of the black? Assuming that, along with Fanon, what is
hidden in Maran's text is how the question of "that within," as memory
and fantasy, comes to trouble Veneuse's claims to a self, we still need to
understand how the experience of racism in the novel seems to be uncom-
fortably like the experience of watching a distraught and anxious child
haunted by isolation and the loss of love.

Immediately after his reconciliation with Andrée at the novel's close,
Veneuse says, "From now on you will know that Negroes are men like any
others [*des hommes comme les autres*] and that perhaps they suffer more than
others, because, when they have the painful good fortune [*l'affligeant
bonheur*] to love a European woman, they can feel bearing down upon
them such reprobation that they really are ashamed to confess or show
their suffering" (Maran, *Un homme*, 248). Painful good fortune? By contrast, when it comes to loving a black woman, Maran can only show

incomprehension: "I am a delicate person, a dreamer, a sentimentalist," he confesses. "I can therefore never understand nor love the indigenous woman, an inert and simple receptacle of disenchanted passion [*spasmes désenchantés*]" (108). How does one tell the difference between white and black women? The former offers dream, sentiment and love as opposed to a receptacle cast as void because it can be repeatedly possessed, again and again. You only have to ask, Maran suggests; "There is never a refusal" (139). The image conjured up is one of hostile and idealized dependence, a splitting that, predictably, takes us back to the black boy forbidden to identify with *les nègres* because of a white ego ideal. In Maran's view, there can be no question of loving the black woman because, being simple and inert, she signifies the absence of passion as well as its satiated surplus or obscene excess. Her sole purpose is to satisfy lust. In her lack of inhibitions and restrictions the debt Veneuse owes to castration cannot be requited. She is life without sentiment, need without desire. In her there is none of that difference driving desire to desire itself in the other. Hers is a presence that will always remain blind to his secretly perverse wish to be his mother's white child. This is why, for Maran, the white woman is a symbol of a desire and the black woman a symbol of sex, body, stench, and dirt, and why both, ultimately, will never be enough for the black who wants to have the phallus (rather than just be it). Hence, Veneuse's desire for the white woman is not really a desire for whiteness but rather for the presence of that object (white phallus) whose absence both she and he designate and want. "I am loved like a white man. I am a white man," Fanon writes, giving the lie to his (feigned) distinction between a neurotic who happens to be black and black neurosis (Fanon, *Black Skin*, 63). This wish both to have and to be the phallus, to be revenged, can one call it love?

———

I began this chapter by saying that *Black Skin, White Masks* was formed around a fantasy of the white woman whose meaning and connection derive from a reading of *Hamlet*. I also said "that within" refers to an existential crisis of desire and recognition that forecloses Hegelian dialectics. In this final section I want to take up again these remarks. More accurately, I want to show how "that within"—that traumatic fissure between being and existence—plays out the spectral histories of race as understood by Fanon. Why is "that within," defined as a traumatic absence as well as an ethics of ressentiment, so important to Fanon's work on the affective disorders of colonial racism? And why does he turn to Hegel to investigate the possibility of a love and an ethics opposed to the drama of misrecognition that ensues in the colony?

Bearing these remarks in mind, it is worth repeating that "that within" refers to something not yet completed, a delayed trace of a loss expressed in the form of an indebtedness within the subject which is not the mark of a repression but of a haunting. What haunts are not the dead, but the gaps left within us by the desires of others. Indeed, "that within" is an exemplary figure of the effect of being haunted by what remains inexpressible or enigmatic in the Other's speech. As a point of attachment marking the desire of the subject and transforming the ego, "that within" is where the self encounters the desire of the other as an enigmatic, even unfathomable message—this something from which the subject finds himself separated but which he sustains insofar as he desires. There is no doubt "that within" is where oedipal desire is experienced as a profound abandoning. The interment of "that within" in the ego points to a décalage that is the effect of a phantomatic haunting; it also points to a loss, unavowed, in which the shadow of the lost object falls on the ego; in which the "I," now mortified and forsaken, is fantasized as the lost object's own.

Now all this requires detailed exposition: let us go back to the opening sentences of "The Man of Color and the White Woman":

Out of the blackest part of my soul, across the zebra striping of my mind, surges this desire to be suddenly *white*. I wish to be acknowledged not as *Black* but as *White*. Now—and this is a form of recognition that Hegel had not envisaged [*décrite*]—who but a white

woman can do this for me? By loving me she proves that I am worthy
of white love. I am loved like a white man. I am a white man. Her loves
takes me onto the royal road that leads to total realization. (Fanon,
Black Skin, 63)

Why is it that the love of the white woman brings (mis)recognition into
representation by acting as the ruination, or interdiction, of Hegelian
dialectics? What kind of love is this that allows Fanon to reinvent the
political and affective life of blackness as the object of a perennially
excluded and so fantasized desire for recognition? And, if it is love, why
does it only appear via an identificatory disappearance of the black? The
naming of Hegel is crucial here. Elsewhere in *Black Skin, White Masks*
Fanon shows how colonial racism detracts from Hegel's master-slave
dialectic and Sartre's Kojevian reworking of it in *Being and Nothingness* and
"Orphée Noir." In "The Negro and Hegel," Fanon shows how colonialism
depends not on reciprocal recognition but on force, on a violent state of
exception where the colonized are neither citizens nor subjects but the
absolute enemy. This absolute hostility between colonizer and colonized is
not only disjunctive of the Hegelian pact between the lord and bondsman;
it also immerses the colonized in a destitution that dethrones the ego and
substitutes an imaginary Other in place of the autonomous, bounded,
separated, individual self. First, contrary to Hegel, the slave "abandons the
object" and the promise of self-certainty offered by work in pursuit of a
desire to be "like the master"; second, the being and politics of this identity stakes itself on an incorporation in which the master remains both origin and end (Fanon, *Black Skin*, 221). What Fanon foregrounds here is an
identity founded on the social and political consequences of a being
denied recognition and whose outcome is the internalization of black epidermal inferiority. Unlike the Hegelian slave, who is able to overcome his
fear of the absolute master—death—and the relative master—the lord, by
risking his life and working: the identity of the colonized reflects a being
that is no more than the fantasy of being reflected, a being whose
drive to be similar remains the sign of a "slavish work" that has lost its

relation to desire, work, and otherness precisely because it refuses the risks and difficulties of freedom (219). If mimesis is the locus, or the process of identification, the desire to be like the master is not an identity but the mimesis of a misrecognition fundamental to the being of the black. In his own desire to be recognized not as black but as white, what Fanon exposes is how this fantasy of the political in the Antilles, this sovereignty in crisis, leads, at the level of affect, to a withdrawal or untying of black identity as black. Far from being the envisioning of a liberated black identity, Fanon presents this desire for recognition as the place of a passivity which has nothing dialectical, nor ontological, about it: this is an identity that excludes itself from what it encloses, formed by the whiteness that surges from within the excluded interiority of the blackness that encrypts it. The black self, according to this instinctual fatality, cannot symbolize itself as a representable loss, but mortgages itself to those "mass attacks against the ego" taking place along the inner and outer frontiers of colonial domination and the subject's corporeal schema.[22] The ethics of recognition and reciprocity insisted on at the conclusion to *Black Skin, White Masks* here gives way to radically neurotic forms of dissociation as Fanon's case studies of "affective erethism" in the Antilles all too readily reveal. As such, they must be contrasted to the 1954–1959 studies of reactionary psychoses set down in "Colonial War and Mental Disorders," the concluding chapter of *Wretched of the Earth*. It is that early focus on the impotence and futility arising from unmourned loss, on the bitter resentments, collusions, and denials of "that within," that concerns me here.

And it is from this standpoint that we can repose Fanon's relation to Hegel and whiteness. In his search for an ethics of recognition—for an ethics, that is, mirroring the vicissitudes of black lived experience—Fanon both resists and reinvents the French postwar rereading of Hegel. What is revealed in *Black Skin, White Masks* is an inner contradiction or aporia in the black that puts into question the self-perficient outcome of Hegel's master-slave dialectic as the foundation of independent self-consciousness and community. For, in the absence of any reciprocity in the colonial relation, the freedom to "assume the attitude of the master" or to eat at his table does not change the systematic actualities of power and domination, nor does it offer blacks a genuinely critical relationship to the metaphysical politics of race (Fanon, *Black Skin*, 219). Instead of producing work, Fanon argues that the Antillean is stuck in a ressentiment that nurtures the unease of a "defect" and an "impurity" that "interdicts all ontological explication," including Hegel's (110). As a result, desire remains aberrated as a dialectical movement. The urgency and currency of Fanon's search for a way out of this existential impasse is what drives his argument with Sartre over the latter's totalizing invocation of negritude as immanently and necessarily self-dissolving. Sartre's *Orphée Noir*, for example, provokes opposition because it makes that experience into a foregone conclusion without any contingency.[23] In his chapter on "The Lived Experience of the Black," Fanon shows why Sartre's discussion of negritude effectively obscures the affect of "that within" in ways which repeat the modern diremption of race and dialectics, black civic life, and colonial sovereignty.

Again, it is the trauma of separation or abandonment motivating Fanon to contest Hegelian dialectics. Fanon says that Sartre has forgotten what the lived experience of the body is; that is, "that the Negro suffers in his body quite differently from the white man," that the black body is not a narcissistic unity that is then alienated from without, but a body that comes into being only insofar as it is driven to encrypt the traumatizing exteriority of the whiteness that inscribes it (134). Certainly, this scenario implies a whiteness already there motivating the black man's wish for love and revenge and one supporting the fantasy of an internally excluded, and so disavowed, whiteness. Very quickly, the desire to be loved becomes part of a wish to make the black body disappear—just as the claim to whiteness comes out of the soul's blackest depths. Does this mean that the black can only be loved insofar as he renounces the desire to be black? In fact, embedded in this scenario are the effects of an unconscious, if latent, masochism inseparably bound up with the workings of a sadistic fantasy. The root of that fantasy is, above all, sacrificial: it speaks to the reapparition of an anxiety-producing imago inside the self, one in whose fantasized scenes the black is both masochistic and vengeful. The black man, writes Fanon, has to obtain revenge for "the *imago* that had always obsessed him: the frightened, trembling Negro, abased before the white overlord [*le seigneur blanc*]" (74). What is at stake in this identification is the racial constitution, then, of the superego, or the black's affective identification with the white overlord, which points to an expulsion (of blackness) that is also a devouring (of whiteness).

And it is at this point that Fanon invokes the love of a white woman as the road to realization: as a phantomatic figure she mirrors the insubstantiality of black self-renunciation. In brief, what Fanon discovers in his reading of *Un homme pareil aux autres* is a counsel of morbid interdiction reminiscent of *Hamlet*. One could say that "The Man of Color and the White Woman" provides an image of "that within" as a permanently depressive state of exception. In Fanon's reading, what is revealed is an ego ever dismal and depressed, submerged by an interminable desire for white appeasement. It is in relation to that alienation that Fanon resituates his commitment to authentic love as a non-dialectical struggle for recognition. Somewhat bizarrely, this is a love mediated by an ethics of transcendence preoccupied with the white other residing in one's inmost depths. Above all, it is the sacrifice of the self to the other as self-relation, which makes love ethical and which brings to an end the calamitous ruins of self-deception. It is this ethical idea of love as the incorporated possibility of a subject without "selfness," as the difficult task of being able to express and work through the intrapsychical inheritance of "that within," that further distinguishes Fanon from Sartre. In *The Transcendence of the Ego,* written the same year as *L'Imaginaire* (1936), Sartre, in opposition to Husserl's concept of a transcendental ego, says that a pure transparence of being can only appear irrepresentable to the subject; that "there is no *I*" outside of the intentionality of a reflective consciousness; nevertheless, there is consciousness without a subject; a consciousness that acts out a role immanent to every possession of a self.[24] It's an insight that admits consciousness itself is an enigma since there is something in it that escapes reflection, something impersonal that recalls the inquietude of Hamlet's "that within." But what is this other scene of the subject whose absent cause is obscured-disguised by the ego and confounds consciousness with egoic loss? Sartre's refusal of the unconscious is no answer here since the scandal of a cogito experienced as unknowable clearly persists: To say of reflection that it simply illumines a prereflective consciousness makes consciousness itself opaque, inscribed by an immanent "ipseity." This dissociative relation does not express a transcendental condition so much as an impersonal and hallucinated ego—that is, a transcendence which is not the contrary of existence or immanence, but which, beyond the ego, appears enigmatic, both mask and veil. Once this dissociation has happened, and even before it happens, the ego is abandoned, and this abandonment, by signifying the impossibility of the I's return to an original transparence, frees the subject-as-actor from having to experience the solidity and opacity of the other's weight; now he is free to choose himself via the absolute clarity of a deed that remains his forever. But the price of that liberation is a self that has "emptied itself of me," to borrow Roquentin's phrase from *Nausea*.

For Sartre, then, the subject is nothing more than the incarnated immanence of its being affected, but this being-affected is the source of acute existential anxiety about the existence of others and the solidity of the cogito. "In my own inmost depths I must find not *reasons for believing* that the Other exists but the Other himself as not being me," he writes.[25] It's a discovery that came to Sartre early. In his autobiography, *Les Mots*, for example, Sartre holds up a mirror to a childhood spent haunted by feelings of nonexistence: "I was *nothing*: an ineffaceable transparency," he writes, defining an existence marked by the acting out of phantoms, personations traced to the early death of his father: "A father would have weighted me with a certain stable obstinacy," Sartre confesses, revealing the connection between his father's absence and his own absence of being.[26] The son cannot do without the solidity that the father gives, since as a phantom he remains tied to an unhappy lightness of being. But since he is a phantom he is fated to encounter the father's heaviness as an enigma; and Sartre goes onto say that his feelings of having an ego with no weight or center, of being possessed by the imaginary, are the consequence of having grown up under the weakened oedipal shadow of a dead father.[27] It is almost as if having died literally, rather than symbolically, the phantasmatic pressures of paternity become less threatening as paternal law, but more worrying as a superegoic surplus policing identity. Here, what begins as an expression of genealogy and filiation returns as a question of spectrality and being, as the enigmatic nature of "that within" becomes linked to an absence that makes it even lighter, stripping the "I"/ego of its density and fullness. What the son's irreality reveals is what appears when—in the words of J. B. Pontalis—"an absolute coincidence with oneself is impossible" and "we are consequently all *actors*" forced to deprive and renounce ourselves but nevertheless maintaining those deprivations as our own.[28]

It is no surprise therefore that Fanon sees in Sartre an idea of self-sovereignty mingling anxiety and paranoia in which the ego first appears, or is made to appear, like a crumpled photograph, which is to say, the projected surface of a destructured form. No surprise, too, that he should characterize the idea of transcendence in Sartre as "haunted," which is to say, the ego emerges here as the doubling affect of an incorporation that encrypts it by emptying it of itself (Fanon, *Black Skin*, 8).[29] No surprise, finally, that Sartre, in his reading of *Hamlet*, should resist this relation of the inchoate subject to its own ego as the experience of being penetrated, and suddenly abandoned by, "a transcendence other than my own."[30] In *L'Imaginaire*, for example, first published in 1940, Sartre writes: "It is not that the character [Hamlet] is *realized* in the actor, but that the actor is *irrealized* in the character."[31] Certainly the actor who is Hamlet knows what it means to be "publicly devoured by the imaginary," to express emotions "fictitiously"; where the irreal is not *"failing to feel*, but deliberately deceiving oneself about the meaning of what is being felt"; where the act, which had been wedded to the real, becomes "a kind of intangible ghost . . . enveloped in the gesture," and having been ossified in gesture, becomes part of the actor's sacrifice to "the existence of an appearance," the

"Hamlet of unreality."[32] This is why the actor trying to lose himself (and to lose himself as an actor) in the part of Hamlet has to "offer *his being* to Hamlet," but with no reciprocity, for Hamlet *is not* the actor; all the actor Hamlet can do is mime "that within" possessing him (Sartre, *The Imaginary*, 191). This is why when the actor playing Hamlet is alone, in the theater, he is not really alone, for he can only return to who he is in the form of the other whom he resembles. The trace of the other is there, when the actor withdraws from himself. The fact of being alone is that he belongs to this "that within" who is not himself, nor anyone else. "*He lives entirely in an irreal world,*" Sartre concludes; in the irreal world there is no one there, but "that within" is there: "that within" as what anticipates, precedes, dissolves all possibility of Hamlet's authentic relationship to himself and the audience (191).

The inquietude of "that within" would seem, then, to reflect the permanent elusiveness of any transformatory relation to the world, a loss that dispossesses and humiliates me (the image recalls *Un homme pareil aux autres*, where desire is the consecration of the ruin that desire makes and the ego is fantasized as the trace or preservative repression of the Other's desiring). And yet, for Sartre, that irreal me is always at a remove from existence, which is why only the act can rejoin the self to experience; only praxis can precipitate the "I" into the "there is." This is also why, if agency is to begin, the subject must negate the imaginary of "that within" and its deceptions if s/he is to experience the political responsibility of freedom. But how is one to effect this movement given that, for Sartre, recognition is invariably thematized as various forms of submission to the Other's gaze whose actuality remains an ungraspable, hallucinatory remnant? Like Hamlet, in other words, Sartre ends with a notion of the deed as both impossible and necessary, in whose staging the subject is both pierced through and overwhelmed, unable to achieve oneness with his dramatic role.

By way of contrast, in his reading of *Un homme pareil aux autres* Fanon addresses the issues and dilemmas of an inability to act marked by an immeasurable, immemorial absence that is neither transcendent nor immanent. For Fanon, the ego emerges via the inaugural movement of a misrecognition that is unconscious rather than a transcendental or immanent structure of consciousness. The black bears the burden of an identification with whiteness which, because of cultural imposition, threatens to rob him of the ability to desire as such. Yet, *Un homme pareil aux autres* presents this dilemma as one of aphanisis: the desire of the other can only be enjoyed in the absence of desire itself which, once again, causes the black to deny himself. Here blackness comes to symbolize the unrelieved mourning of what remains a loveless refusal of love, the remains of which can be neither projected nor disowned. In the novel's endless estuarial mingling of nihilism and loss, what we see dramatized is the emotional and political link between a wish to be loved and the violent misrecognitions of racism.

Now, the fantasy of revenge and the carrying out of murderous pre-Oedipal wishes uncovered in "The Man of Color and the White Woman" (very precisely defined as a rejection that takes the form of an unmourned loss), is always foregrounded as an ethics of recognition that is not dialectical. This is why the recognition offered by the white woman is employed as a critique of Sartre and Hegel. In this reading, the alluring, always appealing fantasy of the white woman is, as Fanon discovers in various stories by black men, invariably a source of longing that is both hysterical and interminable. This is why sexual relations with her are typically described as vengeful, confounded, phantasmatic. Throughout *Black Skin, White Masks*, Fanon shows himself to be an acute reader of such scenes as he passes from the works of Chester Himes and Richard Wright to those of Paul Morand and Boris Vian. What basically emerges is a desolate, perverse image of love in which sex and desire are constrained by myths and longings in which "authentic love" recedes. If "authentic love" is a love freed from "unconscious conflicts" [what could this possibly mean?], it soon becomes clear that inauthentic, or perverse, love is one assaulted from within by masochist fantasies (Fanon, *Black Skin*, 41). In fact,

embedded in Fanon's dialectic of love, recognition, and desire is the sexual
stereotype of the black man haunted by the effects of internal and external
prohibitions and decrees, displaced onto the typically "'maddening'
blonde." Prohibitions and decrees which are revealed in the following
"anecdote":

> Some thirty years ago, a coal-black Negro, in a Paris bed with a "mad-
> dening" blonde, shouted at the moment of orgasm, "Hurrah for
> Schoelcher!" When one recalls that it was Victor Schoelcher who per-
> suaded the Third Republic to adopt the decree abolishing slavery, one
> understands why it is necessary to elaborate somewhat on the possible
> aspects of relations between black men and white women." (63)

This is a strange scene. From first to last, is there not something rotten in
the way that the black man comes, in the way that he is compelled to come
haunted by an entombed ideal? Similarly, why is his coming bound to the
phantasmatic apparition of Victor Schoelcher? At first glance, what suddenly looms up, at the moment of orgasm, is not the black penis but the
apparition of the white man as, perversely, the Father-Protector of the
black man whom he has freed to love white women. It is as if it is not
the black man's fulfillment of his desire that is at stake, but the desire of
the phantom. The idea that the white liberator-father is there, and agitating, at the very inside of the black man's desire for recognition conjures up
a powerfully perverse fantasy at the heart of this scenario. As fantasy, it
also quite clearly exhibits the oedipal dimension of what is otherwise
concealed by the maddening blonde. Hurrah for Schoelcher? What does
this imago, this specter, have to do with that earlier wish for whiteness and
its inverse, the apparently sadistic wish to seduce and so punish the white
woman? Why does the imago of "le seigneur blanc" return at this most
passionate time? And why, at the moment of orgasm, is the black man
inhabited, that is, haunted, by a specter of liberation-enslavement? This
is, perhaps, a mythical narrative, but one which sustains an image of
black desire as host to the violent unfreedoms of culture, as host to the

pleasures, the unconscious pleasures, of masochism. What the black man finds—or conjures up—at the point of orgasm is an unconscious which, it seems, is doubly displaced by Victor Schoelcher, a white man forever associated with slavery and, inversely, its lynching-castration scenes of fear, desire, retribution, and punishment. In other words, it is his apparition—the law-making violence he represents—that supports the black man's discovery of, and wish for, recognition from a white woman who, it seems, is beside herself. But with what—with pleasure, fear, or the fearful pleasures of abandonment? Twice displaced—as object of longing and as source of anxiety—she gives way before the imposing, mythic image of Schoelcher, the father who redeems but also the father who potentially cuts and tears away.

In so doing, the anecdote leaves open the issue of whether, in this little coup de théâtre, the black man's battle for recognition can ever separate itself from the legitimizing violence represented here by the intruding phantasm of the dead white father. His is the law and the violence that condemns the black man to a kind of vulnerable singularity, a kind of spectatorial sadomasochism in which he is both voyeur and performer. (Is this what it means to be loved like a white man?) It is that ideological, fetishistic image that looms up in the story's stereotype of the blonde made more than a little mad (put out of joint) by the terrible, violating thrusts of the black penis. While it could be said that the story privileges the black man's fears of castration—fears that bind his unconscious wish for whiteness to the white man-as-enslaver-liberator—the story also brings together the different representations of the white woman as object of both anxiety and phobia, desire and wish. Naked and abed, what they give each other is precisely the promise of the other as promise, and one that opens up an access to guilt, lust, fear, and vengeance, but also love, recognition, freedom, and gift. That is, the guilty freedom he feels in fucking her is more than matched by what she symbolizes: a just future to come where being black is no longer acting, where being black is an expenditure without loss. (At the same time, her phantasmatic role also puts into production the dramatic disturbance between patrilineal law as sanction and patrilineal law as violence.) This is love as disjuncture, an all-and-nothing love, a love enjoyed precisely because it is haunted by censure and misunderstanding. Nonetheless, what rears up in this tableau, lifting its death's head, is not only the "black sword," but the ghost of the dead white father made all the more powerful for being dead (Fanon, *Black Skin*, 169).

This is a typical, ever-persistent social fantasy that, says Fanon, has "survive[d] through the years" and one which "renews a conflict that, active or dormant, is always real" (64). Certainly it is a scene that plays itself out in the act of writing *Black Skin, White Masks*. Dictating the book to his white wife, Josie (the scene recalls Veneuse and Andrée), Fanon addresses her with his words—the words that, once again, render into writing the perverse eroticism of the negrophobic couple. And those words—the vengeful, persecutory delusions they express—are being heard and transcribed by Josie, who performs the role of witness and accomplice to practices that she can only suffer and condemn. We are left with the impression that the writing of *Black Skin, White Masks* performs part of that struggle for recognition, that wish to be loved, driving the black man. And, once again, that scene is marked by a secret "that within" projected onto the white woman through Fanon's words, part of his restless preoccupation with interracial passion and sex. It is a strange and ambiguous scene of analysis and interpretation, of interracial transference. What we as readers cannot see or hear, what must here be excluded, are the nuances conveyed by tones of voice, the beloved's (the patient's) look, the whiteness of her body. It is therefore no surprise that narrative accounts of interracial sex play such a complex role in *Black Skin, White Masks*. Whether as alienation and engagement, force for psychic and political change or testimony to the affects of racial hatred and/or desire, those narratives are one of the masks to which Fanon returns in order to question and unveil the political and unconscious life of racism (88). It is no surprise that he restates that concern in the course of his discussion of Maran's *Un homme pareil aux autres*, a story that interests him for what it reveals about the attitude of the black man toward the white woman, an attitude and story that has some very powerful things to say about the black man's experience of his manufactured role. It's a role that is elaborate and perfectly imagined, and one that transfigures self-certainty into an envy for self-obliteration. This is why the black is always the perfect actor—acting evokes the impropriety of an "I" detached from the ego's transcendence, a work beyond the person who produced it, an acting out done solely for the purpose of being nothing-but-similar. An acting out in which the other self-related in identity becomes the mask of the ego; an ego that is forsaken and unavowed and the "eternal victim of an essence, of an *appearance [apparaître]* for which he is not responsible" (27). It's a wish to be recognized insofar as one relinquishes any ontology of recognition, a wish to freely remain within the order of representations as the traumatized remains of what remains unrepresentable; and a wish to have the mask so fitted its like wearing a dead person's face. It is through this experience of being-with the dead—one ought to say of the dead within—that Fanon invokes a black sacrificial politics equally condemned by the dead who return and the dead whose shame and distress lingers on within the sovereign authority of the ego: Hamlet's essence always and always the ghost, having no other life than that of the return.

Envoi: The Two Scenes of Abandonment

One makes love to a shadow.

—Frantz Fanon, cited in Juminer, "Hommages à Frantz Fanon" (1962)

One cannot strike the phallus, because the phallus, even the real phallus, is a ghost.

—Jacques Lacan, "Desire and the Interpretation of Desire in *Hamlet*" (1982)

To put all this another way, there is, I think, another figure, aside from Hamlet, haunting Fanon's discussion of loss and Negrophobia in *Black*

Skin, White Masks, a figure irreversibly bound to the dream of pre-Oedipal bliss, but someone driven to turn away from the abyssal depths, "the vast black abyss" [*trou* meaning hole or burial] of the pre-oedipal black-white mother (Fanon, *Black Skin*, 14). That figure is the pining, hate-filled black child whose guilt and anxiety, however disguised, can only restore what he has lost through a confounding repetition. In other words, in refinding the loved object lost he ends up losing himself: he refinds himself as a being-in-mourning. In *Black Skin, White Masks*, the name of that child is, broadly speaking, Orpheus. The following two scenes illustrate, I think, why he remains such a key figure in Fanon's writing on the unconscious vicissitudes of "turn white or disappear" in the black abandonic and his ruinous relationship to "that within" (100).

Scene 1. In *Orphée noir*, Sartre writes: "Since this Eurydice will disappear in smoke if Black Orpheus turns around to look back on her, he will descend the royal road of his soul with his back turned on the bottom of the grotto; he will descend below words and meanings . . . with his back turned and his eyes closed, in order finally to touch with his feet the black water of dreams and desire and to let himself drown in it."[33] A translator's note suggests: "Sartre seems to have confused his images here, since Orpheus was instructed not to look back while he was ascending from Hades, after he had retrieved Eurydice from Plato [*sic*]" (Sartre, "Orphée noir," 140). I do not think this is a confused image despite its metaphor of black creativity as some kind of wished-for burial. For Sartre, the meaning of the myth does not lie in ascent followed by loss but in descent followed by gain. As Orpheus drowns, engulfed by surges of dreams and desire, he assumes a new form and humanity, his "new suns" in consort with a "perpetual surpassing" (127). From burial and exile the fiery vision of his "négritude-object" appears on the horizon of a new dawn (128). As we look back at Sartre's vision of a black "chemin royal," whose ending involves a kind of transfiguring union, we see that, in a sense, Eurydice is not as important for this fusion with the loved object as the journey itself. It is not Eurydice that Black Orpheus wants to look on but the black water of dreams and desire in which he drowns and is reborn. For Sartre the myth reveals an Orpheus bound to the compensations of narcissism, transfigured by a "torrid obsession" rather than by failure or sacrifice—the endless abyss of black negation in which consciousness ebbs away, enclosed in a tight circle that smothers. Here, once again, the Black appears as the remnant of a search for lost unity and, in his search for that lost unity, all sustained efforts to restore the loss, to be loved, to return to the mother as source, take him back to those deep, pre-Oedipal attachments of the abandonic. Black Orpheus's outward journey therefore charts a descent whose essence is a return; it is a journey in which he surrenders his fears of "insecurity and its terrors" as he draws closer to the Source (Guex, "Les conditions," 276). Fanon accedes to Sartre's vision of black expiation and rebirth—the black man "must die to white culture in order to be reborn with a black soul [*l'âme noire*]"—but his approaches to this expiation and rebirth are profoundly different (Sartre, "Orphée Noir," 125).

Scene 2. For Fanon, Black Orpheus is the one who descends into the depths of himself to look for a White Eurydice. The illusion and promise of her daylight is what compels him. He will not discover that her promise is illusionary, dream-filled, until after he has lost her. But in losing her he also loses himself, that is, the promise of himself that was, the becoming intimacy with whiteness that he craves, that allows him to forget himself as black, that makes the essential night of his essence disappear. Without that promise, which he pursues for his own sake, he must then confront the law of the vicious circle—neither white nor black but something in between, inessential. In other words, where Sartre sees the revolutionary rediscovery of black desire and dream, Fanon sees an Orpheus blinded by Eurydice, dazzled by her white-black reflection: her absence completes the inner absence of himself. As Orpheus looks back on the ruins of his longing he cannot repossess it in the way Sartre suggests negritude's "absolute" poetry repossesses the word. Instead, it must be endlessly suffered and endured and tarried with. This is not a search for unity and fusion but a search for renunciation. This is why Fanon writes, "But, when one has taken it into one's head to try to express existence, one runs the risk of finding only the nonexistent [*l'inexistant*]" (Fanon, *Black Skin*, 137). This is also why he states: "I defined myself as an absolute tension of opening" (138; translation modified). This tension cannot be sublated or surpassed, for its creative force is the achievement of negation, an absolute opening to the future *and* the past that is neither white nor black but beyond the Manichean. Hence, Black Orpheus must resist the dazzling lure of whiteness if he is to rediscover that tension of opening within himself. This is, I think, to move beyond what Fanon means by "régressive" analysis, the ability to retrace one's steps, to look back, to reclaim or revendicate what was lost only because never had. Only by returning to himself can he be finally free of himself, free of the self enclosed by the gaze and authority of whiteness. Only by venturing forth into the paths of differentiation can Black Orpheus overcome the insecurities of the abandonic. In short, in Fanon's retelling, it is not Eurydice who disappears after having been set free by the gaze, but Orpheus. But who, then, is abandoning whom? To make Orpheus expose his inner emptiness, to make him open up completely to his nothingness, realize his own unreality by plunging ever deeper into his empty depths—this is one of the tasks undertaken by Fanon in *Black Skin, White Masks*. It is through his powerful unveiling of the power of the negative, both within and outside himself, that Fanon is able to resist the entrapments and lures of Eurydice in defiance of *Orphée noir* and, ultimately, in defiance of that within his innermost self.

3   *"The Derived Life of Fiction"*

RACE, CHILDHOOD, AND CULTURE

It is part of the essence of action to be veiled in illusion.
—Friedrich Nietzsche, *The Birth of Tragedy* (1956)

The derived is never as perfect as the original.
—Søren Kierkegaard, *The Concept of Dread* (1957)

In 1955, the psychiatrist Frederic Wertham published the second of his two key works on the topics of childhood, culture, and crime: *Seduction of the Innocent*. Wertham's well-known (for some, infamous) study of the effects of children's comic books echoes the themes and preoccupations of his previous work, *Dark Legend*, first published in 1941. Taking as his starting point the psychopathology of the everyday life of the child, in both works Wertham brought the violence of the juvenile delinquent into contact with what, in *Dark Legend*, he describes as "the derived life of fiction"—the life which fiction borrows from the deeds, and fantasies, of its readers.[1] At stake, for Wertham, are the connections between reading and acting, wishing and doing, the violence of fantasy and the violence of culture. "Why does our civilization give to the child not its best but its worst," he wonders in *Seduction of the Innocent*, reflecting on the apparent pervasiveness—"on paper, in language, in art, in ideas"—of the *"über,"* or "super," in the forms of representation available to the American child: "supermen, superwomen, super-lovers, super-boys, super-girls, super-ducks, super-mice, super-magicians, super-safecrackers." The repetition, or hyperbole, strikes the note of Wertham's anxiety, his uncomfortable sense that there is something perverse in, *introduced into*, the child. "How," he concludes, "did Nietzsche get into the nursery?"[2]

It's a question which runs throughout Wertham's career as psychiatrist and writer—and one which sustains his remarkable collaboration with the black American novelist Richard Wright. That collaboration is central to this chapter, its exploration of how the idea of fiction and, or in, childhood structures the intellectual exchange between Wertham and Wright; more specifically, their shared preoccupation with the vicissitudes of fiction and therapy, race and crime—Wertham's "derived life." In their different ways, both Wertham and Wright struggle with that life. From 1941, following the publication of Wertham's *Dark Legend*, they struggled together to explore how literature could contribute to a political and therapeutic understanding of the psychopathology of the delinquent child and youth and, in particular, the mythic-hyperbolic image of the black in American culture. To anticipate the argument of this chapter, what Wertham and Wright uncover—through psychiatry, through literature—is a type of fusion between the murderousness of the child's fantasy life and the hatefulness of American culture, a massification of what, in *Dark Legend*, Wertham describes as a catathymic delusion: wedded to the pleasures and efficiency of violence, America demands that its children merge their murderous fantasies with the murderousness of the real.[3] The idea and (at times) the act of matricide is central to that pleasure, its pursuit of a culture founded and sustained by a loving hatred of the mother.[4] That ambivalence can become one of the privileged points of connection or confusion between psyche and culture, internal life and the outside world, as well as the (potentially catathymic) dialogue between Wertham and Wright—a dialogue fascinated, fixated, by the murderous potential embedded in the relation between mother and son. It's a dialogue that takes place over the body of a woman, a mother, murdered by her child, a scene—both fictional and real—which structures the encounters, intellectual and amicable, between Wertham and Wright. That scene supports an account of postwar American culture as one which derives from a massive invasion of self, a possession of the children of America by a culture saturated by images of power, violence, and sexuality.

———

On 24 October 1941 Wright paid tribute to Wertham's *Dark Legend*, his study of a seventeen-year-old youth, Gino, who, possessed by the belief that he has dishonored his family, murders his mother:

> I want to thank you for making it possible for me to read this highly fascinating psychological study of crime. My reactions to Gino, his plight and his crime were so many and so varied that it would be futile to attempt to set them down in a letter. It is enough to say that I think it is the most comprehensive psychological statement in relation to contemporary crime that I have come across. Indeed, it is as fascinating as any novel.[5]

"As fascinating as any novel": *Dark Legend: A Study in Murder* has Wright under its spell, fascinated by its heady mix of fiction and reality, psyche and myth, what Wertham calls his "bio-literary method"(Wertham, *Dark Legend*, 95). That method—"the detailed comparison of a literary character with a living person," as Wertham puts it—supports his decision to tell the story of Gino as an "intellectual detective adventure," which puts the psychiatrist-reader on the trail of Hamlet and Orestes as the mythic-literary prototypes of the modern matricide (12, 95). Merging a psychoanalytic commentary with the noir of true crime fiction—"The cop was standing by the candy store. It was just past midnight on a spring night"—*Dark Legend* seduces Wright with its rewriting of the *ur*-dramas of psychoanalysis as well as its refusal to give up on the enigmatic connection between fiction and action (7). A compelling topic for a writer like Wright, committed to an aesthetic of political change—to what Wertham describes as "the derived life of fiction." Fictions, Wertham suggests in a key move toward the end of his discussion of Gino's murder of his mother, have a "derived life, in the spectator, the reader, and the listener" (87). Part of the problem of Gino, for Wertham, is what drives him to the *act* of matricide, to act out the fantasies that, on one (psychoanalytic) reading, are the common property of every child-man? What is it that allows Gino to move from the *"wish* (and fear of) an act" to its *"execution,"* an execution that condemns the mother for her supposed mistreatment of him, but one that he commits in order to condemn himself, to put to death the unconscious drives driving him? "There was one specific and actual occurrence," Wertham concedes, at the beginning of this discussion, "which, at the last moment, apparently helped Gino to turn his impulse into fact. On the night of the murder he went to a movie" (87).

Let's note the drama of this moment in Wertham's narrative. Gino, a youth possessed by an ambivalent image of his mother, goes to the cinema. He becomes a spectator of the fiction staged on screen, the consumer of a public fantasy which allows him to identify himself with the (avenging) hero of the story unfolding on screen (the film told "a story of revenge," Wertham tells us, "a young man, betrayed by the woman he loves, finds his career ruined by her connivance" [87]). But at the same time, what he sees is already possessed, already haunted, by what is missing from the screen. It's an identification which speaks Gino's displacement from his own imaginings, his preoccupation by a creative act which, though belonging to (coming from) someone else, is able to make his unconscious wishes, and conflicts, more tolerable. More tolerable and so, perhaps, more thinkable, more doable. "I asked myself," Wertham continues, "whether fiction of that sort [cinema] can influence people in this way":

Similar instances are not rare. Immediately before the matricide Orestes heard the Chorus recite in stirring dramatic dialogue the sequence of events concerned with his father's death and his mother's re-marriage. Immediately after hearing the Play-Within-the-Play, Hamlet goes to his mother's chamber and threatens her. In a recent murder trial a father who had performed a "mercy killing" on his feeble-minded son testified that shortly before his deed he had seen a movie called "Murder by the Clock," in which a weak-minded boy was led astray. "This," he said, "had a tremendous effect on me."

It seemed to me just as inexact to say fiction has no influence at all on people's actions as to blame crime on such fiction. Apparently anti-social impulses do not originate in this way. But when they once exist, added impetus may be given them by way of identification with a fictional scene.

This is easily understandable, for literature does not exist in a vacuum. Since stories are read and listened to, it is not even entirely correct to say that they have no life. They have a derived life, in the spectator, the reader, and the listener. (87)

It would be too easy to dismiss Wertham's account of the influence of fiction as a reductive one: crudely, the violence of representation reflects, and repeats, the violence of culture. (That is a common response to his analysis of the effects of violent comics on children.) Clearly, Wertham wants to avoid the dialectic of accusation and defense—fiction as cause, fiction as no cause—which so often dominates discussion, turning instead to the idea of "identification with a fictional scene": identification as a type of *impetus*, a force deriving from fiction or, more precisely, from the *relation* between fiction and its consumers. That is, words become deeds, wishes become actions, in an encounter between fiction and reader-spectator; the derived life of fiction derives from a structure of identification through which fantasy—on screen, in Gino—becomes real. It is as if the odd convergence between impulse and influence, Gino's wish to kill his mother and whatever vengeful scenes he watches on screen, are there to authorize his fantasy, to bring it to life via an identification with the wish fulfillment—the hero who, against the odds, gets what he wants—at the heart of mass cultural forms. Not a repetition but a doubling of fantasy and fiction, then—in Gino, on screen—is what Wertham uncovers in his attempt to identify precisely how, and why, Gino is spurred on from the vicarious pleasures of fictional fulfillment to the *act* of matricide.

That act is startling enough. Gino, Wertham tells us, suffered from an excessive attachment to his mother—an Orestes complex, in the terms of *Dark Legend*—a "fixation on the mother-image," which casts all women as "mother": "In this woman he killed all women" (94, 95). Kills all women, that is, with the thirty-two knife thrusts aimed at his mother ("that agony on the floor behind the door," in the words of the police officer who discovers her) (9). Possessed to death by the image of the mother, Gino finds in the cinematic scene the means to exorcism. In the doubling between spectator and screen there is, paradoxically, a loss of fantasy and fiction; or, more precisely, both are fixated in the moment of identification with a scene which traffics a structure of fulfillment: crudely, I want to be (like) the one who gets what he wants, the superman or *Übermensch*. "In the movie," Wertham specifies, "the young man succeeds," while the spectator is laid open to the imperatives of fiction—Do this! Be that!—in so far as that fiction is able to appeal to what he recognizes already in himself. Gino, Wertham concludes, was "influenced by this picture because it fitted in so well with his own preoccupations" (87, 88). In other words, it is his very preoccupation—the fixation on the mother—which lays Gino open to the coercions of (cultural) fiction, coercions which confirm and encourage the reduction of fantasy to a single scene: the violent death of the mother. Intrigued by that reduction, the poverty of fantasy and fiction in Gino's psyche, Wertham presents the concept of catathymia, or catathymic crisis, as the key to his pathology: a special disturbance in the relation between thinking and feeling, a type of fixation and rigidity in the processes of thinking and wishing. "The thought processes," Wertham explains, "lose their plasticity and become more and more rigid along definite lines as the result of repressed ungratified wishes, unallayed fears or any unresolved feelings" (96). It is as if the mobility of the primary processes—condensation, secondary revision, displacement—supporting the work of the dream, of thought, of feeling, has been lost, the mobility of unconscious life supplanted by an idée fixe which, Wertham points out, casts the catathymic as a subject possessed by the belief that an act of violence is the only solution to the impasse generated by the loss of the capacity to symbolize—and so to bear—the tension between wish and frustration.

When Gino goes to the cinema, then, it is as a catathymic spectator, a youth who finds his obsessions reflected in the (equally) catathymic idiocies of postwar American film in which violence is trafficked as distraction. Fiction allows fantasy to express brutal reality; Gino has no fantasy; fiction comes in because fantasy has become fixated, rigidified. In so far as Gino finds himself mirrored on the screen, in so far as the screen appears to reflect what is already there, so the cinematic scene can begin to direct the very life in which its fictions find their purchase: the life is derived from fiction just as the fiction takes on a derived life in its spectators (no straightforward account of motive or cause here). According to Wertham, the knife thrusts of cultural fiction have, in turn, fascinated and infuriated Gino, provoking him to enjoy his own ferocity in the thirty-two knife thrusts he aims at a mother he believes has betrayed him. But if fiction fascinates, it also allows Gino to avenge himself against a mother-image which has provoked and disempowered him *in the same way*.

A complex relation between pathology and fiction, culture and influence, runs right through Wertham's work and will become central both to his understanding of representation in the life of the child and to his dialogue with Wright. Wright, I think, perceives affinities. *Dark Legend* is (like) fiction. Wertham is telling a story, reconstructing a psyche and a scene which catch at Wright's imagination. Wright is fascinated by Gino's plight, the crime which is a symptom of his fiction from *Native Son*, first published in 1939, to *Savage Holiday*, published in 1954 (the book, it seems, Wright valued most). To put this another way: matricide appears as symptom in the works of one of the most important black modernists at the same time as a matricidal reading of postwar American culture is emerging through the psychoanalytic psychiatry popularized by Wertham in his analyses of crime and race, fiction and film. In this sense, *Dark Legend* fascinates and seduces Wright because it responds to the problem which haunts his life and work. Starting from the son's murderousness toward his mother, that response moves toward an account of fiction as provocative force in the lives of the modern Hamlets and Oresteses: Wertham's Gino, Wright's Bigger Thomas—the protagonist of *Native Son* whose plight, or plot, anticipates the analysis of mother (image) and murder put forward in *Dark Legend*. The question of the mother as *image*, the imago or fiction of the mother in the life of the son, is worked through both *Dark Legend* and *Native Son*, the one embroiled in a real or literal act of matricide, the other bound to repeat the symbolic murder of the mother which thematizes Wright's fiction. It has become a critical commonplace in readings of Wright's fiction that the figure of the mother is used to symbolize the "poverty, the ignorance, the helplessness" of black lives and traditions; similarly, that the body of the mother lies concealed behind the women brutalized through Wright's problematic fictions. But what I'm interested in here is a coincidence between Wright's representation of the mother— as metaphor and fiction, mask as well as masked—and the idea of culture as perverse intrusion on the self identified by both Wertham and Wright. Like the mother, culture intrudes as fiction; fixated by the image of his mother, Gino can be provoked to murder her by the fictions of culture; compelled by a need to understand the fictions of American racism, Wright becomes embroiled in a complex series of substitutions and equations between mothering, childhood, and culture. Figuring himself as Hamlet, say, Bigger Thomas as Orestes, Wright uncovers the logic of racism as a form of sadistic mothering, writing as a way of abreacting (and enacting) the impulse toward matricide at the heart of contemporary life.[6]

"Matricide," Wertham notes toward the end of *Dark Legend*, "is the disease of a patriarchal society"; the murder of the mother by her son has a "social significance in the development of mankind," which, despite the progressive (Wertham's term) forces of repression ranged against it, persists "in life and literature today" (116). At once mythic and political, symptomatic and social, then, the act of matricide explored through *Dark*

Legend becomes central to Wright's understanding of literature and crime as *scenes* which can be used to reveal the repressed of cultural life: the literary and the criminal are the place for that which has no place. One of the key texts here is *Native Son* and, in particular, "How Bigger Was Born," the 1940 preface to the novel delivered by Wright as a lecture at the Schomburg Collection in New York. "The more I thought of it," Wright explains, laying his cards on the table as to how, and why, he came to write Bigger Thomas, "the more I became convinced that if I did not write of Bigger as I saw and felt him, if I did not try to make him a living personality and at the same time a symbol of all the larger things I felt and saw in him, I'd be reacting as Bigger himself reacted: that is, I'd be acting out of *fear* if I let what I thought whites would say constrict and paralyze me."[7] Writing Bigger rather than being Bigger, then; literature rather than crime. *Native Son* takes the place of Bigger's murders, the murderousness directed at the white and black woman sacrificed to the fear generated in a black youth by American culture. This is literature as a defense against the paralyzing effects of white racism, Wright's demand that literature take on the burden of living in a hostile world. The writing of fiction one way of underscoring the fear and freedom from fear that comes from knowing that the "law is white."[8] Fiction, then, one way of making that law's interest and vengeance visible, a law in which any assertion of black virile existence equals a crime against the state. Fiction as a defense, too, against the feeling that to be black is to be already guilty, a feeling that constricts and paralyzes the ego but leaves the whiteness of the law unknowable and undetermined apart from its law-making violence. It is as if Wright is deriving Bigger from a life that might have been his own, the life that Wright has managed to divert through fiction—using fiction to derive another life for himself (fiction as a cure for fiction).[9] What you find in fiction, then, are the traces of a life that might have been, a life avoided, or averted—"an unveiling of the unconscious ritual of death," as Wright puts it, "in which we, like sleep-walkers, have participated so dreamlike and so thoughtlessly" (Wright, *Native Son*, 420).

Like any form of defense, Bigger may not always secure Wright against
the hostile dream that is American racism. Any reader familiar with the
criticism of *Native Son* will know that Wright was quickly identified with
the savagery of his literary character, condemned as the author of this living and dangerous personality. What goes missing here is writing as a
work of transformation, a rerouting of impulse through language: in
other words, writing as that which makes the difference between wishing
and doing (the terms which dominate Wertham's analysis of Gino). How
does one derive from, or stall, the other? This is, in fact, the question which
organizes not only Wertham's reading of *Native Son* but the "experiment"
that both he and Wright undertook to "determine where certain elements
in *Native Son* were *derived from*."[10] Part of Wright's "analysis" with
Wertham—their "discussions," as Wertham puts it, "on the relationship of
psychiatry to literature"—that experiment is written up in "An Unconscious Determinant in *Native Son*," an essay read before the American Psy-
chopathological Association in 1944. Acknowledging an obvious identification between Wright and Bigger Thomas, Wertham is also keen to
emphasize the idea of literature as transformation and disguise. "It has
always to be kept in mind," he insists, that "a literary creation is not a
translation but a transmutation of human experience [*Dark Legend*]"
(Wertham, "Unconscious Determinant," 322). Returning to his earlier
reading of *Hamlet* in *Dark Legend*, Wertham brings his bio-literary-
psychiatric experiment with Wright into dialogue with his analysis of
Gino: black modernism and delinquency, literature and murder, converge
on the topic of matricide (the traces of matricide in the work of literature). At the same time, Wertham refers his readers, or listeners, to two
specific scenes in *Hamlet* and *Native Son*, reading across the two texts to
describe the matricidal impulses of their authors:

> Just as I believe that in *Hamlet* the key scene is the appearance of the
> father's ghost in the mother's bedroom, so the key scene in *Native*
> *Son* is when Bigger Thomas unintentionally kills Mary Dalton in the

presence of her blind mother. (Bigger, as you will remember, is employed as a handyman in the house of the Dalton family.) (Wertham, "Unconscious Determinant," 322)

On Wertham's reading, *Native Son* is replaying the unconscious dynamics of Shakespeare's *Hamlet*, while *Hamlet* is a drama of repressed matricide—"Shakespeare has added in the *Second Quarto* the new motif of matricide"—in which the mother figures as object of both incestuous desire *and* murderous, but diverted, wish. Echoing between *Hamlet* and *Native Son*, the two scenes are supposed to speak a matricidal desire which, however, misses the mother as object. In *Hamlet*, it is a (dead) father's command which stays the son's "bitter business": "Taint not thy mind nor let thy soul contrive/Against thy mother aught" (though, as Wertham points out, Hamlet initiates the circumstances which lead to his mother's death) (Wertham, *Dark Legend*, 88). In *Native Son*, the death of a young white woman comes in place of the (wish for a) dead maternal body that, in Wertham's terms, lies buried in the text of this scene. But where is that body? In what sense is Bigger Thomas—who, at the end of *Native Son* stands trial for the murder of two women, one black, one white—a matricide? "In this woman he killed all women": Wertham's analysis of Gino in *Dark Legend* appears to be reversed in his discussions of Wright's fiction: by killing women, he kills the one woman, the mother. That is, in the transmutation that is Wright's fiction, a son's (wish to) murder his mother is displaced by, re-presented as, the death of a daughter in the presence of her mother. A blind mother, a mother who sees but cannot see: "And the very symbol of the seeing eye that is blind fits the mother image" (Wertham, "Unconscious Determinant," 324).

What is it in Wertham's discussions with Wright which puts him on the track of this disguised matricidal scene? On the one hand, clearly, Wertham is bringing *Native Son* into dialogue with one of the *ur*-texts of Freud's thinking on the troubling relation between mothers and sons; on the other hand, Wertham has been reading, and discussing, Wright's recent "autobiography," *Black Boy,* a text which, Wertham declares, shows up the "special problem" of Wright's identification with his creation, Bigger Thomas (Wertham, "Unconscious Determinant," 322). Let's note that *Black Boy* (first published in 1945), opens with a mother's act of violence against her son: "But for a long time," Wright recalls, "I was chastened whenever I remembered that my mother had come close to killing me" (Wright, *Black Boy,* 13). Maternal aggression is a persistent, and painful, theme, nothing less than an intrusion which threatens the son's capacity to think and dream: "I had once tried to write," Wright acknowledges, "had let my crude imagination roam, but the impulse to dream had been slowly beaten out of me by experience" (272). Part of the world which helps to obliterate her child's impulse to dream, the mother is an equivocal figure in Wright's fiction—source of persecution and desire. A threat to life and imagination in *Black Boy,* she is cast as origin of both in the dedication to *Native Son:* "To My Mother who, when I was a child at her knee, taught me to revere the fanciful and the imaginative." There may be a bitter irony here (the mother who refuses the child's fancy and imagination may well teach him to revere it), but, if so, it's an irony which becomes more apparent when we read across from *Native Son* to *Black Boy,* from "fiction" to autobiography: Wertham is careful to point to the work of disguise—"almost as hard to penetrate as any novel"—in the latter (Wertham, "Unconscious Determinant," 322). Or, perhaps, the mother threatens what she most reveres, censors what she most wants to liberate in her child? In each case, it is the disguise of fiction which allows Wright, finally, to dream: writing is the capacity for dream, resistance to experience. And, it is resistance to, as well as a defense against, the mother, the terror and helplessness she has come to represent:

> My mother's suffering grew into a symbol in my mind, gathering to itself all the poverty, the ignorance, the helplessness; the painful, baffling, hunger-ridden days and hours; the restless moving, the futile seeking, the uncertainty, the fear, the dread; the meaningless pain and

endless suffering. Her life set the emotional tone of my life, colored the men and women I was to meet in the future, conditioned my relation to events that had not yet happened, determined my attitude to situations and circumstances I had yet to face. (Wright, *Black Boy*, 111)

It is in the context of this powerful and miserable statement that Wertham diagnoses the place of the mother in Wright's psychic life—making the connection between Wright and Shakespeare, Bigger and Hamlet. "In Wright's life," Wertham suggests, toward the end of his account of *Native Son* as a complex relation to Wright's image of the maternal, "it may be sufficient to say that the ego ideal was largely *derived* from the mother" (Wertham, "Unconscious Determinant," 324; emphasis added). But, then, what does it mean to derive your ego ideal from a symbol of poverty, ignorance, helplessness, suffering? To internalize, or introject, an inarticulate and brutal cultural legacy, one that, as Wertham claims, is destined to intrude like a "nameless fate" into Wright's oeuvre as well as his dreams (indeed, to intrude on his ability to dream). As symbol, or metonym, for black life in America, then, the mother is a degraded, even abject, figure in Wright's fiction; or, to put this another way, because she carries the riven consciousness, the dereliction, that Wright associates with black culture in America, she is herself a figure of that dereliction: like Bigger, in fact, the mother carries a desperate awareness she can neither understand nor avoid. As Wright describes it in his 1953 novel, *The Outsider*, "Mother love had cleaved him in twain: a wayward sensibility that distrusted itself, a consciousness that was not conscious of itself."[11]

Figuring a violence at once intimate and public—the deeply familial aggression of a mother against her son, the residues of black experience made derelict by racist hatreds—the matricidal attack on the *images* of the mother in Wright's fiction is always also an attack on the racist culture whose effects she embodies. An attack, in other words, on the experience of growing up as a black child in racist culture. A southern childhood in which whiteness equals categorical law and blackness a submissive will to punishment. What Wright learns, in the end, is that whiteness regulates black life with a talionic imperative: whatever the violence done to blacks by whites, blacks have had, a priori, to doubly inflict on themselves as subjects; and this is the debt southern culture (and mothering) passes on to its children. That indebtedness becomes central to the experiment between Wertham and Wright as Wertham begins to probe what he describes as the "unconscious determinant" of *Native Son*, the scene(s)—real or phantasmatic, historical or imaginative—from Wright's childhood in which Bigger is able to find his purchase: "Was he conscious of any fantasies or daydreams from which threads would lead to the key scene and its setting in the novel. The answer to both these questions is "No" (Wertham, "Unconscious Determinant," 322–323). Drawing a blank, Wertham is forced to dig deeper, to bring Wright up against the presence of fiction in the telling of any life. "Did I invent these people?" Wright wonders to Wertham, faced with the uncertain difference between fantasy and memory in relation to the scenes and figures he is uncovering from his past (323). Gradually, against all resistance, against the difficulty of telling the past in a way that convinces Wertham with its "reality character" (an aesthetic, or literary, judgment on the quality of the memories being retrieved?), Wright remembers the scene that, he tells Wertham, "was the soil out of which *Native Son* came" (323):

> As an adolescent of fifteen, Wright went to public school and worked mornings and evenings for a white family. The lady of the house was young and pretty. She lived with her husband and her mother. . . . In his memory the figure of the mother is very unclear. She used to get the breakfast every morning. The daughter, the lady of the house, was friendly to young Richard, and he felt this was a second home to him. . . . Further associative material led to the recollection of a special scene. In the early morning young Richard would carry scuttles of coal and wood into the house. On one such morning when he was carrying out his usual routine, he opened the door and came suddenly

upon the lady of the house before she had dressed. She reprimanded him severely and told him he should always knock before entering. These recollections had great emotional power. They were related to much earlier emotional experiences. (323–324)

It's an abyssal structure of scenes upon scenes: through the (fictional) Dalton family Wright reworks an episode that, Wertham points out, Wright had completely forgotten while that episode, in turn, draws on the power of much earlier experiences. The sexuality, and shame, of the adolescent is projected back into earlier experiences—Wright's powerful, and ambivalent, tie to his mother—and forward into the literature through which Wright reinvents himself, refinds his life. Let's note, again, that in this "adolescent" scening, the mother remains a shadowy figure, "nebulous" (Wright's word) in his memory and apparently not able to be further delineated in his discussions with Wertham. Shadowy, and therefore, in terms of the psychoanalysis to which both Wright and Wertham are indebted, a significant and overdetermined figure. What does the shadow of the (white) mother represent here? Mother of a woman on whom Wright may have looked with desire; however accidental, the black boy's look at the naked body of the white woman transgresses the racist laws governing those "painful, baffling, hunger-ridden days" of Wright's childhood. Put the mother in the shadows and you cannot quite see her: more important, perhaps, she cannot see *you*. She cannot say "no" to whatever it is you are doing which she cannot see (looking or murdering). It is not the mother who issues reprimand or prohibition here but the object of the look herself. (Compare Wright's memory of his own mother: a woman who reprimands him for looking at a naked white girl—"Once he saw a drove of white Mexican children on a road. One little Mexican girl was nude. His mother commented on Mexicans" [Wertham, "Unconscious Determinant," 324].)

It could be that the mother in the shadows is one way to deflect the maternal reprimand that Wright so fears (not only because it comes from

the supposed source of life and love but because that source is equated
with the hatreds of racist culture). But, as Wertham's complex reference
to *Native Son* suggests, we also have to read this memory *forward* into
Bigger Thomas's murder of Mary Dalton; that is, there is another mother
in this text (another unconscious determinant of Wright's identification
with Bigger). In *Native Son*, a blind woman, a mother, is standing on the
edge of the scene, looking on at the murder of her daughter. Looking
without seeing: a technique of vision which makes for a curious form of
witnessing, one belonging to what Wertham calls the blindness of the
"seeing eye"—the very symbol of the mother in Wright's text. "Who is the
woman who is blind but not blind enough," Wertham muses (Mrs. Dalton
plays a key role in uncovering Bigger as murderer), "who does not see but
who watches the secret acts of the hero? In Wright's life it may be
sufficient to say that the ego ideal was largely derived from the mother,
and not from the father. And the very symbol of the seeing eye that is
blind fits the mother image" (Wertham, "Unconscious Determinant," 324).

   Certainly that uncanny seeing eye becomes, in *Native Son*, a predicament of both memory and fiction. First of all, the inverse mirroring
between Wright and Bigger is repeated by Bigger's first conversations with
Mrs. Dalton. In response to her delicate questions and his curt replies, Bigger feels her eyes upon him; he wants not to have to look at her but, as he
succumbs to feelings of going blind, he knows that her vision has been
doubled by him and in him. "He had the feeling that talking to a blind person was like talking to someone whom he himself could scarcely see"
(Wright, *Native Son*, 100). Bigger, like Gino, can only turn away blind
because he has already been unconsciously blinded by the unseeing eye
that sees; the gaze that, in the absence of the paternal word, makes internal reflection impossible and so nonsymbolizable and, like a catathymic
mirror, entraps him in the necessity of violence. Here fantasy is rigidified
by a look, a glance, that undoes the ability to see beyond its sinister repetition. Bigger is struck dumb by the symbolic power of the (white) mother
because he is already blinded by the fantasy he has of her, a fantasy he can

neither avow or disavow. Just as the blindness of mother-love is blinding, murder becomes one way of knowing what is inside and what is out, what is reflected and what cannot be seen. Murder, that is, one way of making visible the dialectical relation between blindness and castration, matricidal wish and its awful repetition in catathymia. Murder, in sum, as a defense against those unbearable feelings needling him, forcing him to act so as to avoid servitude and dispossession, guilt and envy.

No limit, then, to what a blind mother can look at. The secrets of a murderous and incestuous soul: Bigger, certainly, is convinced that Mrs. Dalton "knows" what he has done—the fear of her knowledge drives *Native Son* toward its fatal conclusion. Throughout the opening scenes of *Native Son*, the seeing eye that is blind is a figure of censorship and prescience. "Like Bigger himself," Wright comments in "How Bigger was Born," "I felt a mental censor—product of the fears which a Negro feels from living in America—standing over me, draped in white, warning me not to write" (Wright, *Native Son*, 24). Again, the mother is being identified with the exigencies of racist culture; this time, however, it is a white mother who censors the (black) son into the dereliction of black life in America. Like the censor, Mrs. Dalton is a figure in or of white: "He was thinking that perhaps Mrs. Dalton was standing in flowing white and staring with stony blind eyes in the middle of the floor"; "He turned and a hysterical terror seized him, as though he were falling from a great height in a dream. A white blur was standing by the door, silent, ghostlike. It filled his eyes and gripped his body"; "He clenched his teeth and held his breath, intimidated to the core by the awesome white blur floating toward him" (Wright, *Native Son*, 123, 125, 126). Reading *Native Son*, Wright seems unable to mention Mrs. Dalton without the qualifier "white": she is the luminous blur at the navel of Bigger's world, overseeing the transformation of matricidal wish into the murder of a young white woman. As such she is both censor and playground, the woman who in bearing witness to the act in which Bigger for the first time "creates" himself, opens him up to the violence of the law: "He had the feeling toward her that was akin to that which he held toward his mother. The difference in his feelings toward Mrs. Dalton and his mother was that he felt that his mother wanted him to do the things she wanted him to do, and he felt that Mrs. Dalton wanted him to do the things she felt that *he* should have wanted to do" (Wright, *Native Son*, 101). In short, whereas the black mother wants submission, Mrs. Dalton wants Bigger to experience the forbidden pleasure made possible by his own transgressive feelings. Her categorical imperative might just as well be: enjoy! the pleasures made possible by white cruelty and punishment. Enjoy, because America demands it.

It would be impossible to overstate the ambivalence and complexity of the imago of the mother (black and white) in Wright's fiction. After all, what does it mean for the white mother to stand in for the cause of her daughter's demise? (Bigger kills Mary because he does not want her to call out to her mother; however innocent, as a black man he cannot afford to be discovered in the bedroom of a white woman: the weight of American history casts its shadow over the relation between the three.) Part of the challenge of Wright's fiction is the way in which it runs that imago into the very modern problem of "Bigger": symbol of a black delinquency athwart American national life and the matricidal relation between black mother and son. "I wanted the reader to feel that Bigger's story was happening now, like a play upon the stage or a movie unfolding upon the screen," Wright explains in "How Bigger Was Born." "I wanted the reader to feel that there was nothing between him and Bigger; that the story was a special première given in his own private theatre" (Wright, *Native Son*, 36). Not only Wright, then, but his readers are asked to occupy the place of Bigger, to be him in order to know, from the inside out, what it feels like to suffer from and to wage war against American racism. Again, this is an understanding of literature—cinema, drama—in terms of its derived life: fiction can take up its place on the inside of its readers, grappling with, even combating, the formations of fiction and fantasy which already reside there. It's a derivation which, in the case of Wright's aesthetics of commitment to political change, can be used to generate a therapeutic action against the violence of American cultural life (a derivation which cuts both ways?). "Like a scientist in a laboratory," Wright continues, "why should I not . . . use my imagination and invent test-tube situations . . . work out in fictional form an emotional statement and resolution of this problem?" (Wright, *Native Son*, 36).

Identification, derivation, fantasy: Wright will bring these three terms together in one of his last, and most curious, works, *Savage Holiday*. The matricidal scene which structures this novel is at once apparent and displaced; uniquely, in Wright's fiction, this is a novel populated by white characters. Not a Bigger or a black boy in sight. "As I told you," he writes to his agent Paul Reynolds on 6 March 1953, "this deals with just folks, white folks" (Wright's attempt to universalize the pathology which will unfold through the book [cited in Fabre, *Unfinished Quest*, 379]). Described by the critic Bernard Bell as a "melodramatic Freudian tale of the repressed sexuality of [protagonist] Erskine Fowler," *Savage Holiday* has been read as the most psychoanalytic of Wright's novels; it is also indebted to Wertham's *Dark Legend* (see Fabre, *Unfinished Quest*, 376–380). From letters he wrote to Reynolds in 1952 and 1953, Wright appears to have considered the book to be "a rather simple little story," one that deals with "crime *per se*" (cited in Fabre, *Unfinished Quest*, 376). Given the tortuous, and deferred, temporality of *Savage Holiday*, Wright's comment may well be ironic. This is a novel in which the identification between Erskine Fowler and a young boy, Tony Blake (the son of his next door neighbor Mabel Blake), the identification between Fowler's mother and Mabel Blake, is going to call into (dizzying) question any certain distinction between memory, fantasy, and reality. On one level *Savage Holiday* is the story of a successful businessman suddenly made redundant, or retired; a man who does not know what to do with himself on an enforced "holiday." The incident which opens the book— Fowler manages to lock himself, naked, out of his apartment—is quasifarcical but it generates the tragedy which drives the plot. Running out onto his balcony to reach his bathroom window, Fowler's nakedness terrifies the young Tony Blake, who, shrinking from the sight of the naked man, falls to his death ten stories below. The death of a child, then, is central to the strange story which follows: Fowler's brief but intense love affair with Tony's mother, whose sexual promiscuity unleashes violent feelings of attraction-repulsion in him. In this he follows the model of her (dead) son, whose Oedipal anxieties remind Fowler of his childhood self. It is that identification which prompts Fowler's furious and fatal attack on Mabel Blake—a murder which releases a moment of deep self-revelation in the form of a childhood memory.

> With slow feet, as in a dream, he walked into the bathroom and stared at his white and sweaty face in the mirror above the washbowl, and he seemed dully surprised to find that the face he saw was still his own. . . .
>
> . . . *he was looking in the mirror to see how bad he was, for his mother had said: "Go and look in the mirror at yourself and see how bad you are!" And he was looking at his face and the face he saw was his own and it wasn't bad. . . . His mother had lied to him. He hadn't changed; he could see no bad in his face . . . .*
>
> *Yesterday he had been playing with the little girl next door—Gladys was her name—and he had taken her little doll and had "killed" it and had told Gladys that the doll was his mother and he had "killed" her because all the boys had said that his mother was bad. . . .*
>
> *He had taken a dirty brick bat and had beaten the doll's head in, had crushed it and had told Gladys: "There's my mama. . . . I killed her; I killed her' cause she's a bad woman . . .".*
>
> *And Gladys had cried and had told her mother and Gladys' mother had told his mother and his mother had asked him if he'd said it and he'd refused to answer. And his mother had said: "Look in the mirror and see how bad you are!" And now he was staring at his face in the mirror and it was his own face and it had not changed.*[12]

Only after Fowler has discarded the butcher knife on Mabel's ruined body does the memory of "killing" the doll return. As if in a dream, the act of looking at himself in the mirror throws him back into a childhood in which the wish to kill his mother—"because all the boys had said that his mother was bad"—is played out in the destruction of a young friend's doll: "He had taken a dirty brick bat and had beaten the doll's head in. . . . 'There's my mama . . . I killed her.'" Reading from this point in the story, then, the murder which has just been committed is presented as a kind of repetition, derived from the wish to kill the mother. The strange career of a matricide: kill a lover in order to kill a mother; kill a dead child's mother to abreact the return of one's own Oedipal crisis. Once again, there is a structure of identification enabling a convergence between impulse and action; in this case, however, it is the dead child who authorizes the fulfillment of Fowler's criminal wish. In Wright's imaginary, mothers die because they murder their sons: "YOU KILLED TONY!" Fowler yells at Mabel Blake. "How? Like this . . . You had let Tony see you naked many times, naked and making love to men, *many men . . . Tony told me so*! I swear it!" (Wright, *Savage Holiday*, 199–200). Is this the speech that Fowler should have made to *his* mother, the speech that would have saved the broken doll and, years later, Mabel Blake? Certainly, it's the speech which forces the readers of *Savage Holiday* to confront Wright's persistent association between (identification with?) matricide and the life of a damaged, or dead, child. But Wright does not leave his readers there. From this "dimly remembered, far-off scene," Fowler goes to hand himself in at a police station nearby. "I just killed a woman," he tells the officer behind the desk:

> "Well, what happened?" the policeman demanded. "Don't you remember what you did?" The policeman smiled ironically. "You're not playing a game are you?"
>
> The word "game" made Erskine start slightly. . . . Slowly his eyes widened. He no longer heard the policeman's voice; he was staring at yet another memory from the dusty past, a nebulous memory whose return stunned him even more than had his recollection of that battered doll, for this memory now told him that his previous memory of that battered doll was but the *memory of a dream he'd had!*

He'd never "killed" the doll, really! That memory was but the recalling of a
shameful daydream of revenge which he had pushed out of his mind! . . .

How could he ever explain that a daydream buried under the rigorous fiats of duty had been called forth from its thirty-six-year-old grave
by a woman called Mabel Blake, and that that taunting dream had so
overwhelmed him with a sense of guilt compounded of a reality
which was strange and alien and which he loathed, but which, at the
same time, was astonishingly familiar to him: a guilty dream which he
had wanted to disown and forget, but which he had had to reenact in
order to make its memory and reality clear to him! He closed his eyes
in despair. (Wright, *SH*, 220)

"How could he ever explain?" It's a question which belongs to the
unique perversity of *Savage Holiday* as it shuttles backward and forward
in its quest to discover Fowler's story—to find the "real" childhood scene
(memory, dream, daydream) from which his murderousness is derived.
Quite literally, finding that scene is murder. Like a nodal point in the
dream, or nightmare, of this book, the idea of a "game" throws Fowler
back into the time of another "nebulous memory" (remember Wertham's
description of Wright's "nebulous" memory of a key figure of the
mother), opens him up to the shock of a dim and dusty past: "this memory now told him that his previous memory of that battered doll was but
the *memory of a dream he'd had!*" No wonder Fowler closes his eyes in
despair. The memory of "killing" the doll is a false one, coming in the
place of a vengeful daydream that, it seems, can force its return over the
body of a dead woman. Like a picture, Fowler *stares* at this dream-mem-
ory, rediscovering the image of the desire he has had to "reenact" to make
it real. A wish so powerful it provokes—derives—a reality.

A fictional reality, of course. Fowler is not Gino, and Wright's conjur-
ing with words defends him against the hostile world which overcomes
Bigger. It may be that matricide—as fiction, as act—comes as a defense
against the effects of that hostility (the mother identified with the racism

of cultural life) as well as the unbearable pain of a conflicted inner world. "Regarded from the point of view of the development of his personality," Wertham concludes in *Dark Legend*, "the act of murder appears to have prevented consequences far more serious for Gino's mental health" (Wertham, *Dark Legend*, 99). The question of matricide always, finally, derived from something else? A happy matricide, Gino *acts* rather than *wishes*, obeys his mother in the very act of murder: "I killed her, I took her life away, but no one can say that I ever disobeyed her" (99).[13] What price the mother? How do we start to reckon her guilt in the filial imaginaries explored by Wertham and Wright? Is it always her fault?

──────

"It must be my fault": at the very end of *Seduction of the Innocent* Wertham confides a compelling story about his encounter with a young woman, a mother, at Lafargue Mental Hygiene Clinic (New York's first racially integrated, and free, psychiatric clinic which Wertham cofounded with Wright). Wertham is tired from his evening clinic, but he listens to this woman's distressed, and distressing, account of life with her son—a "juvenile delinquent" who, having been referred to Lafargue some time before, has now been picked up again for possession of a switchblade. Now the boy faces reformatory and, at her wit's end, his mother pleads for Wertham's help. He does what he can: calls in a social worker, makes plans to contact the authorities about his young patient, and tries to reassure the mother—a "hardworking woman," he tells his readers—that she has done the best she can (Wertham, *Seduction*, 395–396). "I know your boy," he assures her, "and the Clinic will take full responsibility for him again" (396). Apparently consoled, the woman thanks him and leaves.

An hour later, the clinic is finally closed. Leaving his office, Wertham catches sight of a woman, sobbing on a bench, and recognizes her as the mother he has so recently seen. "It was late," Wertham recalls, "and I was tired, but I went over to her and took her back to the office" (396). It is some time before the woman is able to speak to him but Wertham attempts—once again—to comfort her as best he can, reiterating his promise that Lafargue will intervene on behalf of her son and that he—Wertham—will do whatever he can. "I know what you have done for this boy," he reminds her. "Don't think that it's your fault" (396). Commonplace words of consolation, perhaps, but words which appear to arrest this woman's attention. "It must be my fault," she insists to Wertham. "I heard that in the lectures. And the judge said it, too. It's the parents' fault that the children do something wrong" (396).

"It must be my fault." Wertham could not have wished for a clearer expression of the thesis that *Seduction of the Innocent* is written to refute: namely, that what is wrong with the children is their parents. "Not at all," he interrupts the woman to say. "You have done all that you could." Parents are no match, in Wertham's view, for what he describes as the "other influences" to which children are exposed: comic books, crime programs, "adult influences" in general (396). Once again the woman seems reassured. Once again she thanks Wertham and gets up to leave. But, halfway through the door, she turns back. "'Doctor,' she said in a low voice. 'I'm sorry to take your time. But please—tell me again'" (397).

Tell me again that it isn't my fault: the pressure of mother-blaming on this woman is all too evident. "And I did": Wertham's final words of reassurance in *Seduction of the Innocent* confide in a mother impotent in the face of the seductions of culture. But it's a reassurance that the book cannot finally sustain: after all, who can forget Wertham's opening question: "How did Nietzsche get in the nursery?"

"Nietzsche in the nursery": everything seems to be said in this phrase, yet the intimate connection between the mother's worry that she may not be good, or good enough, for her wayward son and Wertham's revelation that American culture is to blame, leads me to wonder who or what is at fault here. The mother's worry is not about what she has done or did not do but about being blamed: that is, condemned for the mother-love that, on one narrative, is the very source of the criminality of which her son is accused. Wertham's response, that what lies beyond her is a prior cultural seduction of her son, raises the question of what he thinks ought to be her role regarding her son. Or: realizing that she can only confirm her parental love by disparaging it—that is, confirm it as an object of doubt, either displaced or absorbed by the superegoic hatreds driving her son—Wertham's reassurances necessarily end up with her playing an inessential, secondary role to culture. As such, seeking reassurance is more than she has a right to do, because on Wertham's reading her love can only ever be a derived or displaced response to the Nietzschean forces of culture driving her son.

Guilty or displaced, then, mother love only exists as its own negation. Indeed, there is always something beyond her, something made manifest by her delinquent child. In this sense, it is the clinical image of delinquency that concerns Wertham and not her scruples as a parent. That clinical image is, as we've seen, one of a child who has little or no resistance to the hateful pleasures of culture. A child who is so catathymic, so rigid, in the contentments of his fantasy life he can only block the path to the emotional "balance" (Wertham's word) of a fully integrated ego. This is a child who yields to the fascinations and cruelty of culture as a way of making real the pure and perfect joys of a jouissance not his own. As such, this is a child ever eager to shinny up the pole of his own undoing: in this embrace he declares a war on the world from the intimacy of his own fascist imagining. Fascist hatreds, then, are not only the point of pleasure but also the novel exciting element present in the child's ongoing solidarity with America's perverse and sovereign cruelty. What does the child want? Not the mother or psychiatrist, argues Wertham, but the spontaneous pleasures of a Nietzschean childhood, one in which when you get older and stop playing, the game does not escape the mind but completely takes it over, endlessly performing the "adult" pleasures of hatred. In this, the child is carried forward by an affective movement beyond fantasy, induced to recognize his own desires in the violences of culture, to see himself reflected (and perfected) there: the act by which he becomes who he is enough to incorporate him and all the vengefulness of his desires, be it thirty-two knife thrusts or the occasional work of a double murder, since without this act he is doomed to remain in the twilight of his neurosis.

In light of this, we needs must ask just what is it about Wertham's work with juvenile delinquents that engenders in Wright feelings of uncanny familiarity? To what common fantasies can we refer this shared pleasure—murderous, punishing pleasure—in Wright's writings with their violent and merciless attacks on the mother? In this chapter I have suggested that Wright saw himself, or at least one possible version of himself, in those children impregnated with nihilism, presenting narcissistic or depressive disturbances in uncontrollable acts of violence and delinquency. What Wright discovers in *Dark Legend* is the confirmation of *Native Son*'s significance; that is, Bigger only finds himself, realizes himself, through the act of murder. Before this act exists, not only does he not know who he is, but he is nothing. He only exists as a nothingness whose fate is to be nothing, but then he can only make of himself a reality by becoming one with the racist fantasies others have of him—that is, by identifying entirely with the derived life of fiction, by becoming the inessential essence of a fascism defined by the value, truth, and reality of negating everything that exists. *Native Son* ends with Bigger grappling with the meaning of murder while awaiting execution for what he's done: "What I killed for, I *am!*" "I didn't know I was really alive in this world until I felt things hard enough to kill for 'em" (Wright, *Native Son*, 461). Murder, or more accurately, the murder of women, allows Bigger to know himself. This being-toward-death, this claim of life in death as the self's own most dignified possession—everything suggests that this confession, spoken while awaiting execution, is Bigger's execution of the verdict on himself. Like Erskine Fowler's final confession, this moment is not so much a submission to the law's vengeance, but a wish to inflict the greater harm and cruelty of a superegoic law that has already judged and decided the self to be irredeemably guilty. The murder of women gives both men a glimpse inside that superego that drives the transgression that brings its punishment into being and for which the self must sacrifice itself by being forced to confess and bear witness. Through this self-execution the two men are brought together in deep completion: their killings lay bare their own sacrificial victimization made to seem ever more fixated because suffused with a reverence for America's sovereign cruelty.

Just as *Native Son* mirrors and anticipates *Dark Legend*'s focus on a kind of catathymic resistance or breakdown through which the superego exerts its pressures on the psyche, Wright's writings also helped Wertham recognize, as in a mirror, how catathymia could not be grasped, much less spoken about, without seeing how racial subjects carry the hateful traces of culture. Accordingly, their collaborative turn to psychiatry and psychoanalysis during the 1940s—a turn to fiction as therapy and the therapeutics of fiction—was an attempt to understand the affects on children of that superego and its derivations. In this sense, the politics of therapy in Wright's fiction cannot be separated from his protest aesthetic. Nor can the role he played in Wertham's understanding of the democratic possibilities of the clinic be separated from his fictions on how racism plays out a superegoic law within the mind.

I'd like to conclude this chapter by going back to the Lafargue Clinic Wright cofounded with Wertham in Harlem in 1946. Set up to provide, in the words of *Time* magazine, "pinpointed, no-nonsense psychotherapy" to Harlem's poor, mostly black, people regardless of race or ability to pay, Lafargue's main clinical initiative was to offer a more pragmatic, more direct, more humanist counseling sensitive to all forms of social exclusion while being more demanding in its ethical choices.[14] Located in the basement of St. Philip's Episcopal Church on 215 West 133rd Street, the most immediate and notable impact of the clinic, again according to *Time*, was to showcase black minds and black neuroses: "Negroes are no more happy-go-lucky—or neurotic—than other people," the article concluded, their "mental troubles, though aggravated by their underprivileged status, are essentially no different from those of [Dr. Wertham's] wealthy private patients." "The only difference," according to Wertham, "is that here in Harlem the trouble is much more naked and obvious. . . . What the Negro needs, and what psychiatry must help him find, is the will to survive in a hostile world" ("Psychiatry in Harlem," *Time*, 1 December 1947, 24).

The social importance of that will to survive is underscored by the profile of some the patients of Lafargue. On the one hand, we read of the black G.I. fidgeting in his chair, muttering: "Daid. . . . He's daid"; on the other, a civilian engineer "whose violent dreams of military battles (with sexual symbolism)" are rapidly decoded by Wertham's "machine-gun questions" as "a deep-seated fear that he was homosexual" (24). To read the *Time* article is, I think, to see how the aggressions and coercions of culture have already crossed over into the dream life of blacks. Lafargue was designed to take up arms on behalf of that life, that unconscious, distorted by such threatening hallucinations. And yet to read this *Time* article is to come across an uncertainty as to where the battle lines are drawn. If there is no difference between white or black neuroses, how does one explain what is specific to the racist aggravations of black life? Can the issue of cure and therapy, by definition, contain or delimit the black psyche at war with itself? These questions were at the centre of Lafargue's attempts to extend the democratic rhetoric of illness and cure to the effects of American racism, the conviction that a black will to survive was America's postwar battleground.

This realignment is made explicit in the profile of another patient mentioned by *Time*, "a moon-faced ten-year-old," called Midgie, whose problem, according to the reporter, is stealing. The article continues: "Because Harlem, with only one-fifth of Manhattan's population, accounts for more than half of its delinquency, Dr. Wertham concentrates on neurotic youngsters" (24). Or compare the affecting story of a boy called Billy, a Lafargue patient filmed during the 1957 NBC TV program *The House I Enter*, who, Wertham tells us in a voiceover, "could not tell where his own body left off and where some other object began. He could not recognize his image in a mirror. He was tortured by dreams and fantasies."[15] This is a boy who cannot justify or visualize his existence, since for him no mirror image exists. The mirror belongs to other people, people who can see themselves reflected—but what does it mean to live without a mirror image? To look into the mirror and be surprised to find that the face you see is still your own? How does one counter this (catathymic) withdrawal into an enclosed and foreclosed intimacy? Although the history of Lafargue is yet to be written, one can say that Wright's interest in the clinic stemmed from a wish to understand the "shadowy outlines" of such a mind that is the "undeveloped negative" of itself (Wright, *Native Son*, 16, 20). Young minds for whom a fantasmatic world comes to stand in for the missing (motherly?) consolations of the self misrecognized in the mirror; the self that has not yet come into being, and nothingness is all that, in him. A phantasmal existence swaying under the weight of the psychic devastation brought on by racism. It was as a correcting mirror for those unable to symbolize the world before them that Wright conceived of his fiction as a kind of therapeutic praxis. That is, fiction as a cure for a mind incapable of separation and so unable to tell the difference between wish and fantasy, act and fiction.

As a director of Lafargue as well as a renowned Afro-American writer, Wright wrote two articles in aid of the clinic, signing over his royalties: "Phychiatry [*sic*] Comes to Harlem," first published in *Freeworld* in September 1946, which was reprinted along with "Juvenile Delinquency in Harlem" and "A World View of the American Negro," in *Twice a Year*, 1946–1947, under the title, "Urban Misery in an American City."[16] Relatively ignored in the literature on Wright, "Phychiatry [*sic*] Comes to Harlem" refers to Lafargue's origins as *sub rosa*—that is, secretive, confidential, clandestine. "The *sub rosa* methods of establishing the Lafargue Clinic," Wright suggests, "amount in the main to a complete reversal of all current rules holding in authoritative psychiatric circles" (Wright, "Urban Misery," 351). Those circles—dismissive of the claims of the black mentally ill on time and conscience—also discriminated against the training of Negro psychiatrists. It was to address the realities of a psychiatry in which "Negroes are not allowed the luxury of neuroses," that Wright believed Lafargue had something of value to add to the affective pressures of black life in America (351).

"Urban Misery in an American City" returns us to the preoccupations of *Dark Legend* but also looks ahead to the psychoanalytic concerns of *Savage Holiday*. Drawing on the rhetoric of black anomie developed by the Chicago School of sociology, Wright traces a vicious circle from American culture to black neurosis, black mothers to their offspring: "The delinquent children of disorganized families tend to grow up and propagate children who, having been reared in delinquent homes, will in turn also tend to grow up to be delinquents" (Wright, "Urban Misery," 341). It's a legacy compounded by America's "consistent sabotage" of black "democratic aspirations." Poor, segregated, bereft, fatherless: "the ties that bind Negro families together are far weaker than those that bind white families," Wright concludes (350). The aptitude and ease by which Wright adopts the conclusions of Kenneth and Mamie Clark's *Dark Ghetto* and E. Franklyn Frazier's *The Negro Family in the United States* (1939) seems to me to derive from that mother-complex uncovered earlier in *Native Son* and *Black Boy*: two novels demonstrating an intimate link between the mother's suffering and the son's suffering world. It is a familiar narrative, not least of all because part of a more pervasive anxiety about the decline of paternal authority in America, the so-called emasculation of black men by a culture of nihilism whose meaning is the overdominating or phallic mother. For some critics—black and white—matriarchy, rather than racism, is at the root of what is wrong with black men.

Wright's reading of black juvenile crime is, however, more nuanced and perhaps less accusatory than this implies. "At the core of almost every delinquent Negro child," he writes, "is found *emotional deprivation*" (Wright, "Urban Misery," 346). That disavowed core relates to the child's unconscious recollection of sexual fantasies of the mother—but it is the sense underlying those memories that leads Wright to see a correspondence between the child's matricidal wish and the egoic drive to screen out a more originary and traumatic *racial* seduction. One memorializes, repeats the other. If the child's deprivation is inseparable from the black mother who, in this typical story told about the pathology of black family life, in bringing up her children alone cannot defend them against the pressures of culture, that is because her loss testifies to an altogether more dark realization: that her failure joins with the racial work of culture that the child comes to recognize as its own, but only via the perpetual enticements of a racist vilification and violence familiar because it is working in all of us. Matricide, in short, as a revenge for the foremost sense of never having managed to even be born. Or as a kind of ominous answer to the feeling that, no matter what he does, no matter what he has been able or not been able to do, the son can only recognize himself through her, can only make a claim to a self through the tortured dreams and fantasies in which she is both target and cause. The sacrifice of her perversity, poverty, and helplessness siding with a childish wish to lay waste to the rest of the world.

This can be seen in the following case history of Boy C that Wright takes from court records. No surprise, perhaps, that Boy C is also a (failed) matricide:

Boy C lives with a mother whose husband has left her. . . . Boy C notices that several men visit his mother night and day, and he knows that these men do not visit other homes nearby. His playmates taunt him for having so many "fathers," but he does not quite realize the implication of their words. Finally he learns that his mother is doing something terribly bad.

His mother is all he has; he loves her and is emotionally identified with her. But the awful thing she is doing makes him ashamed of her. At the age of ten he inherits a traumatic conflict which he cannot master or understand. . . . His feelings become double-edged, dual: He loves and hates his mother . . . .

One morning he is home playing irritably with his toys. His mother lies languorously abed. A knock comes at the door and a strange man enters. His mother asks him to go out and play. He refuses to move, staring with hatred at the man and his mother.

"You do what I tell you!" she yells at him.

"I wanna stay in the house," he says.

"Go play and don't talk back!" she says.

He leaps to his feet, spits at his mother, kicks his toys, and runs out. His mother does not suspect the fury that burns in him. Later he returns hungry. The man is gone and his mother is still abed. He rummages in the kitchen for food and finds that none has been cooked.

"I'm hungry," he tells his mother.

"Wait a while," she grumbles at him.

"You get up and feed me!" he shouts at her.

"Don't you talk that way to me!" she yells back at him.

He grabs a pair of scissors and stabs her in the breast. She grapples with him, taking the scissors. He then grabs a knife: he is possessed with the feeling that if he kills her he will banish the conflict that tortures him. His mother is stronger than he and she wrestles the knife away from him, drives him into the street, and screams for help. The boy screams back at her, vowing that he will kill her if he sees her again. The mother spreads the alarm and the boy is caught by the police. (Wright, "Urban Misery," 344–345)

"It is quite clear to the judge that the mother has done great harm to her son," Wright concludes, "but he cannot make the mother realize this." "She is unaware that perhaps she has spoiled her son for life" (Wright, "Urban Misery," 345). A harm done for posterity: the price of having no father and so too many and so the price of the mother's "fault." What all this amounts to is a focus on the mother as the unconscious and derived source of her son's psychic ambivalence, a focus from which the son's cure, his sanity, depends. Similarly, it is her legacy that unleashes a murderous and unmanageable psychic conflict in Boy C. But only insofar as the suddenness of the matricial blow impacts on and so realizes the psychic devastation of memory—that is, makes visible (and reflects) the psychic implication of the missing paternal word. Once again, there is no

straightforward account of motive or cause here, only a heartfelt identification with a game in which there are too many, and so no, "fathers" (a
game in which the boy is charged to take on and so identify with the meaning of his fatherless state by playmates quick to taunt him. The big lesson,
though, is the one that tells him that by acting out his stupid, blind, matricidal rage, he can commemorate the father otherwise missing from the
adult men who visit her to play. When he strikes at her with all the venom
he can muster, isn't this also a perhaps understandable wish to stay in and
play "fathers"?).

Two issues arise from this filial drama, both with relevance for how
Wertham and Wright think the psyche and the social in relation to the
question of literature and fiction. If we see "Urban Misery in an American
City" as yet another example of Wright's Orestes complex—that is to say,
as a condemnation of mother love—then we miss what he is also trying
to say about the transformative work of fantasy, about literature as the
denial and destruction of that work. What is striking is that in Wright's
(matricidal) literature, Wertham discerns the sickness of catathymia but
also the possibility of fiction as a way to health and sincerity. When
Wright's literature gazes into the abyss of black existence it not only
makes the subject's fantasmatic world recognizable and so treatable, it also
represents the catathymic work of American culture. In an unpublished
letter to Wright sent on 27 May 1942, Wertham says as much in the following poem:

Underground

The Freudians talk about the Id
   And bring it below.
But Richard Wright took off the lid
   And let us see the woe.[17]

There are many reasons why Wertham calls this verse "Underground":
it's a complex figure for Wright, denoting repressed elements and id-like

representations, but also a topography of black desire as a place where eros and the death drive are intimately linked.[18] The underground is the place where good itself or happiness is foreshadowed by "the haunting impression" of a "gigantic shock . . . which one could not forget or shake off," "creating in one's life a state of eternal anxiety" (Wright, *Eight Men*, 68). The underground defines a realm of unreality and unreason and transgression in which "the accused" is already guilty, "had always been guilty," and where one oversteps the bounds without knowing what they are (70). The man in the underground knows he is guilty, but he is in the void, the void where law and punishment realize the obscene pleasures of the superego and the only choice left is freedom or nothing. Wertham's title therefore does not define Wright's importance in terms of the honest conscience with which he addresses the psychic work of blackness both politically and creatively. Rather, Wright lets us see the woe. By taking the lid off, Wright allows others to see how they too are propelled by the implacably hostile but seductive forces of racism which increase in severity with each black demand for equality, with each black demand for the desirable and respectable goal of citizenship. These demands should not, however, be confused with a simple masochistic relation to superegoic law. For Wright, black masochism comes into being as the demand that blacks have a right to enjoy the obscene pleasures of the law that whiteness forbids them from having: the black masochist, far from being a nonviolent subject who gladly submits to the law, demands that the law punish him severely so that he too can then experience the satisfaction of desire that derives from the law's forbidden intimacy to himself.[19] What Wright is describing here—in dialogue with Wertham—is a temptation that takes the form of a violent seduction in which the black sacrifices himself. This is the meaning of his unconscious guilt—he needs to be punished so that he can proclaim himself a citizen with access to the forbidden pleasures of freedom. It is because he is deprived of being and forced to renounce desire that the black experiences the whiteness of the law in terms of what both allows and commands his rebellious servility.

The point is further underscored in a letter Wertham sends to Wright on 16 March 1945, concerning *Black Boy*.

"Black Boy" describes certain bad features in our society. Pointing these things out in the way in which you do is an act that has revolutionary implications. It should arouse the reader to the wish and perhaps the deed of changing these things. Now the paradox comes in in [*sic*] the fact that hundreds of thousands of people buy and read this book. The vast majority of these readers are of course the persecutors themselves, and not the persecuted. In other words, the people read a book that in a revolutionary sense is profoundly directed against them. . . .

There are several possible ways to interpret this: (1) Maybe these works of art have no fundamental revolutionary significance because they do not point out a specific way to act, as for instance the movie "Professor Mamlock" by Friedrich Wolf did. (2) Maybe they do affect the (guilty) people who read it. (3) Maybe they give these people, the readers, the wrong impression that they are actually doing something by just reading about these things, which gives them the satisfaction of leaving everything as it goes and feeling at the same time that they are righteous.

The question of whether it does any good when papers like *PM* expose something or other belongs to the whole problem.

I do not have "Black Boy" in mind particularly, but all this is an example of a problem that interests me for my studies in "Marx and Freud."[20]

In many ways, of course, Wertham's letter brings us full circle. Should fiction offend or be stricken by the catathymic terrors of American culture? Should it threaten or confirm the narcissistic-masochistic pleasures of both persecutors and persecuted, or should it bring us back to ourselves by offering something other, by becoming other, a spur to revolutionary wishes and acts? Unlike the comic book that is no more than a regressive reflection of America's violent culture, Wertham looks to literature and psychoanalysis to carry out a more transformative work of negation. The writer must not only destroy language and the hateful "fictions" of culture, but also negate those feelings of guilt and remorse denying the need for action. For Wertham, then, the political thought of Wright's literary realism is one way out of the seductive pleasures of catathymia. The book, the written thing, enters the world of freedom by revealing the repressed elements of what lies *hidden*, forced underground, by race hysteria. If blackness is felt to be a kind of demonry, a spreading taint or curse, Wright's works lifted the lid on how blacks and whites remain bedeviled by the fearsome power of this fear. It is at this point that the affinity between Wright and Wertham begins and ends. That affinity comes into being on the back of psychological tales of male murder: Hamlet, Orestes, Bigger Thomas, and Gino—overwhelmingly male tales of matricide and revenge. But tales, too, of how the child is subjected to a seeing eye that is the blind (and blinding) work of race, an imaginary that sees the father expelled from the symbolic realm and the mother-child dyad as ruinous.

Certainly Wright shared Wertham's concern with how literature ought to realize the work of the imaginary. In 1946, for example, alongside cofounding Lafargue, Wright published a review of Jo Sinclair's prizewinning novel *Wasteland* for *PM* magazine, under the title "*Wasteland* Uses Psychoanalysis Deftly."[21] In this review, Wright praises Sinclair—the pseudonym of Ruth Seid—for her novel about Jewish family life as told through a character in analysis. Sinclair, he writes, has done a rare thing "in our anxiety-ridden, postwar-America," which prefers its novels to be "more grimly optimistic than revealing, more cheaply moral than truthful"; she has written a novel "that challenges our assumptions and compels us to accept a reality which we have been all too prone to reject or misinterpret" (Wright, cited in Fabre, *Unfinished Quest*, 245). *Wasteland* "contains a quality of reality that simply could not have been imagined or contrived" (245, 246).[22] Further, she has done so through an adroit use of psychoanalysis. "Many writers," he writes, "are led astray by thinking that they can use the seemingly easy device of the psychoanalyst in novelistic structure"; *Wasteland* succeeds because it "depends, for much of its effect, upon subtle repetitions." Miss Sinclair, he continues, has managed to blend psychoanalysis with a sound literary principle: "Repetition that never quite repeats" (246–247).

"Repetition that never quite repeats": it's a phrase we can use to revisit the fateful child whose death and delinquency is at the heart of this chapter. What is repeated but never quite repeats, above all, is the fantasy and dream of a memory that never in fact happened (*Savage Holiday*). A memory, in turn, that derives from the resistance of the child's symptom: the memory of a mother who is the starting point of *everything*, whose stage is the lie of her disheveled bed, her white hair shining in a region that is not beyond the world, but the world itself, but the world as veiled, disguised, displaced by the spectral genius of childhood (*Black Boy*; *Native Son*). In killing her the son kills the representation that possesses him, the racial-Oedipal law with whose violence he identifies, and with whose rage he submits as to an enchantment (*Dark Legend*). Repetition is here the child repeating a catastrophe that never happened, and that keeps on happening insofar as it never happened. The terror he personifies does not come from the death he inflicts on the mother but from the death he repeatedly inflicts on himself. All this the appeal of a fiction whose utter strangeness presents itself as the best way of putting to death the black child already killed by culture. Is it any wonder, then, that Wright connects the political work of literature to the repetitive fantasy of a structure in which blackness equals a (maternal) death that kills? A fiction that turns back into a fantasy of the mother become the memorial-to-be destroyed by the mortiferous child as revenant? As an answer, I think what is at stake here is the disquieting, anxious return of an inheritance in which the black child can only begin to desire insofar as he is the object to be murdered. Only then can he begin to live. Live, that is, like a mother, yes, a mother blinded by the lesser betrayal of Oedipal law and eros: the child her shadow, in death.

4   *Black Narcissus*

ISAAC JULIEN

The power to look is not the power to fuck.

—bell hooks, *Reel to Real* (1996)

In "Undressing Icons," the late Essex Hemphill describes why literary works by postwar black heterosexual writers are the "wrong places for black gays and lesbians to seek *true* reflection and affirmation."[1] Seeking that reflection Hemphill turns instead to a 1989 work by the black British filmmaker Isaac Julien: "By creating *Looking for Langston,* Julien gives us the first black gay film to articulate black gay desire"(Hemphill, *Looking for Langston,* 182). It's a claim that implies *Looking for Langston* offers a true reflection and affirmation of black gay desire. Having undressed the black cultural icon, Langston Hughes, Julien has, Hemphill argues, eased Hughes out of his cultural and historical closet: "those closets are ancestral burial sites that we rightfully claim and exhume" (183). True reflection, then, emerges through the exhumation of repressed desires; it's a way of seeing that literally transforms the filmic image into a graveyard of desire.

I'd like to ponder Hemphill's comments alongside what Julien himself says in a 1989 interview with Hemphill concerning the film: "I didn't want to deal with just gay issues," he states, "I wanted to talk about the role of the black artist in relationship to the black community and specifically the role of the black gay artist" (175). "The idea was to have desire exist in the construction of images," Julien continues, "I wanted to dwell on the psyche and the imaginary as well as the factual" (176, 178). While *Looking for Langston* is not "just" a reflection, or affirmation of "gay issues," it is a meditation on the role of the black gay artist in black communities. It's a theme that emerges through images of dream and desire and one sustained by an imaginary reconstruction of black aesthetic history (i.e., the Harlem Renaissance).

Many commentators on *Looking for Langston* have applauded it for its queering of the Harlem Renaissance and for its lyrical, formal beauty. Amanda Cruz, in her introduction to *The Film Art of Isaac Julien,* says that the film has garnered a "cult following" ever since its first screenings at international film festivals.[2] Manthia Diawara describes the film as "doubly scandalous" in its outing of homosexuality in the Renaissance and in its confrontation of the avant-garde with its Other—that is, race.[3] According to Henry Louis Gates, *Looking for Langston* "compels its audience to participate in this rewriting [of Afro-American modernism]" by enjoining us "to go behind the mirror, as Wilde urged."[4] In support of this enigmatic statement, Gates cites Wilde's "The Disciple":

> When Narcissus died the pool of his pleasure changed from a cup of sweet waters into a cup of salt tears, and the Oreads came weeping through the woodland that they might sing to the pool and give it comfort.
>
> ... "We do not wonder that you should mourn in this manner for Narcissus, so beautiful was he."
>
> "But was Narcissus beautiful?" said the pool [...] "I loved Narcissus because, as he lay on my banks and looked down at me, in the mirror of his eyes I saw ever my own beauty mirrored." (Gates, "Looking for Modernism," 205)

"My own beauty mirrored": it is hard to read this as a wish to go behind the mirror. Instead of Narcissus seduced by the image of a beauteous youth, what we see is a pool entranced by its own beauteous reflection as seen in the mirror of Narcissus' eyes. This is a story about a reflection seduced by the image of itself, mourning the fact that when it looks it now sees nothing. "The Disciple" raises the question of what happens when we look in a mirror and do not see ourselves reflected: is this a failure to see ourselves looking or a failure to see ourselves mirrored, reflected in the eyes of the other? Rather than reflecting Narcissus, the pool sees itself reflected by him, but the transfer offers no secure, or stable, site of reflection: the reflector is always in need of reflection. Ask the pool what it sees and it will answer: a beauty mirrored, yes, but also a reflector in mourning; the pool realizes that behind the image which now fails to appear there is, in fact, nothing. The critical intervention of the story, part of its shock, is that Narcissus, and we as readers of the myth, have not considered the pool as anything other than a means to reflection. This realization derives from the nonidentity between the visible (the object seen) and the visual (the experience of seeing): both Narcissus and the pool are the mirror reflection of each other; they reflect the other's act of looking in ways which suggest mimetic reflection but subvert it. It's an experience that confounds pleasure and loss with the threat of annihilation. Endowed with a fleeting life that appears to be the double of both the subject reflected and the image received, a dissemblance seems to have slipped into the pool's resemblance: "But was Narcissus beautiful?" asks the pool. For a moment it sees itself through Narcissus's eyes, but then something else— a grief born out of loss, an unwillingness to abandon its former semblance, takes over. But what this illusion veils is the absence lurking behind the mirror—the lack in whose vision the gaze of the other can be seen. What is terrible about this, however, is that this is all one sees.

But how does this distorting vision illuminate the spectatorial pleasure of *Looking for Langston*? If *Looking for Langston* offers us a "true" reflection is it because we see our own beauty mirrored on the screen or because we are compelled to seek our true image behind that mirroring in the wake of its loss and dissolution? And why imagine this moment of "self-recognition"—behind the mirror?—as one of exhumation, one that happens to coincide with a vision wherein the beautiful stands revealed as a corpselike reflection? (Wilde, cited in Gates, "Looking for Modernism," 204). A form of looking that threatens identity with the loss of the mirror as both object and subject? If anything, what *Looking for Langston* presents to black gays (and lesbians?) is not a *true* mirror image, but the representation

of a black desire to look as a subject (and not an object) in front of the mirror. It's an exhumation and retrieval of a black spectatorial pleasure otherwise missing from the gaze of racist homophobia. But then the film also
leaves us with the feeling that Wilde's pool leaves us with—that the screen
also wants to be seen, to see its own reflection in the spectators gazing
upon it, and in a way that allows it to escape the emptiness of the mirror.

What remains obscured by Gates and others is that *Looking for Langston*
crucially stages scenes of looking through scenes of interracial gay desire
(really—the eyes that look and are looked on are never simply black or
African American, but white and black British; eyes that, at the same time,
are not only disappointed by what they see, but also profoundly frustrated
by what they fail to see in the eyes of the white or black other). For me,
Looking for Langston is a meditation on the failures and pleasures of misrecognition—let's recall that the pool in Wilde's "The Disciple" is mournful not because Narcissus has died, but because of the loss of Narcissus's
capacity to reflect back the pool's own image, a loss valued more than the
original which cast it; and even here desire is stricken not by death but by
the deathliness of the reflected image whose reflection is so beautiful
because so deadly. That is, what is mournable about the image is that it can
only be secured against an always absent world, and hence its forming
is always the experience of an endless dying, and that in some ways the
image reveals what it necessarily lacks, because loss and absence is the
quintessence of its being. Looking back, the pool mourns what is lost in
the loss of this object—that is, the capacity of the object to reflect what
gives it "life"; but what the pool also loses is the fiction, or at least the fantasy, that the beauty reflected was its and its alone. That is, what is lost is
the fiction that the image permits a relationship (of identity and not alterity) of the pool to itself. Narcissus has died, but it is the loss of the reflected
image—not the image itself, the image of the self when it was there in his
eyes—that is dreadful (and deadly). The mirror image now becomes the
eidolon of the body that is no longer here, its phantom or double, but also
a passageway to what one doesn't see—the ghostly double of the departed,

a simulacrum of the dead person after death.[5] It is this awareness—of the mirror, or image, as an insubstantial resemblance of life as lived; the mirror, or image as inseparable from its eidolon (from this body whose reflection or simulacrum it is)—that also recurs in endless stories of blacks pursued by persecutory doubles or imagoes.[6] One soon becomes aware of how racism is experienced as an encounter with a mirror image in which one sees one's double, one's simulacrum, one's ghostly semblance— a specter which you greet with frustration and impotence, because of its inseparable hold on one's life. I would suggest that if *Looking for Langston* is compelling it is because what we see is a screen in mourning, a screen on which the looker finds himself having to offer atonement for, or denial of, or excuse for, what is unobtainable and lost, a game in which the desire to look—gay *and* interracial—finds itself mirrored by the seductive, ultimately vicious, lure of racist reflections.

Perhaps this is why *Looking for Langston*'s portrayal of black gay art and interracial gay desire is so infused with grief and loss? Or why this filmic mirror—this reflection on love and loss—appears to be so passionless in its mourning for the dead? *Looking for Langston* opens with a burial. After some documentary footage of Hughes's funeral, the camera tracks slowly over banks of calla lilies, peers through decorative choir screens and clouds of incense, lingers on a group of male and female mourners and angelic attendants who brandish portrait photos of the deceased, until it takes in the open casket. Lying in state in the casket with eyes closed is Julien himself: "the corpse in the casket" (Gates, "Looking for Modernism," 202). In *Looking for Langston,* "every sequence in the film is juxtaposed to the scene of mourning [that opens it]," writes Diawara (Diawara, "The Absent One," 222). Death, burial, looking: every sequence of *Looking for Langston* arouses in us the desire to look at the image as if it were the cadaverous remains of a dead body. To look on film itself as if we were gazing on the strange beauty of dead bodies, the "here lies" of the opening sequence itself the (film or mourning) work of exhumation and commemoration. But what we also see in this opening close-up are *eyes no longer able to see* or reflect us;

Figure 3 Julien, the corpse in the casket. Courtesy of BFI/Sankofa Video.

what we are made to see is literally the *death of vision* via the condensed, displaced figure of Julien, the corpse in the casket, the passive object of our reflections: i.e., the filmmaker as inverse mirror-image of the dead poet; the corpse as a representation of what happens when mirror image can no longer be identified as mirror reflection.[7]

In "A Lovesome Thing," David Deitcher describes this funeral scene as a "disturbing, densely symbolic" evocation of "longing" and one which "extends in various forms throughout Julien's project as a whole."[8] For him, this scene symbolizes "the loss and deprivation and unappeasable desire" afflicting the lives of black gay men prey to both racism and homophobia (Deitcher, "A Lovesome Thing," 11). All this is true, but this stress on longing and desire: why show this as a corpse-image? Why begin with the image of Julien himself as dead and thereby as an impossible witness? The opening image of the artist in death addresses no one; it falls short of a demand, even though it presents the artist as a figure to be mourned because, first of all, he is dead or missing.

What this image immediately gives to be read is the way we live with and memorialize the dead because of our own need to keep on living: making the dead account, in other words, for the presence or work of mourning. *Looking for Langston* begins with an attempt to render present the one who is other, absent; the one whose death makes possible these exchanges of grief and ritual. The film is the event of this missed historical encounter. The encounter with the fatal emptiness of the other as image, the reflection that brings death into the game of desire, its double or ghostly image. It is not in the name of longing that the film opens but with this encounter—that is, with the death that haunts the film's visibility and in which reflection is no longer an animated and living form (as in Wilde), but the effigy of a corpus or *corpusculum*, the manifestation of something hidden that has no mimetic equivalent *in* representation.

"Death and desire are linked in *Looking for Langston*," bell hooks suggests in *Yearning*. "Beauty merges with death and decay."[9] Referring to the opening funeral scene, she writes: "Death is no longer nightmare; it is an elegant transformative ritual, an occasion that demands, requires even, meaningful recognition and remembrance" (hooks, *Yearning*, 196). Rather than longing, then, *Looking for Langston* is an attempt "to resurrect and bring back to life what has been lost"; and at this funeral what we witness is the loved one resurrected and "collectively embraced, held in the arms of memory" (195, 196). In truth, what is striking about the funeral scene is not resurrection and embrace—there is no evidence of either— but the strange, passionless identification between Julien and Hughes; it is a meeting that emerges from the other side of death and, as such, designates a profound disjuncture. It is that encounter that encounters us. To again refer back to the scene, the mourners show no pathos or affect, neither recognition nor embrace. What they show is precisely the absence of reconciliation, an essential discordance between the corpse in the casket and the voice or documented absence of Hughes. Julien's wake does not abolish Hughes's footage or voice, but takes place in an unsituatable space—of loss and desire—that immediately disturbs what we see and know of the poet. We encounter Hughes's second death: he remains doubly absent from both the documentary footage of his funeral and from Julien's imaginary wake. All we see of him in *Looking for Langston*'s opening scenes are recorded televisual images and his photographic image held aloft by angels.

What does all this signify? Black gay desire does exist in *Looking for Langston*, but as an enigma, as the enigmatic encounter with a look in which desire withdraws as soon as it shows itself, destined to depart, slip away, to steal itself away without leaving any trace other than this fascinating encounter with one's dark reflection in the mirror. If "seduction begins with the look" in *Looking for Langston,* what also announces itself is the way in which the interracial desire for intimacy, between white and black men, is always laced with danger and exposure to the terrible fantasies wherein the real is articulated (197). "History, the smiler with the knife"—as Stuart Hall reminds us again and again.

"The ghost of Robert Mapplethorpe haunts the *mise-en-scène* of the gaze in Julien's film," writes Kobena Mercer in "Dark and Lovely: Black Gay Image-Making."[10] To illustrate this point Mercer refers to a scene in the nightclub where an exchange of looks takes place between Alex (played by Ben Ellison) and his object of desire, Beauty (Mathew Baidoo). This provokes a hostile, contemptuous glare from Beauty's white male partner (John Wilson). "As he turns away to face the bar," Mercer writes, "Alex drifts into reverie and imagines himself kissed by Beauty, their bodies coupled and entwined on a bed as if they had made love" (Mercer, "Dark and Lovely," 225). "It is important to recognize," he continues, "that this coupling takes place in fantasy, because it underlines the loss of access to the object of desire as being the very source of fantasy itself" (225). What haunts the filmic gaze, in other words, is a black desire to look structured by an inability to have the desired (black) object. I cannot enjoy what I see because what I see remains inaccessible to my visual pleasure, censored by the white male gaze. Or *"we want to look, but do not always find the images we want to see"*: a phrase taken from Mercer and Julien's coauthored response to Mapplethorpe's photography in "True Confessions."[11] Racism, in short, introduces a certain opacity, or violence, into the recognizability and desirability of black images. Because blackness is marked as the difference—or tain—in the mirror, what cannot be seen is precisely the gaze that opens up this gap between image and desire. Consequently, the black spectator's relation to the image is disturbed or lost.

This is a crucial insight into the role of fantasy in the film's mise-en-scène. The tension between eye and desire in this scene is, according to Mercer, not the same thing as racial fetishism even though *Looking for Langston*—the wish to look?—remains haunted by its logic. Another way of reading this is to say that black gay desire just can't be found outside of Mapplethorpe's perspective; there is nowhere else you can look in Julien's film that is not already haunted by racialized structures of fetishism and / or its revocation. Because whichever nightclub you go to play, sex, or film, racist homophobia is gathered outside the gates, waiting to break up the party. Unlike the racially "fetishized" look of Mapplethorpe's photography, Julien's filmic representation of black male desire "reposition[s] the black subject as the desiring subject, not the alienated object of the look" (Julien and Mercer, "True Confessions," 133). (Does this mean that alienation is located only in the exchange of interracial looks?) Fantasy may come in response to the "eroticized antagonism and rivalry" between white and black men, but what is haunting Alex's desire to look (at another black man) is his own object cause of desire; the fear that if he looks in the mirror he will see nothing, or nothing will be seen looking back (133). This anxiety is not, it seems to me, about the alienation of identity in the objectifying look of others, but about the very ability to symbolize and / or recognize a self in representation. It is precisely this fear of symbolic loss or repudiation that informs Alex's need to seek recognition in his mirror image. It is important to note here that Alex's reverie comes after his encounter with his reflected image in the mirror above the bar. Although Mercer fails to mention this detail, it is only after Alex's encounter with himself as a reflected image—as object of the look—that the illusionistic space of the film opens onto the "wish-fulfilling" sequence of Alex's dreams, desires, and fantasy (133). That is, it is the mirror that invites the eye to cross through to the fantasmatic mise-en-scène looming behind it. The mirror unveils, like a dream, that which escapes the visible. This is not so much a "mirror that looks back" (Mercer), or a mirror reflecting the loss of the object (Wilde), but a mirror that signals a detachment between racist gaze and black self-image, between the black as the imaged embodiment of the white castrating gaze and the black as what precisely escapes this mirror image (even though his dreams and desires remain haunted by it).

There is a frightening irony here. The forbidding gaze that awakens Alex's reverie and desire is also the censor that withholds it, and one that remains invisible, unlocatable, even ghostly. To look in the mirror, as a black, is to become aware of a separation between one's reflected image and one's image as publicly monitored or watched; you see yourself both from without and within, in the doubled mirror of an eye rendered see-able—but also impenetrable—by the gaze observed. When you gaze upon the mirror you are never alone, you are also surrounded by the many *imagoes* and phantasms projected onto the being that is black. Accordingly, and despite the loss to narcissism incurred, black visual pleasure does not transgress the racially fetishizing gaze but acts as a regressive substitute for it precisely because of this loss; and it is this combination of seeing and castration that becomes the source of fantasy and mourning in *Looking for Langston*, scenes of looking and sexual love that always seem fenced in by the figurative and formal mirroring between looking and masochism, desire and loss. This is the "true" scandal of *Looking for Langston*: what we see on screen is a black wish to see, and to derive libidinal pleasure from, a culture of racist violence driven by the desire to punish such looking. That is, we want to look *because* there is no meeting-place between image and desire except through fantasy; after all, the image that separates me from myself (as a free, desiring subject), is also what allows me to discover and answer that absence.

To his credit, Julien has refused to present *Looking for Langston* (leaving aside for now his use of documentary images) as anything more than an imaginary history of the Harlem Renaissance. In the interview with Hemphill, Julien admits that the controversy surrounding Hughes's sexual identity intrigued him: "it seemed to me to be a very important area to dwell in, even if it meant being at odds with different audiences and different sections of the black community. I thought it was imperative to at least suggest and visualize some of those anxieties" (Hemphill, *Looking for Langston*, 179–180). So instead of documenting the enigma of Hughes's "sexuality," Julien wanted to visualize the anxieties associated with Hughes through a meditation on his poetry; "I was trying to comment on how I imagined this lifestyle would have existed" (180). This is why *Looking for Langston* takes the form of a poetic "meditation" rather than the form of historical biography and why the enigma of Hughes's sexual identity is presented in terms of the sensuous exchange of enigmatic words and looks. In brief, *Looking for Langston* is an encounter with Hughes the icon—that is to say, with the phantasm reflecting public anxieties about black sexual and artistic life.

The response of Hughes's literary executor, George Bass, to *Looking for Langston* is a notable case in point. Objecting to the film's homosexual content, Bass and the Hughes estate twice blocked the screening of *Looking for Langston* in the United States while withdrawing permission for the use of Hughes's poems in the film's soundtrack. Behind this response can be glimpsed ever present anxieties concerning racial art and positive images; the demand that black art be "representative," that it act, as a delegate does, on behalf of black communities as a whole; that certain images are more "representative" of black political interests than others; that "black" art should authentically reflect these archetypal (straight, Oedipal) forms. In "De Margin and De Center," a 1988 essay coauthored with Kobena Mercer, Julien describes this process of "delegation" as an "exclusionary practice."[12]

Delegation, whether by whites or blacks, reduces blacks to a representative *type*, a reduction that is then taken to stand in for and correspond to the heteronormative "reality" of race, and by virtue of which white ethnicity remains invisible—that is to say, always the measure of other peoples' visibility but one that is disavowed (Julien and Mercer, "De Margin," 201).

Julien borrows the term "delegation" from Paul Gilroy and Pierre Bourdieu. For Bourdieu, writing in "Delegation and Political Fetishism," delegation is always a "magical" act of citation and usurpation: to speak on behalf of someone is to speak in place of that person, just as to say "I am the group" is also to say "I am, therefore the group is"; the delegate is he who is fully aware of the disguised violence that this "symbolic power" over the represented represents, and who exploits this fetishistic manifestation of the group "*in effigy.*"[13] The self-sanctification of the delegate makes it so that his power appears more real than magical, thus appearing as the requisite measure and embodiment of the alienated lives he professes to signify or represent. In "Cruciality and the Frog's Perspective," an essay first published in 1989, Gilroy alludes to delegation when describing the relationship between black art and community in eighties Britain. To see artists as public representatives of a homogeneous blackness is, for him, to miss the point. The critical task for black art, he suggests, is to dismantle the "constructed differences, not just between black and white but within black communities too."[14] The implications of this "antiphonic" relationship are as follows: "race" is depicted not as type, ideal or essential trait, despite the political desire for icons and idols, but is shown to be symbolically complicated by "gender, sexuality, generation and class" (Gilroy, "Cruciality," 111). It's an attempt to remove black art from its reduced mimetic role as delegation, while nonetheless making it deconstructive of what in effect excludes it: the racially "symbolic act" of delegation that limits black art to the role of the sociological, the denotative, and the documentary (Bourdieu, "Delegation," 59).

Bourdieu's suspicion of delegation informs Julien's account of why the black artist should tear himself away from any idealized or imaginary wish to represent the black community. In opposition to delegation—the iconic devaluation of certain images as unrepresentative and disfigured—Julien turns to what he calls "depiction." Black art must refuse delegation so as to depict the imaginary and unconscious need for racial representatives. This emphasis on showing over telling is also aimed at Gilroy's belief in the "redemptive uniqueness" of black "vernacular" art and his moral insistence that black art "can only be produced by *representing* black life in terms of active agency" (Gilroy, "Cruciality," 110; emphasis added). Julien concludes with two questions that return us to Mercer-Wilde's Lacanian mirror: "*What* does the black spectator identify with when his/her mirror image is structurally absent or present only as other?" "What if certain social categories of spectator do not have access, as it were, to [Lacan's] initial moment of *recognition*?" (Julien, "De Margin," 205). Aside from the mistaken slant here on recognition—recognition in the mirror phase is always misrecognition—these questions underscore the link between narcissism and mirror image, but also anxiety, usurpation, and representation. Hence the many scenes within scenes in *Looking for Langston* of desire and rivalry represented by men looking at other men; of men looking symbolically—longingly—at themselves, like counterparts, in the reflective surfaces of eyes, pools, mirrors. Looking here acts as a symptom (of desire, self-love, shame, and aggression), but also of complicated feelings of mourning that have neither address nor destination—that is to say, delegation—and that only hint at the interracial dreams, fantasies, reminiscences that they represent.

In *Looking for Langston* images of black men looking into mirrors betoken a wish to have access to a form of reproductive mimesis no longer haunted by the white racist (male, gay) gaze. Mirrors in the film act as indexes of a beautiful black interiority otherwise missing from the iconography of black men as types: oversexed, feckless, indigent, nothing but cock and drive. Typing represents a form of delegation that gives only a veiled image of black gay desire. And so one's projected reflection is not the same thing as one's likeness; the image that one sees is not reflective of how one is seen.

In contrast, the film addresses the viewer with the desire to see another kind of likeness; this is a wish not for sameness (the desire for a representative "true reflection"), but to have the mirror image prop up, in the process of representation, a contiguity between black gay image and black artistic desire. Because racism darkens the mirror, rendering it opaque, the black desire to look becomes equated, in *Looking for Langston,* with a wish to restore one's lost resemblance or history. In this sense, the film offers us new eyes with which to see our mirror images or to represent our otherness to the phantasms of culture. Recall the scene in the nightclub where the viewer sees Alex first stricken, then completely absorbed, by what he sees beyond the mirror as his gaze pierces the mirror's—the camera's—surface. Or the repeated image of Beauty lying face down with eyes closed on the mirror's surface, split-off from his resemblance and yet driven to embrace it precisely because he has lost sight of his image. Both are telling images of this focus—the impossible wish to touch and be one with the gaze.

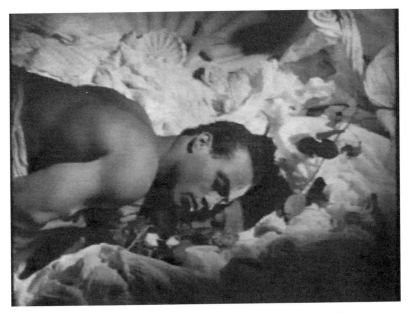

Figure 4   Beauty's mirror. Courtesy of BFI/Sankofa Video.

This is why *Looking for Langston* is not a documentary, but an imagined history of repressed desire. The voiceover states, "I long for my past"; a longing reiterated when we are told: "It's not wrong for the boy to be looking for his gay black fathers." As a "counterhistory" of the Renaissance—a word I borrow from Gates—*Looking for Langston* is fascinating to me precisely because it queers the familial Oedipal tropes of race and literary history that dominate conventional accounts. And so Houston A. Baker, in his seminal *Modernism and the Harlem Renaissance,* while questioning the prevalent reading of the Renaissance as a "failure," offers, instead, the analogy of a paternal *filiation*: "I knew, to be sure, that my father had not been a failure either in my own eyes or in the eyes of the community" in order to record the Renaissance as "a comprehensible moment in a distinctive, family modernity."[15] The image of success here merges with a memory of paternity. In this brief recollection, Baker presents history via the recollected order of family life, with African American modernity literally part of the family. He makes that history visible as a case of paternal inheritance, but nowhere is the work of the queer felt or seen. In another important reinterpretation, George Hutchinson, in *The Harlem Renaissance in Black and White,* writes, "As opposed to the method of the theorist who looks for purity of origins and the continuity of a tradition identified with a given stock, my method will be that of the satirical genealogist tracing the illegitimacy of origins."[16] Between Baker's consciousness of legitimate paternity and Hutchinson's contrived, satirical illegitimacy, there really is not that much difference. Their collapse of black modernist history into family life, history into genealogy, seems oddly blind to the opposed notion of a queer Renaissance and, for this reason, their accounts appear to be extricably caught up in an intricate web of descendence and genesis that is deeply heteronormative. In both texts what remains constant is an altogether familial model of genesis, origin, and filiation, and one quintessentially removed from questions of sexuality and desire.

That the issue for Julien is not one of legitimacy, but of the joys and pains of sexual desire is a useful corrective, as is his self-image (homosexual, black British) that is already distant from conventional historical narratives of genesis and filiation in Renaissance scholarship. It's an awareness in keeping with Hughes's understanding of black *life*, most especially the intimacy with which we greet the perverse mimicries of our projected selves. It is a practiced intimacy, and, between what is projected *onto* and what is ejected *outside* the self, there is no clear line from which to clarify what is parodied from what is being acted out—that is, no (il)legitimacy.

Looking for Langston, then, is a counterhistory, but it is also a work of mourning which is linked, for Julien, to a certain relinquishing of self and responsibility for otherness. In the 1992 essay "Black Is, Black Ain't," Julien says why a working through of repressed desire can relieve us of a need to abuse others because of a need to deny the otherness in ourselves: "I want to raise ambivalent questions about the sexual and racial violence that stems from repressed desires of the other within ourselves. . . . Racial anxiety is projected onto black subjects in the scopic register. It is the repressed desire for this other that surfaces as violence."[17] It is to avoid a complicity with such violence that Julien wants to "have desire exist in the construction of images" and why he "dwell[s] on the psyche and the imaginary as well as the factual" (Hemphill, *Looking for Langston*, 176, 178). This, then, is why depiction is, for Julien, both an ethics and a politics of responsibility concerning the power of racial images. Julien's remark—*interracial violence is a way of dealing with the repression of the other in one's innermost desires*—presents us with an image in which what is seen is the return of the disavowed now conceived as violence or threat. Behind the image can be glimpsed fear of violence of the Other, which ultimately refers to the sexual-racial violence of the self. What is important to Julien is that his films, at the level of image and desire, openly contest such presentations of otherness. I would like to conclude this chapter with a consideration of why, for Julien, interracial desire, through whose hostile, alleywayed territory we are often obliged to pursue the "inauthentic" desires and interests of blacks, becomes, for him, a transgressive sign of both gay sadomasochism (s/m) and black queer desire. It is a debate that will oblige us to take a look at gay interracial s/m, before coming back to Julien's equally radical questioning of racial sameness and sexual difference through the figure of black male masochism.

———

In 1993, Julien published "Confessions of a Snow Queen: Notes on the Making of *The Attendant*," a film where he examines interracial s/m in all its paradoxes: "could not the representation of interracial s/m," he asks, "be read as a practice of a racial and sexual dynamic which, in displaying the codes of a (Fanonian) master/slave dialectic, presents a transgressive simulacrum, one which parodies and disrupts the codes of societal and racial power?"[18] Or, in the more concise words of the late African American gay writer Gary Fisher, "racial humiliation is a real turn-on."[19] "I enjoy being your nigger, your property and worshipping not just you, but your whiteness," he adds. "I really wanted your cum and more of your piss" (Fisher, "Confessions," 231). Black masochism, for reasons that will require the rest of this book to explain, is a provocative subject, especially when the question of racial violence is linked to a black identification with a white sadistic gaze, as it is here in the work of Julien and Gary Fisher.

The starting point for *The Attendant*, a short video, is François-Auguste Biard's nineteenth-century painting *Slaves on the West Coast of Africa*, with its scenes of torture and trade, white lords, black bondsmen. The film re-creates a number of tableaux vivants drawn from the painting but "repositions" them—Julien's word—to signify interracial gay s/m and closeted queer desire. "Our gaze," writes Julien, "is repositioned through the eyes and fantasies" of the black, closeted, and middle-aged museum attendant who gives the film its title (79). As the attendant (Thomas Baptiste) checks in a white, leather-clad visitor (John Wilson) their eyes meet in mutual recognition and longing. Once again, as in *Looking for Langston,* seduction begins with a tantalizing, interracial look. These two looks become metaphors of one another in the film: the attendant discovers his repressed image in the white other's eyes; it's not so much that he sees a self that he doesn't recognize but an identity reined in and suppressed. In the gaze of the other he discovers a place of fantasy and play between what he is and what he is not, a theatrical stage where he can act out queer sadomasochistic fantasies. Seeing and imaging here merges with seeing and imagining via scenes of reminiscence and of fantasy. As spectators, looking on outside the fantasy s/m scenarios, our voyeurism is solicited: as the attendant and visitor perform their respective s/m roles, we see their investment in a fantasy, a fantasy that can neither fully represent them nor their desire, for the latter remains in excess of the fantasy that grounds it even as it is transgressed by the mise-en-scène of camp interracial s/m. It is in that space between fantasy scenario and the parodic, gay interracial gaze—a space that the film constructs purposefully—that the spectator is addressed and that a subject position is figured out between heterosexual and homosexual interracial desire.

In the window of fantasy framed by the visitor and tableaux vivants the attendant becomes aware of a self abjected; of his loss, so to speak, of that which he never had. "Abjection informs the attendant's new identity as he laments the passing fantasy of his white male visitor and contemplates his own mortality" (Julien, "Confessions," 79). Once again, the desire to see oneself reflected is in some sense a testimony to the proximity of death. But what is being repudiated or abjected? Julien's comments on abjection refer us to a politics of sexual identity. And so he draws on Craig Houser, who writes, "homosexuality becomes 'abjected' in the construction of normative heterosexuality. Abjection is a position assumed by gays and lesbians in defining their difference" (80). It's a self-representation in which black and queer subjects come to question and challenge the cultural laws that prescribe them by inverting the meaning of abjection from within. In this reinscription transgression gets a foothold, so to speak, because it mimics the fragility of heterosexuality by subjecting it to the perversity of the sexual drive. However, in *The Attendant* what comes across as abjected is the anguished work of mourning ("mourning is never very far away from abjection," Julien adds) for the lost desired object; what we see and hear is the attendant's mournful gaze and aria as he bemoans his age and loss as death approaches. What we also see is what happens when the object of fantasy appears to be too close but never close enough. In *The Attendant,* interracial s/m gives way to the story of a man humiliated by his own desires—a black man who desires to observe himself subjected to the gaze that everywhere surrounds him, but from which he is excluded.

The outcome of this "Fanonian master/slave dialectic" is not, then, liberated work or desire, but the grievous awareness of what *exceeds* both domination and dependence, otherness and desire. Let me return here to Julien's phrase "passing fantasy of his white male visitor": I read "passing" as passed away, gone, no longer, but read diegetically back into the film we also see repeated images of the attendant passing in front of paintings as he walks through the empty galleries. He never looks into the paintings even when they become mirrors to his fantasy life via the acted-out scenes of the tableaux vivants. (What this suggests is that he is excluded from the imaginary realm of desire that eludes him, which the s/m fantasy serves to cover up or hide.) It's a missed encounter made palpable by color and editing as the film switches from the monochrome black and white of the empty rooms to the brightly lit colors of the repositioned paintings. Passing here becomes a metaphor for a self emptied-out, evacuated—a self ghosted, in effect, by the representations that surround him but do not address or invoke him. This leads me to ask whose fantasy is this and who is doing the repudiation that inaugurates mourning? As it turns out, the connection between abjection and mourning has nothing to do with the interracial fantasy of seeing oneself beaten and quite a lot to do with the repudiation of a thought that is both wanted and prohibited. When the attendant sings Dido's aria "When I Am Laid in Earth," from Purcell's 1689 opera, *Dido and Aeneas,* it is the identification with death that resurrects itself; it is a death that has already taken place and that he performs in his desire to be beaten and punished, which is why just before we see him meet the gaze of the visitor, we see an image of him performing this aria in which Dido laments her death from the place of the other's desire. This is an aria about loss and remembrance, but also about the loss necessary for the representation of lost desire and the return of its insubstantial semblance. It isn't, in truth, about parodic or transgressive desire, but about an impossible love that transcends death, in whose failure we witness an incessant, interminable mourning ("remember me" in my dying; never renounce the pain, the agon, of my suffering; remember my grievous fate, but never forget that I am gone).

It is in this commandment to bear witness to endless dying that *The Attendant* rejoins and reaffirms the absence that shimmers on the surface of the pool in Wilde's "The Disciple." Dying here appertains to the cold dissolution of the self in the depths of its own emptiness. The best one can do is to *pass* through this interminable loss without, that is, memory or desire and without, at the same time, any assurance as to the "presence" of life. For precisely these reasons, Julien's films strike me as strangely passionless, closer to still lifes than to the unforeseeable movements of pain, anguish, and sexual desire.

To explain why this is the case let me now turn to another text haunted by interracial gay s/m. Gary Fisher's *Gary in Your Pocket*—a posthumous collection of diaries, poems, and stories—offers a striking contrast to *The Attendant*. Knowing himself to be dying from AIDS these writings begin as a memorial, a posthumous memorial to the body's former likeness now gone, ravaged by both treatment and disease. The writing down of words is part of that memorialization and the attempt to symbolize the unsymbolizable threat of death. In contrast to the beautiful male bodies on display in Julien's tableaux vivants striking their leather-clad poses in *effigy*, Fisher's diseased body is meditating—writing—on the living body as effigy of the carnal body that was and is no longer. In her afterword, Eve Kosofsky Sedgwick writes of how Fisher, alone in his apartment, "would spend hours, sometimes whole days of months, paralyzed in front of his mirror, incredulous, unable—also unable to stop trying—to constitute there a recognizable self" (Fisher, *Gary*, 281). According to one of Fisher's sisters, "that's how Gary experienced being black, too" (281).

It is the anguish of seeing, and knowing, oneself disappear. All one sees is absence as one peers mournfully at the dissemblance now haunting the mirror (the difference of the image less traumatic than the uncanniness of the resemblance). Despite references to the AIDS crisis and aging in "Confessions of a Snow Queen," in *The Attendant* there is no real attention to the fact that the loss of resemblance to oneself might induce terror rather than abjection, fixation rather than beauty or parody. That terror and fear is definitely there in *Gary in Your Pocket*, as indicated in the following long passage on the ruin and fear and threat carried by the surface of the pool:

> black x gay x (black x gay) for some kinky sexual gratification built on
> and fueled by self-hatred. That's not simple enough, I know, but which
> came first: the sex or the hatred? Indeed, I believe it was none of the
> above. It was FEAR. Fear of being hurt (because I am black) leads to an
> excitement which strangely mimics the excitement I feel when a man
> (particularly—[?] though I have precious little variation to contrast this
> with the general—especially—[?] (particularly a white man, although
> I know, have known, few black men [fewer brown (and no yellow)]
>
> (particularly a white man—though the word, if not the idea of *par-
> ticular* comes out of an imagination—or lack of it!—or out of a strat-
> egy for a sexual future that includes mainly, if not only white
> men—because certainly little or nothing in my past would require me
> to imply distinction between or to qualify or to filter out the white
> man from the pool. [. . .]
>
> [. . .] little or nothing required that I distinguish him, qualify him or
> filter him from the pool, since pool here (for him and for me) implies
> no variety, no turbulence, no movement, not a ripple, no nothing: pool
> doesn't imply at all, it doesn't *do* anything except watch itself
> unwatched (?) . . . ahhh! then perhaps it does im-ply, that is M-ply like
> white narcissus—or like the tv serial that tests its own worth [. . .] by
> dangling its own suspense week after week, foreshadow unresolved,
> unresolvable—like what narcissus remembered, suspended and con-
> stant, though always in ecstatic jeopardy of folding in on himself;
> the face in the pool threatens to imply. And if it threatens to imply

something not itself then it risks breaking the silence, risks revealing me to me, know if not . . . no I don't know what a white man sees below the surface of himself, if not me, 'cause certainly I've been taught that I'm this way through and through, a dark dense star, horribly attractive, irresistible, a lodestone, the plunge at the very heart of . . . what now can only be perceived as ripples. Unresolved till unresolvable. [. . .]

So, particularly (especially or primarily) a white man, when he holds and protects me from others like him, brings me an excitement which strangely and uniquely parallels that which he causes me when he threatens or frightens me. Of course, if my white man goes he takes his protection and his comfort. . . . Obviously, then: without him, why would I need him. Want might be another problem, but want's based on memory, on fantasy, on the way things might have been. Without these I couldn't want him, but I could have created him anyway as something to avoid, as a barrier to desire and hence its fixation. (236–237)

"Unresolved till unresolvable": clearly, for Fisher, the pleasure of being taken and mastered as a "nigger" is not just about being brutally fucked by cum, piss, whiteness. It is the risk or threat that past ruination may be repeated but, even so, one must give oneself absolutely (without relation or self-identity) to that risk if sexual pleasure and excitement—the "ecstatic jeopardy" of folding in on oneself—is to become more than impotence, self-hatred, or black ruination. Unlike the attendant, what Fisher sees in the pool is not the empty infinity of desire, or the endless serialization of guilt, but the risk of the other to oneself, a threat that must be embraced and borne precisely because sexuality is the meaning of this risk. And so it comes to pass—and this is a way of seeing oneself as neither active nor passive, neither the dark star around which the ripples endlessly reassemble on the surface nor the narcissism drawn to project its emerging in the depths of the pool—that Fisher's masochism is a defense against self-loathing and represents a desire to be shattered beyond fear. From the pain of a self shattered to breaking point he gets the excitement he needs; in the process what is publicly abolished is the indignity he feels as a nervous black man (and, by implication, the serialization of fixed self-definitions, i.e., black x gay). In the book, especially the entries dealing with serial conquests, what is awful and disturbing is not Fisher's resolve to be shattered by law, but the American "lords" who play upon this emotional and political confusion to satisfy their own vulgar racism. Between Fisher's will to be the desirable object of law and their own pretensions to embody that law without risk, without staking their own collusions, we see a world of difference. In a way not seen in either *The Attendant* or *Looking for Langston*, here the white man/pool is fantasized and admired because of the "threat" carried by his obsessive self-absorption. Such is the deathly singularity of the self submerged in self-reference, withdrawn from the uncanny turbulence of the other's desire or sex, the expanding field of drive or movement is unresolvable as either suspension or deferral, it remains a pressure threatening to *impress* or *breach* the surface of the pool with a jouissance that is intimately alien. Watching itself unwatched, the implications of that threat are inseparable from the pool's attraction and fascination; the refusal of the surface to harbor, and so protect the other's image, is felt, paradoxically, to intensify, relative to the strength of the narcissistic ego, the projected image against which the ego projects being attacked—implications that are narcissistic in the most rigorous sense of this exacting term, a merciless overvaluation that excludes all otherness. No variety, no movement, no nothing.

Without sentiment or voyeurism, Fisher shows himself to be far more punishing and perversely cruel than the white men he burdens with his powerful fantasy of the big Other. As such, *Gary in Your Pocket* induces a crisis of identification in me because it brings me up flat against a black will to be humiliated and the personal and political depredations at stake. It is this "strange parallel" between the gaze that holds and protects and the gaze that wounds and cuts that bears on the vicissitudes of the black when faced with the racism of representation. "I could have created him anyway as something to avoid," writes Fisher—that is, hate *me* in him, persecute *myself* as him, experience the libidinal excitement and pain of that barrier to desire. To recognize that I resemble the white racist other, that I resemble myself in him even in my own desire, would be tantamount to admitting the inadmissible: that I am not myself and that my most proper being is over there, in that reflecting double who enrages (shames, despoils) me. Whoever encounters the pool risks this oblivion, but this is not a "barrier to desire" because of Fisher's need to avoid hurt, the fear of never being anything but the recognizably black (abject) self. Hence his fixation on being abolished beyond representation, even if the resemblance offered coincides with an imago that is inimical and gives reality to the "nigger" as the site of an irresolvable psychic conflict: black x gay, a libido conventionally read as fueled by self-hatred and the overprominence of fear. What Fisher wants above all is for the white lover-master to assume his full strength and potency and to test his force on his orifices and skin. The idea of being beaten as much a demand that the other bear witness to one's narcissism as the pleasure in bearing witness to his cruelty.

It also occurs to me that Julien's slave-as-simulacrum is not the same thing as Fisher's nigger-as-identity. A black devotee of interracial queer s/m may enjoy neither the image nor idea of "nigger," despite being turned on by the idea of himself as a slave. The role of "slave" can, argues Julien, perform a transgressive "parody" of power; but what is transgressed belongs to the order of appearance wherein fantasy encounters the simulacra-phantasms of discipline, and the law reveals its secret, obscene underside. As such, *The Attendant* is meant to provide a visualization of such spectatorial positions and their reverses in desire and fantasy. This should not be confused with Fisher's s/m pleasures that are neither semblances nor parodies, but denote a drive to be *the* nigger rather than transgress the image of it. He *has* to be the nigger, *whether he wants to or not.* The only way he can satisfy this "will to enjoyment" (Lacan) is to become a nigger for a white man. So, though Julien says he is not interested in "correct notions of sexual practices from a world devoid of fantasy," his portrayal of black gay masochistic desire/white sexual domination very much remains within the world of fantasy, simulacra, self-performativity (Julien, "Confessions," 81). What tends to go missing is any sense of a self imprisoned by the terrors and fears, the hatreds and stigmas that also form part of the drama of interracial s/m and where being a "nigger" signifies racial aggression in the scene of seduction itself. What goes missing, in other words, is the drive to love and be loved as a nigger. It's a scene where the nigger, needless to say, finds the real of his desire, not in fantasy but in the pleasure of choking on his master's cum and piss. This distinction is found again and again in *The Attendant* and *Gary in Your Pocket*.

There's more. In the course of *The Attendant*, "auditory pleasures of aural voyeurism are explored" (Julien, "Confessions," 79). Whereas the downward strokes of the whip are always about to fall on the attendant/visitor's prostrate bodies, what we literally see is the whip always held in suspense, its effects never seen only heard. Further, the only diegetic audience to the interracial couple in the film is the attendant's wife, who Julien refers to as the attendant's straight "alibi." "She is the accomplice, the knowing participant and partner in an unspoken agreement that is sealed with a hetero-kiss" (80). "The rhythm of the whiplash is heard forlornly in the rhythm of her clap," he adds, the strokes of her (heterosexual) "resentment" interpenetrated by the strokes of the attendant's groans of desire. The representation of interracial s/m is consequently a mix of complicity and resentment grounded in sexual difference. If the s/m scenes are reenacted in a sort of frozen progression, the roles shifting from the attendant to the visitor, the frozen quality of the exchange is, I think, equivalent to the arrested movements of the conservator as she overhears the reality of their pleasure. It is through her arrested image that we encounter the arrested movement of suspended desire and the attendant's masochistic use of Dido as a mirror to his humiliation. Since sadism has no "realistic" presence, or visual evidence, it is the conservator's clapping and looking that serves to distinguish spectatorial pleasure from the visual s/m fantasy, aural voyeurism from the images and "codes" of domination. Those codes become metaphors for a fissure in both Oedipal law and legality allowing transgression to get a hold, for when an active black gay desire for humiliation meets a consensual white desire to humiliate, then the "satisfying of the sexual libido [certainly] does not come within the category of *good* reason," as argued by Lord Chief Justice Lane in the infamous 1992 Spanner Case: the trial and conviction of five middle-aged gay men for practicing extreme homosexual sadomasochism, a case Julien cites in "Confessions of a Snow Queen" as representative of his concerns (81).

Once again, Julien's comments direct us to the racial politics of gay s/m and the place of interracial desire within queer s/m discourse. But how does this play out in the film? Whereas racial difference connotes desire and mourning, visually it is sexual difference that enables us to hear and visualize the transgressive play of interracial gay desire; it is the wife's response to the attendant's aria that makes us aware of his abjection; her clapping that echoes the performance of sadomasochism (its suspenseful strokes of desire); and her waiting and suspense that ensures the advent of pleasure and expected pain in the tableaux vivants. For me, it is the female conservator's role in *The Attendant* that "displays" the codes of a Fanonian master-slave dialectic. I understand that display, because of her aural voyeurism, as a problem of representability—that is, what lies beyond the frame and the field of vision. Significantly, it is her inability to see that underpins her displacement from the place of perverse desire even as her "resentment" grounds it. She is the mirror to the attendant's closeted desire; she is the echo to the strokes of sadistic desire evoked and covered over by her spectatorship. What we see is her inability to see, to envision. Because she is a screen—an alibi, a decoy, a mask, a prop, a double—she cannot become part of the spectacle in which the interracial homosexual subject projects himself and is held. As the representative for the Other of the gaze her role is to be the image/screen outside the picture and not the specular subject inside the picture. On the desire of the conservator, one could say, replaying Fanon, that Julien's film has nothing (i.e., everything) to say about her. The spectacle of *The Attendant* is all about the attendant's crisis, his morose disquiet that "passing," even in s/m, can never void the void of castration: "remember me, but ah forget my fate."

But there is yet a further dimension. Throughout this chapter my intention has been to explore a typical scene in Julien's films in which black desire is frozen before its reflection in the mirror. Black narcissism is frozen by virtue of being stereotyped and suspended, a freezing relating to the ruination of its resemblance in the fictions and images of culture. We have seen why this pool is filled by a combination of abjection and pain and yet drained of all passion by the image of an endlessly deferred pleasure, work, or mourning. But was Narcissus beautiful? It is a question that already requires the pool's dark waters to answer for the other's absence and to account for its own frozen, arrested, cadaverous quality—a responsibility that is difficult, interminable, and necessarily unresolved. For the mourning that is at issue is indistinguishable from the pool's own misrecognition of loss. In *Looking for Langston* misrecognition conveys an otherness that is disavowed and in suspense; to this end we see countless scenes of men totally absorbed in their own reflections trying to find, like Orpheus, their lost Eurydice. In *The Attendant* this search becomes, by analogy, a death without end, the loss of the other's absence become *the* masochist fantasy of interracial desire. If, in *Looking for Langston*, it is the incommensurability of interracial gay desire and racist homophobia that takes place as a narcissistic crisis; in *The Attendant* what is abject can only be resignified as unending loss that cannot be overcome or overturned by the self's transgressive possibility.

5   *Letters to Langston*

Too great a cost this birth entails.
—Countee Cullen, "The Shroud of Color"
(1925)

Because this chapter is intimately related to my previous chapter, and therefore each reflects the other and their reflections, as in a parallel play of mirrors, this chapter is also about black visual history and the frozen, arrested, fetishistic image of blacks invited to study themselves within the orb of abjection. This chapter returns to what happens when blacks, suspended and enraptured by the orb, appear to be pleasurably affected by what they see, or fail to see, in their reflection. I'm not sure whether seeing is here a consequence of terrible clarity or blindness, the better to shield the imagined self against similitude or to secure the ego against a despoiling which is itself suspended in fantasy? It's a question that, because I cannot see all that clearly myself, returns me to the language of art and film and the issue of delegation.

In *Looking for Langston*, Julien features several gay historical figures of the Harlem Renaissance, including the poet Countee Cullen and Alain Locke, the Howard University philosophy professor and editor of *The New Negro* (1925). Their appearance adds to the appearance of Hughes both formally and dialectically. Julien pays more attention to the iconicity of Hughes, during which his homosexuality is implicit but never identified as such, than he does to literary history. Instead of turning to the *real* Langston Hughes, the life outside the work as its supposed model, let us take Julien's cue and turn to Hughes the icon, the enigma of his sexuality. As we shall see, that enigma affected strong sexual desires in Cullen and Locke, a desire suspended and postponed but all the more intense because of this painful inhibition. What follows is the story of this missed encounter, one that takes place through the image and act of writing letters. It's a story in which Alain Locke also "looks" for Hughes, a search characterized by his views on art and queer desire: the wish to see a new order, a new culture emerge from the act of men loving other men. The main difference from Julien is that Locke will elaborate a narrative of delegation that will transform it from within by way of a model of procreation rather than representation. In Locke's writings on philosophy and aesthetics, the role of criticism is defined, more or less, as one of nurturing art through the experiences of elation and deprivation into the painful delivery of critical judgment. It's a view of criticism based not so much on self-consecration as a model of self driven by the need to bear the labors borne by others: the office of midwife preferred over the legal fiction of delegation. It's a vision that has not, to my knowledge, been previously studied for what it says about Locke's homosocial investment in black aesthetics and the connecting thread of manly love.

In Statu Nascendi

Washington, 17 January 1922. In a letter to Hughes, Locke writes of thought and art in terms of implied homoerotic exchange and intimacy; but he also describes a kind of inner intrusion, or unconscious instinct, running away with him, driving him on, welling up within. The language used is one of desire and anticipation but also one of seeing; it's a mental picture or projection, an *insistence* supported by much anticipation and one that has forcibly taken him over: "Everybody it seems who is a particular friend of yours insists on my knowing you. . . . Some instinct, roused not so much by the reading of your verse as from a mental picture of your state of mind, reinforces their insistence." "Their" refers to Jessie Faucet and Countee Cullen, who "are the friends who insist" and whom Locke thinks "ought to be good enough introduction" for Hughes stationed onboard the *West Hassayampa* in Washington harbor.[1]

Locke's ardent invocation of Hughes, the first of many, is occasioned by his wish to know, now, the young poet, his state of mind. But, on the other hand, the wish to marry up the two—inner urging, outer insistence—is already the result of urgings by others: "everybody it seems who is a particular friend" of Hughes. One of those "friends" is Cullen, who in January 1923 wrote to Locke urging him to approach Hughes: "Write to him and arrange to meet him," Cullen suggests. "You will like him; I love him; his is such a charming childishness that I feel years older in his presence."[2] That tempting picture is framed, in turn, by Fauset's glowing accounts of the poems she has selected to appear in the *Crisis*. Against such advertisements, Locke was defenseless. No surprise, then, that he is "roused" by the "mental picture" of Hughes; or that his initial, ravished response to that picture is made even stronger by such insistence. (This fascination with the fascination of Hughes—shared by Julien—not only concerns the enigma of Hughes's sexuality but also turns to the poetry as the enigmatic appearance-disappearance of that sexuality.) The sequence, driven first from without and then from within; the self-image—a certain passability, a vessel waiting to be filled up by the seminal words of others— suggest a desire and longing precipitated into being by Hughes's reflected beauty. But if Locke feels replete, awash with the pressures of instinct, he is also frustrated, for the picture of Hughes can only offer anticipation.

"I glory in your creativeness," Locke writes to Hughes again on June 13. "I am so hopelessly academic and sterile it seems—still I can vibrate once in a while."[3] The double effect of this imagery—engorgement and vacancy, erethistic pressure and depletion—figures poetic creativity as phallic power and the quivering homosexual body as the passive instrument waiting to be struck. In contrast to academic sterility, in which parturition is expressed as loss—that is, estrangement—the opening up of a chasm between the meditative self and the creative self, the vibrations set in motion by Hughes's poetry results in an ecstatic rendering of the self. Locke entwines eros and the aesthetic here as the sensuous promise of male friendship and collaboration, but he also unfolds the drama of what it means to be engorged by the poetic imagination when all one is conscious of is vacancy and aporia.

"Still I can vibrate." Shelley's famous analogy of the poetic mind to a "harmony, [that is] by an internal adjustment of the sounds or motions thus excited to the impressions which excite them," is echoing here, as is his likening of the poet to an Aeolian harp whose music (the poem) results from the affecting presence of the wind on the strings which it vivifies into melody or harmony.[4] Another echo would be Hazlitt's "the natural impression of any object or event, by its vividness exciting an involuntary movement of imagination and passion, and producing, by sympathy, a certain modulation of the voice, or sounds, expressing it."[5] It is this Romantic view of the imagination as the accord of nature and sensibility and the harmonious reciprocation of form and aesthetic idea that is echoing in Locke's metaphor. It's a view of the imagination as spontaneous self-affection—that is to say, the imagination as the informing power of a universe of representation in which the self immerses itself in order to unburden itself of the authoritative pressures of affect within it. In this coalescing will and sympathy, the boundary between what is given and what is bestowed, knowing and the known, is a sliding one. Again, mind is not active over and against nature but within it, a natural force or harmony shaped by and within a natural and cultural environment. There is no polarity between mind and world, but a mutual engendering of one in the other in which the image, or picture of Hughes, comes to stand for the point of indiscernability between what is imagined and what desired, the actual object and the more irreal, undetermined, feelings of sympathy through which the object is expressed.

On the other hand, Locke's allusion to sterility—"I am so hopelessly academic and sterile"—suggests that such harmonizing is less authoritative, somehow, than the romantics conceived of it. Epistemologically, that sterility expresses an anxiety over the possibility of reaching the world as it is. Spiritually, it expresses itself in anxiety over the enclosedness of the individual self, the isolating uniqueness of a self. This anxiety is not about being a self, or whether there is a self, but the anxiety of being itself—namely, that which finds itself burdened with a self and above all wants to escape from itself and flee its suffering, or, at any rate, it wants to transform itself, to turn itself into something more bearable. It wants to be unified with poièsis, and it wants to be immersed in facticity in order to rid itself of this ghostly disincarnation, which the burden of oneself is. It is as though, after all the sensuous correspondences and analogical metaphors, Locke found his own nature and sensibility bodied against him; the fear of never being able to bring to term what connects, for him, the poetic life of spirit to the rhythm of his own instincts: the experience, the danger of losing contact with that self-image. "Poor me," he writes to Hughes on 10 February 1922. "I am all leaden intellectuality and have to content myself with being a friend of poets . . . Like Banquo, though I am none, yet do I like being in at the feast and watching the succession of the spirit."[6]

Locke as the ghost at the feast?[7] It's an odd self-deprecation given the role of Banquo's ghost in *Macbeth*: murdered because of the prophecy that he will beget kings; murdered because of the threat posed by his paternal legitimacy to Macbeth. Yet if Locke's progeny can only be known by proxy and by a spectral genealogy, then the father's role in the ever-renewed revelation of spirit can only be claimed as the suffering of a separation from its own genealogy, which is to say, as the ghost of spirit. Further, the apparition of Banquo's specter in *Macbeth* is not only the unbearable harbinger of a traumatic message but also the interruption of Macbeth's claims to succession. To regard Locke as Banquo thus opens up quite a complex narrative of filiation. If Banquo is the watcher at the feast, he is also the horror upon which Macbeth's eyes scarcely dare rest, the specter whom he acknowledges by turning away from. What appalls Macbeth is the fear that the specter is not real but the manifestation of what is most intimate to him and from whose traumatic and uncanny innateness he cannot free himself—that is to say, the specter as the eerie representative of what is unrepresentable to the subject that is its own most becoming. Yet if we return to Locke's stress on friendship with poets, the aesthetic is where the real encounter between genealogy (spirit) and paternity (specter) takes place, where spectral apparition enters into relation with the fraternal community of spirit.

Once again, poetry emerges as the process that converts what has grown leaden and inert from being abstracted from experience into some new, vital form that reanimates experience and thereby literally gives birth to a new succession of spirit. As such, the poem is the manifestation of the sensuous inner workings of spirit that is itself haunted by the separation between intellect and experience, paternity and generation, life and death. That said, if too much intellectuality results in a morbid simulation of life, it also leads to a strange form of intimate witnessing that is both conjoined and disparate, a process of consciousness that is passionately aware of the virtuality it actualizes and of its own resemblance to the ghostly simulation of such actualizations. In other words, as the ghost of spirit, Locke is able to see how art and literature are ghosted by the virtualities and imitations of interiorized experience that they recast as spirit.

Locke's background in pragmatism led him to transform what is here experienced as estrangement and loss in the sundering of ties between knowledge and the world, into a pragmatic requirement for the rebirth of art and spiritual progress. In his aesthetics, Locke was trying to account for what William James, one of his philosophy tutors at Harvard, refers to as "all those indefinitely radiating subconscious possibilities of increase *that we only feel without conceiving*, and can hardly begin to analyze."[8] But unlike James, Locke did not try to defend himself against the anxiety produced by such feelings via a manly reliance on "sheer force and will and fight."[9] In "Pragmatism and Humanism," James writes, "In our cognitive as well as in our active life we are creative. We *add*, both to the subject and to the predicate part of reality. The world stands really malleable, waiting to receive its final touches at our hands. Like the kingdom of heaven, it suffers human violence willingly. Man *engenders* truths upon it."[10] In his commentary on this passage, Jonathan Levin argues that aesthetic creation was primary for James, which was why he dismissed "forms of esthetic seduction" as "quite diminished."[11] This comment doesn't quite get at the anxiety aimed at such seduction, nor at James's exclusions and displacements of both the homoerotic and the feminine from the virile "engendering" of truths on malleable nature (and its willing submission to violence). Lockean midwifery should be understood as a reaction to such engendering and anxiety, one facilitated by a homoerotic flight from a "feminine" orientation toward art and a rebirthing of the poetic knowledge of the world as androgynous masculinity. For Locke, the philosophical midwife not only stands midway between the male engendering consciousness and feminized nature, but is also both subject and predicate of the phallocentric freedom of aesthetic feeling, the mediated receptacle of its pragmatic truth.

Locke's metaphors recall the pool of Narcissus, that dialectic of impressing power and sensuous passivity shimmering on the mirror's surface. But one also gets the impression that what possesses is the image of the beloved as seen by others rather than his own beauty mirrored. It's a self-image—sterile, academic—so disappointed by what it sees or fails to see in the mirror that it seeks to see itself reflected in the creative life of others. In this drama of shame, concealment, and exhibition underlying the worship of poetry as a phallic art, the desire is to be understood and reflected, to be seen by what is missing from the mirror. Crudely, what one loves in the other is the image of creative genius that one sees in him, that he possesses, and that one wants to be loved by. This is a narcissism that can only desire itself from a point beyond the mirror. But what is also conveyed is the fantasy that the ever-present pressure of the sexual instinct can only be allayed when the satisfactions and promise of the desired "mental picture" are unified with the *I* and its representations. True life lies elsewhere in the unrepresentable thought that makes the self vibrate with the feelings and passions of affective life. It's a wish to reflect and be reflected by that fertile creative spirit that, Locke writes elsewhere, "pregnantly develops in our youth." "It has so many analogies with birth," he continues, "that I often think that from the pangs of the developed of their personalities, men of talent achieve vicariously the experiences of

motherhood, and with it the intuitive understanding and spiritual clairvoyance of women."[12]

What is one to make of this language? Why does homoeroticism rely
here on analogies to childbirth and reproduction? Locke's vision of himself as "the nurse-maid of genius" is not a metaphor: "I do not shirk the
metaphor—I believe it is literal" (Locke, "To the Young Friend").[13] Here,
in an unpublished text, "To the Young Friend on Reading *Jean Christophe*,"
Locke suggests that the "problem of life" is to "culturally keep alive the
spirit of that personality which pregnantly develops in our youth"; to
deliver the self "from all that would confine, cramp, and constrain it"—
forces such as racism and sexual repression. The "genius born in every
adolescence" must be nurtured, he urges, if that spirit "born in youth" is
to survive through "to manhood and expression"; that spirit must become
"frankly pagan" and anti-imitative in its expressiveness if it is to "live creatively" rather than "imitatively." Words must be impregnated with eros if
they are to endure beyond the forces constraining them; if they are to be
disseminated as a potentially generative bond between youthful immatu-
rity and creative adulthood. It is important to note here that the distinction
between drive and constraint corresponds and is the foundation of Locke's
view of the artist as he who embodies the spirit of eros and reproduces its
mimetic fecundity, he who under the sway of inspiration or impulse
becomes the medium for the negation of normative sexual morality and
the ego. What is involved here is not just an evolutionary movement from
adolescence to manhood, constraint to spiritual clairvoyance: creative
genius is not just a stage of life but that which adulthood (that is, discourse, signification, reason) represses via the workings of culture. Spirit
is, within the adult, that which cannot be reduced to racial or gendered
mimesis, not because it refuses to reproduce masculinity and femininity,
but because it emerges as some other thing irreconcilable to such relations; it is the pagan outside to such identities, thus always appearing
more as a remainder than as the working of representation. Spirit is not
representative; it is the seminal effect on art and language of the force

exerted by unconscious homoerotic life. In brief, if black gay art is to be productive it must not be imitative but a medium for those manly passions having their source in drive and nature. "Imitativeness has its shallow end in early sterility and unproductiveness," Locke concludes (Locke, "To the Young Friend").[14] Imitation is false appearance; the pursuit of simulacra rather than procreative life. The artist who imitates is sterile because, like the mirror, he only copies forms rather than creates them and is therefore incapable of engendering life. The "true" artist neither imitates nor copies: he imagines and creates.

The mental picture of Hughes so important to Locke—the letters reveal how much—seems to embody this imaginary, unseemly, libidinal force at work within and against discourse and representation—this radical division or cleavage between the wish to conceive and the power to imagine. It is an homoerotic vision in which Hughes becomes an emblem for both what is imagined and what remains incommensurable to that imagining. The intervention of puberty not only introduces a disarrangement of genius in the birth of erotic experience from spiritual idea but also becomes the site of a tension in the unfolding of artistic life: gendered identity as the dissipation of desire finally lived; puberty as the awareness of this possibility of separation and loss. The experience of art—a gap through which the nonunity of gender and desire can be glimpsed—denotes an interruption meant to free us from the conditions of stability and security—that is to say, sexual-racial repression—so that one may live once again those heightened moments of life beyond all communicable-mimetic reality. Accordingly, the twin task of gay art and love emerges—in Locke's letters to Hughes in "To the Young Friend on Reading *Jean Christophe*"—as both a defense against masculine culture *and* its consummate aesthetic fulfillment as homosocial self-cultivation.

If meditative life is barren that is because it lacks affinity with poièsis, with spirit. The only way to think thought is not barren is to conceive it as a fecund relationship between two men, as an anal fantasy of procreative birth. The poet is a receptacle likened to a mother because of his receptivity to impression, but he is also the father as source or spring for the artistic form of spirit which enters him and stirs and informs him. The child is the artwork which is formed through their union: the androgynous body of art. In Locke's account, the artwork is itself a child of the union of spirit and form. But it is the philosophical midwife and not the mother who works on and shapes the effective and active element, who transforms the poet's insemination of spirit. The feminine element here connotes receptivity rather than reproduction. All that is fertile or spiritual—the romantic's vibrating Aeolian lyre, the harmonizing of drive and desire in the plasticity of the imagination—belongs exclusively and entirely to the poet's androgynous creativity (at least on first reading). It is the poet's sympathetic entanglements with the world, Locke suggests, that truly respects the object—that is, what allows the variety of the world's meanings to unfold without coercion or too-focused interrogation. Unlike the poet, for whom the feminine and masculine merge and vibrate in a harmony or concert of mutual interpenetration, the philosopher's role as midwife is the revisioning of this articulated kinship; he divines the hidden harmonies and relations of the sympathetic imagination. The midwife is, then, Locke's metaphor for the range of forms and intensities of male homosocial bonds, for a masculine form of self-cultivation avoiding both culturally defined "femininity" and the muscular heterosexuality of Jamesian pragmatism. The exclusion of women from the romanticism of genius and from male intimacy is seen here as virilizing those bonds rather than perceiving the choice of a male object as feminizing them.

In brief, given that thought is set in vibrating motion by the poetic syntheses of spirit, and that the philosopher is solicited by a being who is the symptom of male and female principles interweaving, it is the task of maieutics (as an obstetrics) to sever these two halves of the truth—the midwife's work is the movement of their separation but also the reanimation of their unity. Poetic thought (sympathy), in first following this enveloping (from the outside to the inside) and then gestating it (from the inside to the outside), then turns to the midwife as the limit that links one to the other, a pragmatic limit at the level of utility and technique, but also a metaphysical limit to poetic labor, or generation, at the level of "intellectuality." Locke needs the labors of poets/artists for their generation gives birth, in turn, to philosophical aesthetics. Throughout all, Locke is twice-born, father and mother to his meditative self, this time as the engineer and architect of his own separation from the barren body of speculative reason via his reunification with the phallic eros of male poetry. He too becomes both a receptor and receptacle in the wake of the ordering and shaping forms of Hughes's poetry.

It is this emphasis on homosexual eros that informs Locke's letters to Hughes. It's a virilizing, classicizing, political ideal; a queer version of Du Bois's Talented Tenth; a philosophical attempt at a black homosexual community based on the masculine passion of *paiderastia*, to borrow J. A. Symonds word.[15] It is also a deeply romantic conception of masculine friendship, restricted to the spiritual and sensual causes of creative power. All of this is communicated, too, in Locke's letters to Hughes. The tone struck is one of initiation. The offer of patronage is made unambiguously clear: "You have my best wishes—wishes commensurate with the interest in you that has developed, and that I wish you would allow me the opportunity of developing further." Locke not only presses Hughes for a rendezvous in Washington—in the hope that the nervousness he was feeling was "either through anticipation or some deeper instinctive feeling about our first encounter"—he also declares his wish for a friendship based on an intimate footing.[16] Under these circumstances Locke undertakes to share with Hughes his German ideal of male friendship, or *Lieblingminne*— "which cult I confess is my only religion, and has been ever since my early infatuation with Greek ideals of life."[17] "You see," he continues, "I was caught up early in the coils of classicism." Sparta and Athens, Heidelberg and Berlin: Locke's models for a philosophy of culture in which homosocial institutions (aesthetized pedagogy and male gentility) and homosexuality are fully continuous and fully exclude the world of women from the ideal of cultivation. Out of this language of nurturing and interest, homosexuality and learning, an invitation is being essayed for a collaboration, mostly sexual, but also engaged with artistic matters. "Eventually certainly there will be some literary and educational plans to be worked out," Locke suggests, just after inveigling Hughes to supply "medical particulars,—you get the idea, I am sure." The request for particulars about Hughes's medical condition suggests, once again, artistic creativity is the experience of male pregnancy (connected, here, once again to phallic jouissance).

Even though barren himself, Locke is able to bring to term the labors of others because of his ability to nurture the pains and disturbance of the artistic spirit. In "To the Young Friend on Reading *Jean Christophe*," Locke alludes to the *Theaetetus* and the *Symposium* to describe how he assists in the birth of homoerotic "truth" from beauty. "You see, my friend," Socrates says to Theaetetus, "it is a secret that I have this art" [of midwifery].[18]

> Now my art of midwifery is just like theirs [female midwives] in most respects. The difference is that I attend to men and not women, and that I watch over the labour of their souls, not of their bodies. And the most important thing about my art is the ability to allay all possible tests to the offspring, to determine whether the young mind is being delivered of a phantom, that is, an error, or a fertile truth. For one thing which I have in common with the ordinary midwives is that I myself am barren of wisdom. The common reproach against me is that I am always asking questions of other people but never express my own views about anything, because there is no wisdom in me; and that is true enough. And the reason of it is this, that God compels me to attend the travail of others, but has forbidden me to procreate. So that I am not in any sense a wise man; I cannot claim as the child of my own soul any discovery worth the name of wisdom. But with those who associate with me it is different. At first some of them give the impression of being ignorant and stupid; but as time goes on and our association continues, all whom God permits are seen to make progress—a progress which is amazing both to other people and

themselves. And yet it is clear to me that this not due to anything they have learnt from me; it is that they discover within themselves a multitude of beautiful things, which they bring forth into the light. But it is I, with God's help, who deliver them of this offspring. (*Theaetetus*, 150b–d)

Locke uses the Socratic maieutic to avoid heterosexual reproduction and borrows the image of the uterus to make noble and useful-seeming the otherwise dead-end of the anus. (Does this portray the maieutic as an answer to the uterus?) As a midwife, in matters of art and ethics, Locke (like Socrates) relieves, by giving thought to, the confusions and delinquent labors of other men. Pregnancy as an art of dialectical instruction defines his legacy; but it also gives savor to his philosophical self-awareness, his multiple roles in black, homosexual, theoretical culture. In a sense what he offers (again, like Socrates) is knowledge as seduction or lure; knowledge as a way of embracing the void that possesses each of us in turn; knowledge, in short, as a ceremony of the newborn bringing forth new, potentially fertile truths. In *Theaetetus* true wisdom is painful mediation, the quality of bringing out into public life the secret, unsuspected life of others. The idea that truth is a child and dialectic the midwife imagines the maieutic in parturient terms. It may just be a male fantasy, but the above passage also succeeds in giving a picture of Socratic wisdom as an obstetrics compelled to allay the pain of others.[19] They, the young men wracked by the throes of childbirth, anxiously waiting to be delivered, now learn that the maieutic will make their birthings (into wisdom) as beautiful as possible. Socrates' administrations will not only lead to scenes of progress and beauty but will also deter false pregnancies and phantom births. For Socrates, the "greatest and noblest function" of his midwifery is to "distinguish the true from the false offspring"; the secret life of wisdom from the self's fraudulent refuge (*Theaetetus*, 150b). With Locke, one suspects, along with the birth of New Negro art comes a new sense of black aesthetic beauty freed from the phantasms of racism and homophobia.[20] Like Socrates, he could also say, "this pain my art is able to bring on, and also to allay."

But, because what is involved here is first a question of delegation or proxy, it is not always easy to tell apart true from false births, especially when the relation of art to culture is conceived as a corrective mirror— that is, when racial art is seen as holding up a nonracist mirror to American culture.[21] Hence Locke's opposition to imitative art. Deploring what he sees as Afro-America's "protective social mimicry" and "psychology of imitation," Locke looks to Negro art "for group expression and self-determination."[22] For Locke, great art is a sign of racial and national maturity. The creative effort of the New Negro is part of America's wider self-discovery and self-definition. Or, as he writes in the foreword to *The New Negro*, troping Booker T. Washington's 1895 Atlanta address, "Separate as it may be in color and substance, the culture of the Negro is of a pattern integral with the times and with its cultural setting" (Locke, *The New Negro*, xxvi). To correct racist ways of seeing art has to reflect back to American culture a nonrepresentative but culturally integral vision of itself. Because racism substitutes phantasms for reality, black art must distinguish true likeness from false resemblance. Locke, like Julien, wants black art and writing to produce a picture that goes beyond the statistical—read: symbolic, synecdochic, indexical—properties of racial types or traits; but, unlike Julien, there is an essential discordance between his ideal of a procreative art and his wish for art to be racially representative. Locke's writings on Afro-American poetry offer yet another aspect to this attempt to generate a black modernist project out of racial typicality. For Locke, poetry typifies black aspirations to art and culture; poetry is exemplary because it calls forth the purest example of what is typical. The poet makes his type into an artistic thing, he begets it, impregnating and disseminating his own typicality through works of art. Emulation, and not imitation, is thus what typifies the New Negro art of racial resemblance.[23] It's not that the mirror of art must be empty so as to return a true likeness, but, like the pool in Wilde's "The Disciple," Locke conceives of beauty via the internalization of what extends and so haunts it: the spirit of youth reflected in the tarnished mirror of uncreated being midway between sexuality and procreation, or, more generally, paternity and generation.

And so, when he and Hughes finally do meet in 1924 on a cold, frosty midwinter morning in Paris; after they take a stroll together in the Parc Monceau ("Mother and I have spent such happy afternoons there"); after they hear *Manon* and *Samson and Delilah* at the Opéra Comique and are mortified to have missed *Tristan*; disillusion and then decay become the supports upon which Locke enlarges his fantasy of a momentarily fulfilled erotic vision whose intensity fades due to the disappointments of delayed expectations.[24] "As to the joy of having met you and of being able to be with you," Locke writes a few days later, "I can only say that it is intense enough to be sad and premonitory of change or disillusionment" (Rampersad, *The Life of Langston Hughes*, 92) Unable to endure his own intense desire or its deferral, Locke's "great passion" appears stretched between the opposite abysses of reserve and unreserved surrender, alternately driven by the involuntary and imperative sway of passion and the sense-giving form of sublimated things. He no longer speaks of erotic consummation but of the danger of being disfigured by its need. Indeed, Locke would later write of feeling an "almost suicidal depth of despair and discouragement" at Hughes's failure to respond to his overtures of passion (92). Locke's relation to Hughes's refusal to raise the veil shrouding his sexuality and artistic labor results, inevitably, in a kind of pseudocyesis, or phantom pregnancy—that is to say, a failed maieutic.

The two men agree to meet in Italy later that summer. Hughes has been in Turin a few weeks when he receives the following from Locke, who had remained in Paris. After a "trance-like walk" up the Champs Elysées and a ramble in the Bois de Boulogne, Locke confesses: I am writing "to tell you how I love you" before going on to give an account of his hopes for some intimacy, "before America with her inhibitions closes down on us."[25] Give him that moment, Locke pleads, "and then perhaps through prosaic hours we can keep 'the gleam of the transcendental thing I believe our friendship was meant to be.'" And, as before, it is the wish to

be reborn into the world that underpins hopes of rescue: "let our association breed beautiful things, like children, to hallow the relationship." The
letter ends with a hope for tomorrow: the experience, that is, that goes
beyond the prosaic world in search of the transcendental gleam of desire.

It should come as no surprise that Locke's encounter—more accurately
nonencounter—with Hughes returns us to *Looking for Langston*. What we
see in both instances is the loss of self that occurs when the outline
between self and a wished-for mirror-image becomes blurred or distorting. Hughes's final refusal clearly upset Locke, who, in a petulant note to
Cullen, advises him to "discontinue pampering his [Hughes's] psychology."[26] Aside from implicitly accusing Hughes of being too selfish to invest
in the homoaesthetic work of racial uplift, the word "pampering" also suggests a less indulgent nurturing of the pregnant male artistic spirit. That
ambivalence emerges in Julien's film. In *Looking for Langston* Locke appears
only once. He is briefly shown introducing a black artist to a white female
patron at a Harlem gallery opening. The voiceover asks us: "were they
[Locke, Nugent, Cullen] seeking the approval of the race or of the black
middle class and the white literary establishment?" The voiceover also tells
us: "White patrons of the Harlem Renaissance wanted their artists and
writers to know and feel the intuitions of the primitive. They didn't want
modernism; they wanted black art to keep art and artists in their place."
It's an ambiguous appearance, condensing the many images we have of
him. In 1940, for example, Hughes, in his autobiography, *The Big Sea*,
names Locke, along with Jessie Faucet at the *Crisis* and Charles Johnson at
the *Opportunity*, as the three people who "midwifed the so-called New
Negro literature into being. Kind and critical—but not too critical for the
young—they nursed us along until our books were born."[27] The geniality
of Hughes's remarks stand in stark contrast to Zora Neale Hurston's view
of Locke as a "malicious spiteful little snot," or W.E.B. Du Bois's dismissal of
Locke's aesthetics as "decadent" in his 1925 review of *The New Negro*.[28]

In these instances, Locke's potency as a symbol of the Renaissance
endures: he is doubly the nurturing midwife to an artistic generation of

black men and their decadent bourgeois representative. It's an unwitting dualism that persists in more recent criticism. Arnold Rampersad's references to Locke's "dainty," "conspicuous sophistication," and "malicious wit," in his 1986 biography of Hughes, while lucid on Locke's "petulance," fails to see how that petulance hinges, in turn, on feelings of inadequacy or how Locke's many testimonies of sympathy were nourished by romantic visions of homosexual love, images based on Greco-German ideas of art and sexuality (Rampersad, *The Life of Langston Hughes*, 67, 68). The Hughes letters have been crucial to that symbolism, to the production of Locke as, in Michael J. Cobb's words, a "convenient figure" of "literary repression and obsession"; the "icon who needed to be broken."[29]

And yet the letters to Hughes also reveal, through images of sterility and birth, why ambivalence plays such a pivotal role in Locke's cultural racialism. There is a dissymmetry, in brief, between Locke's ideal of the midwife, whose skill consists in converting the passive heteronomy of sensibility back into the virile bonds of homosocial friendship and his idea of racial art as representative of "race feeling." The moralizing approach to male aesthetic beauty as racial uplift does not sit well with the transvaluative possibilities of homosexual desire. Locke's pragmatist politics thus exceeds the very homoeroticism it is founded upon. This discordance was never resolved: if the creative rebirth of black art was part of a more collective reaffirmation of Afro-America, the role of the midwife ruins this narrative of descendence by not being part of, but nonetheless central to the racial reproduction of the manly "succession of spirit." Why else are Locke's writings on masculine friendship so taken up with the deformations—the phantom birthings—of homosexual desire? And why his persistent representation of himself to the artists and writers of Harlem as "at least realizing by proxy some of my own unfulfilled ambitions"?[30] Locke's conception of the poetic mind was, as we've seen, bound up with an aesthetic of homoerotic procreation derived from Greek ideals of *paiderastia*. The Socratic figure of the midwife symbolizes this aesthetic of "beautiful things" borne out of homosexual union. But in other respects, Locke's vision of the New Negro movement as made, shaped, and quickened by black homoerotism never entirely escaped the modernist primitivism that remained its symptom and put its realization at stake.

As such, the outing of black gay desire in *Looking for Langston* would, I believe, have struck him as both revelatory (as an example of depiction) and embarrassing (for its refusal of racial uplift and the symbolic satisfactions of delegation). And so the story of Locke's pursuit of Hughes is not just the old story of a wanted intimacy never wanted: Hughes's rejection forced Locke to look at himself, to measure his homoerotic aesthetics against the sexual and racial "inhibitions" of America. It was a painful undertaking, and in the altercation between his cultural midwifery and his pedagogical-erotic vision of the New Negro, Locke emerges as an ambivalent philosopher of art, mimicry, and value. In that clash, masculine eros was not so much bound to lose, replaced by the 1920s vogue for racial art, as set to become the suppressed, queer standard for Afro-America. That standard has to be looked for not just in New Negro aesthetics but also in the philosophy of culture, where, from 1923 onward, Locke records the beginnings of "cultural racialism"; the birth of a new psychology in Afro-America as witnessed in the depth and value of black gay art and culture. The same year in which he's attracted to and rejected by Hughes, in other words, Locke was also absorbing new work on race and culture by Franz Boas and others, work resulting in the strategic racialism that became synonymous with the New Negro.[31] Philosophy and racial aesthetics, then, are deeply intertwined in Locke's Socratic midwifery; and, while the former causes him to question seriously the "genteel traditions" and inhibitions of white America; the latter allows to him to struggle toward the possession of a gay and black identity in all its reflected beauty. It is to that mirroring that I now turn.

The Psychograph

The issues above are all reflected in the "psychograph" of Alain Locke, first published in 1935. The story behind this piece of writing is a tightly knotted piece of resentment, envy, disgust; indeed, the story returns me to my opening questions: what does the black do when he sees himself, as it were, in an orb of abjection, and this is all that he ever sees? Does he embrace the image, *reconciling* himself to its vision; does he insist on his *difference*, his otherness from what he sees? Or does he put out his eyes the better to see and enjoy what behind the image is never seen—that is, what can only be looked on when the eyes are opened in blindness? It's a question that, as we will see, lies at the origin of Locke's musings on the imperative values of race and sexuality, but also his writings on cultural pluralism as a flawed answer to those imperatives. The question is embedded in Locke's "psychograph" as well as some letters (to and from the philosopher, Horace Kallen) in which his ideas on art and aesthetics (as places where truth and semblance undergo upheaval and convergence), leads him to a cultural politics of difference. I need to ask, once again: if what we see in the mirror, as blacks, is always wishful, then who can pinpoint the moment wherein the false is as unreal as the wishes that disturb the viewing?

I should like to claim as life-motto the good Greek principle,—*"Nothing in excess,"* but I have probably worn instead as the badge of circumstance,—*"All things with a reservation."* Philadelphia, with her birthright of provincialism flavored by urbanity and her petty bourgeois psyche with the Tory slant, at the start set the key of paradox; circumstance compounded it by decreeing me as a Negro a dubious and doubting sort of American and by reason of racial inheritance making me more of a pagan than a Puritan, more of a humanist than a pragmatist.

Verily paradox has followed me the rest of my days: at Harvard, clinging to the genteel tradition of Palmer, Royce and Münsterberg, yet attracted by the disillusion of Santayana and the radical protest of James: again in 1916 I returned to work under Royce but was destined to take my doctorate in Value Theory under Perry. At Oxford, once more intrigued by the twilight of aestheticism but dimly aware of the new realism of the Austrian philosophy of value; socially Anglophile, but because of race loyalty, strenuously anti-imperialist; universalist in religion, internationalist and pacifist in world-view, but forced by a sense of simple justice to approve of the militant counter-nationalisms of Zionism, Young Turkey, Young Egypt, Young India, and with reservations even Garveyism and current-day "Nippon over Asia." Finally a cultural cosmopolitan, but perforce an advocate of cultural racialism as a defensive counter-move for the American Negro and accordingly more of a philosophical mid-wife to a generation of younger Negro poets, writers, artists than a professional philosopher.

Small wonder, then, with this psychograph, that I project my personal history into its inevitable rationalization as cultural pluralism and value relativism, with a not too orthodox reaction to the American way of life. (Locke, "Values and Imperatives," 312)[32]

Locke's comment—*paradox is the key to Negro life as lived in America*—offers us a mirror of inversion. But what else does one see?

In 1935, Locke wrote a "psychograph" of himself (the word connotes phrenology and spiritualism, psychobiography and automatic writing). His author's note first appears as a preface to the essay "Values and Imperatives," in Horace Kallen and Sidney Hook's *American Philosophy Today and Tomorrow*. What comes across most is a failure to fit in, a feeling of being barred, kept outside in, resulting in a kind of "dubious and doubting," "not too orthodox reaction" to the circumstance of being born black and gay in America. Unable to claim nothing in excess—the Greek aphorism *meden agan* written on the temple of Delphi by Cleobolus and alluded to by Plato in *Protagorus*, an aphorism denoting reservedness and something held in reserve or retained—Locke has had to wear "all things with reservation" as a badge of circumstance or a life-motto for being Negro, a motto combining Aristotle's idea of temperance, or *sophrosyne*, with the psychic effects of life in a racist state, or the right to oneself reserved or retained by the legal powers and interests of race segregation. Once decreed Negro, it is obvious that one has to give way on one's desire, forced to negotiate all claims of admission into the nation via the certificates of legitimacy (the "badge") that the selfsame nation uses to bar and exclude (disinherit) you.

That disinheritance remains the symptom of Locke's life: paradox is the key to the unreconciled systems and beliefs causing him to switch between race loyalty and nationality, gentility and protest, humanism and pragmatism. Paradox is the tone, too, for the equally desperate wish to make the "more of," "yets," and "buts" reflect value loyalty and conviction rather than the "inevitable rationalization" of the decrees of circumstance. Shorn of those claims to aesthetic cultivation and inner unity ["self-culture," or *Kultiviertheit*],[33] the life is reduced to its lowest common denominator: a "pragmatic" assimilation to racial intolerance, where all that is left is a life held in reserve.[34] In the "psychograph," every existential countermove—black cosmopolitan culture for bourgeois provincialism; "paganism" for puritanical morality; Europe for America; but also every political and institutional decision; national liberation movements over British imperialism; philosophical midwifery over professional philosophy—is used to question the limits and exclusions of one position by another. If America represents a self held in reserve, in restraint, then by outing himself in Europe, Locke was able to discard the discards of circumstance, since repression, as the main metaphor for the paradoxical realization of self, is here theorized as the key to his psychography. The "psychograph" is an attempt to understand this (repressed) link between conservation and constraint (*sophrosyne*); or, what happens when one is forced to recognize that one's fantasies and desires mirror the decree or duty—the libidinal position—of one's unending public humiliation.

This reading becomes even more feasible if we fold back into the "psychograph" Locke's *Harvard Class Reports* from 1914 and 1933. In June 1914, Locke wrote the following:

> For three years (1907–1910), I was in residence at Oxford University as a Rhodes scholar from my home state, Pennsylvania. There . . . in the

midst of a type of life that is a world-type simply because it is so consistently itself, one had every facility for becoming really cosmopolitan—it was a rare experience in the company of many foreign students to pay Englishmen the very high tribute of not even attempting to be like them, but to be more one's self, because of their example: third, is a brief corollary, for me the same fact was the very rare opportunity to choose deliberately to be what I was born, but what the tyranny of circumstances prevents many of my folk from ever viewing as the privilege and opportunity of being an Afro-American.[35]

Compare the class report from 1933:

From the influences of Royce, James, Palmer, Santayana and Perry, you see, I have drawn a not regretted vocation—a decent livelihood teaching philosophy; and from Wendell, "Copey," Briggs and Baker—an avocation of mid-wifery to younger Negro poets, writers and artists, who in these years have been struggling through to self-expression. I am sure it has all been due to Harvard, at least where there has been creditable and productive; and would rather pay tribute to the inspiration and original stock-in-trade which was stored up in those formative undergraduate years than talk about any subsequent events more personal.

One thing to be regretted has been the comparative isolation that separates Negro life and institutions from even academic and cultural interests and circles at large; but I have done what I could in an interpretative way to bridge some of these barriers.[36]

The last reference to theoretical practice echoes back to that wish "to be what I was born," an echo that leads back to queer midwifery and the cultural politics of black imitation. Thus, a distinction is posed that cannot be avoided: emulation, when it betokens a search for who one is not imitation, but a way of seeing oneself as an identity rather than as an unreproductive copy of others. Unlike illusionistic mimesis, philosophical mimesis consists in an inward assimilation of oneself to what is other and radically alien (the English), with the aim of undergoing change in oneself. It is a projection and an incorporation, but also an expulsion and a devouring. The play of same and other (as in imitation) is inverted when one passes from seeming to assimilation to being who one is. In the first case, the image relies for its resemblance on what in the model confirms self-identity by going beyond it; in the second, imitation includes the recognition of the otherness of the model and poses it as other in its desire for semblance, precisely because the model is that which always remains the same as itself. (Is this a shift from self-love to love of the other in the same?) Actually, this affection of an inside by an outside (the ego imaging itself outside itself) produces division and the reciprocal interpenetration of self and other as the key to identity—which is why Locke is engaged in a postromantic drama of sameness and alterity, what was earlier invoked as the harmonizing of the imagination and nature. Here the ego appears to be trapped between what it cannot leave and the ideal of what it cannot yet be. As such, Locke is most cosmopolitan when he refuses to imitate the English and insists instead on emulating "the privilege and opportunity of being an Afro-American": that is, the "true" birth of black nationality emerges from a wish to see oneself and to be seen as who one truly and actually is.

But how does one reconcile the ideal of the self that *was* with the assertion that the ego conform to the ideal that it *would like to be*? How can we conceive of the ego that forms its ideal in its own image and forms itself in the image of its ideal, that identifies the ideal with itself and itself with the ideal? In this paradox the image (self) that precedes the model or ideal (world-type) presents emulation as the emissary of an exterior authority that reopens the gap between self-image and wished-for reflection. This admiring, identifying, envious love of the English is, in the end, narcissistic. The mimicry of the world-type, where one loses oneself in order to recover and represent oneself in them as in a mirror, is a rediscovery of the narcissistic ego in the specular other that already inwardly haunts and possesses it. The desire to assimilate the world-type's mastery and potency, to become him by devouring him, consuming him, is a desire to possess because the being of the Afro-American is felt to be sterile, empty; barren, he is unable to become a self, an ego, unless he devours his rival's mastery. As in the tale of Hughes, Locke, when faced with the value of the other, is driven by a will to possess; only he who has value can be loved and desired, which is to say Locke loves and desires that which he lacks and has not got (which means that he cannot love those without the value of male eros and self-cultivation: women, say, or the noneducated). To extend this problematic of narcissistic desire to the politics of racial identification and assimilation—the decision to become who one is aporetic—black homosociality arises, alas, only as the coexistence of sameness and alterity, abjection and mimicry. More, the appeal to world types, some of whom have had to repress who they are in order to conceal the fault of not being English, remains enigmatic; how, in effect, does one accede to world typicality if one must transgress the imperial (read: white racist) model in order to conform to it, if the fault of not being English defines that identity, since its fault a priori is its indebtedness to the imperial model that escapes it? If cosmopolitanism is a "bridge" between Negro life and the forms and values of art and culture, why is the struggle to choose it read as a "very rare opportunity"? Is this not because of the interdiction through which racist imperial authority both orders and forbids the emulation of itself, orders and forbids conformance to this interdiction by enjoining colonial black subjects to identify with but, paradoxically, not assimilate the objects of white cultural privilege? So how do the world types correspond to such emulation, if not in guilt and malaise, self-denial and "comparative isolation"? As Locke discovers in his Oxford paneled hideaway during 1907–1910: the beautiful mirror of cosmopolitan *Kultiviertheit* could only ever be a complaisant observer to the racist *Wertgebeit* that pursues him like a ghost from America; it is a knowledge that presents itself there and whose essence he is enjoined to repress in order to conceal the fault of being a Negro. Here, his role is not so much that of midwife, ministering to the progeny of other blacks, but that of a despised, empty mirror.

As the celebrated first Negro recipient of a Rhodes scholarship to Oxford, Locke was, from the first, exposed to very public debate over his representative qualities and achievements as a gentleman scholar and "race man." And yet, in letters home to his mother, he states: "I'm not going to England as a Negro"; "I am not a race problem. I am Alain LeRoy Locke."[37] And in other letters home he shows himself appalled by certain black *types*: the "typical Southern niggers" he meets at Harvard, men and women who are "niggers in everything they wear." I am "mightily thankful," he writes, "for the training that has separated me from them."[38] While in the midst of Boston's black bourgeoisie intellectual prestige gives him proof of his worth as a man, his superior fellowship and connection. In England he discovers that elite culture fails to whiten his refined black self-image. His cosmopolitan training means little to the condescending English, and even less to the southern Rhodes scholars who abuse him repeatedly. They even insist on excluding him from a Thanksgiving dinner given for American Rhodes scholars.[39] As Fanon would say, Locke discovers his "true face" at Oxford: no longer able to love his mirror image as the means to class sociability, or as what secures superior ties of resemblance and race equality. It was a painful lesson and a shock. It's also a story that returns us to Locke's psychograph: if paradox is the key to the alienated self, it is also one of its disguises in Locke's touched-up portrait. Both the disguise and the portrait return us to racism's own distorting mirror; it all comes down to Locke's renunciation and reclamation of his black bourgeois identity. At Oxford, Locke is able to recast his associations of racist typicality as a disguised, displaced conformity to white symbolizations of black desire; only then is he able to rebuild it as "the privilege and opportunity of being an Afro-American." It is this reclamation and denial that leads to his rethinking of cultural pluralism as racial homosociality, to which I now turn.

The Corpse in the Pluralist's Casket

New York, 29 October 1955. The philosopher Horace M. Kallen is reading "Alain Locke and Cultural Pluralism" at the Memorial Meeting to Locke held at New York University. Locke had died a year earlier on 9 June 1954. The essay subsequently appears in *The Journal of Philosophy* in 1957–58.[40] "How did the author get this way?" asks Kallen, opening his reading of the psychograph for "what it postulates *en philosophe*." "How came Locke—a proud and sensitive man who was penalized by 'whites' for his darker skin, in matters of spirit an incidental difference—to give up the idea of equality as identification, as sameness with whites, and to urge equality as parity in and of his difference from the whites" (Kallen, "Alain Locke," 121).

The turns of this single sentence are somewhat vertiginous. First, the idea of equality as identification is related to the belief, the presumption, that being black is the *same* as being white. This is to confuse equality with likeness; and then, because Locke believes himself to be alike, he thinks, he presumes, an identification *as* white. It is that identification that, according to Kallen, leads Locke to mistake parity for identification. But even before distinguishing identification and parity, Kallen presents democracy as the equal sharing of racial differences that are unconditional and absolute. If the perception of parity between two distinct and different ethnic groups is true democracy, the perception of equality between racial unlikenesses is seen as politically authoritarian. And so the tension between the two equalities (identification or parity) is constituted by the prior determination of race as an essence that is beyond calculation or measure, and which includes within itself the incalculable inequalities of whites and blacks, who are both assumed to be equally endowed with differences that are, incommensurably, incalculably, unconditionally, *raced*. Why does this mutation take place? Because racial particularity is conceived as the democratic ground for any universal claim to equality, and racial difference is universalized in terms of a formal logic of equivalences. It's a catachrestical reading of the "psychograph" as a tale of two differences which yet remain the same, and of two equalities *inversely and yet integrally raced*: the incidental difference of a darker skin once penalized and outcast, now indivisible from "equality as parity" in and of one's difference from whites. (Why is the word "whites" in quotation marks here but later without? As if the whole difficulty of race is denied and yet simultaneously disclosed by these marks and their *unequal* distribution in Kallen's articulation of equality and difference. And why "parity," "equality," "reconciliation" instead of "paradox"?). The shift, Kallen implies, places difference on either side of a wish to be white, for now Locke stands apart, witness to the equal difference of his blackness. As Kallen imagines him, Locke has become indifferent to his former need to be the same *as* whites; no, now he recognizes his darker skin for what it is and, as he raises it from penality to equality he again grasps his difference *from* whites. Difference, then, the unconditional kind of equality that brings Locke back to himself: by purging him of the wish for sameness, the emulation of difference brings back the man he was born to be. (Pluralism, then, a guide to how one resembles who one essentially is; or how one discovers an "inalienable right" to difference while remaining essentially not the same, for we are all alike equal in our differences.)

All this is underscored by Kallen's belief that pluralism, the right to be different, "reconciled" Locke to himself: "Now this is what Alain Locke envisioned from the time that he became reconciled to himself. He became a cultural pluralist. It took him some time" (121). The word "reconcile," according to the *Oxford English Dictionary*, means "to bring (a person) again into friendly relations *to* or *with* (oneself or another) after an estrangement; to win over (a person) again to friendship with oneself or another; to set (estranged persons or parties) at one again; to bring back into concord, to reunite (persons or things) in harmony." Reconciled: to distinguish a hunger for the falsely different—to be the same *as*—from the readjusted, reintegrated self different *from*; a balance accomplished by Locke's reconciliation to Kallen's (liberal, Jewish, heteronormative) model of cultural pluralism. Taking the "psychograph" as the main source for his portrait, Kallen continues:

Locke presents himself here with the passions and powers of his individuality. His singularity is evident, and he gives hints of his idiosyncrasy. But he accepted neither, although he couldn't reject them. He felt, in sense and intellect, a human being the same as other human beings, especially white ones who denied the sameness. He knew that in his ideals, his intentions, and his works and ways he was not inferior, nor otherwise different from those people who held themselves to be better than he was, and there were intervals—one was certainly his undergraduate days at Harvard—when he did not appear to live under any penalty for his difference. He seems not to have in Philadelphia. I know that at Oxford—I was there at the time— he was penalized. There were among the Rhodes scholars at Oxford gentlemen from Dixie who could not possibly associated with Negroes. They could not possibly attend the Thanksgiving dinner celebrated by Americans if a Negro was to be there. So although students from elsewhere in the United States outnumbered the gentlemen from Dixie, Locke was not invited, and one or two other persons, authentically Americans, refused in consequence to attend. You might say it was a dinner of inauthentic Americans. Now, the impact of that kind of experience left scars. The more so in a philosophic spirit. (122)

Locke's "idiosyncrasy" (a euphemism for his homosexuality?) is also part of this tale of rivalrous proximity having racism as its symptom. What does not get told in Kallen's 1955 recollection of the 1907 Thanksgiving incident—around which a whole mythology of the origins of cultural pluralism has arisen—are his own feelings of professional rivalry and conflict mirroring those of the "gentlemen" from Dixie. Locke resembles him too closely, but not close enough, a fact pointing to a resemblance that is much more rivalrous than sexual. How else explain the rapidity and ease with which Kallen claims that Locke accepted neither his singularity (as a Negro) nor his idiosyncrasy (as a homosexual)? Where Kallen speaks of the "penalty of difference," the narcissistic injury referred to attests to his own ambitions and jealousies (but he does not say so in 1955). Thus it is necessary to stress racial difference, displace the accent, inflect the rivalry from one of sexuality to that of race. It amounts to saying, finally: I, Kallen, have succeeded (I have accepted my difference) where Locke initially failed, an error due to his singularity and idiosyncrasy. That understanding comes later in Kallen's 1973 interview with Sarah Schmidt where he recalls the significance of the 1907 event for his relations with Locke.

> It was in 1905 that I began to formulate the notion of cultural pluralism and I had to do that in connection with my teaching. I was assisting both Mr. James and Mr. Santayana at the time and I had a Negro student named Alain Locke, a very remarkable young man—very sensitive, very easily hurt—who insisted that he was a human being and that his color ought not to make any difference. And, of course, it was a mistaken insistence. It *had* to make a difference and it *had* to be accepted and respected and enjoyed for what it was.

> Two years later when I went to Oxford on a fellowship he was there as a Rhodes scholar, and we had a race problem because the Rhodes scholars from the South were bastards. So they had a Thanksgiving dinner which I refused to attend because they refused to have Locke. [The imprint of that event in "Alain Locke and Cultural Pluralism" is somewhat different: "Locke was not invited," Kallen recalls, "and one or two other persons, authentically Americans, refused in consequence to attend. You might say it was a dinner of inauthentic Americans."]

> And he said, "I am a human being," just as I had said it earlier. What difference does the difference make? We are all alike Americans. And we had to argue out the question of how the differences made differences, and in arguing out those questions the formulae, then phrases, developed—"cultural pluralism," "the right to be different."[41]

What difference does a difference make? When "we" are all alike Americans. That "we" includes those petitioning for Locke's inclusion and those dogging Locke to exclusion; at the same time Kallen redefines national belonging in terms of those who elect to exclude—self or other—and those who suffer from that "same" election. *In both instances it is*

Locke's difference that difference makes. Kallen's "we" only becomes possible because racial difference is no longer seen as a national but as an "incidental difference"; or, when the black other becomes a *good* other, that is, *the same as we are* (to borrow Alain Badiou's phrase): the all alike Americans. ("There is no real respect for the one whose difference consists precisely in not respecting the differences," Badiou rightly concludes.)[42]

Despite Kallen's insistence—with all those hads—that it took time for Locke to learn this lesson, it is he who insists that race just *had* to make a difference for Locke, that it *had* to take precedence over his being human —that is, that wish for recognition in the face of the racist incivility that suppresses it. Indeed, that discrepancy is never openly addressed. Kallen's judging, judging Locke guilty of racial delusion, becomes a question of something else entirely in the reckoning: Kallen can only ever see Locke's difference from whites, what he fails to see is Locke's own comprehension: of an impossible conformance to whiteness because of a necessary nonconformance to blackness, a struggle which withdraws the black subject from the life of culture and which Locke presents as the paradoxical legitimacy of being black in America, an identity defined by an always prohibited desire deferred, symbolized, and exchanged. It is this insight that informs Locke's thinking, and which I intend to track in his philosophical writing, but also trace in the silences and disguises behind Kallen's decision to lay bare Locke's thought. As we shall see, the tale is bound up with how Locke's thought on race is essentially a complaint against the pluralism as conceived by Kallen, a liberalism that participates in the very forms of domination that it claims to overthrow. In contrast, Locke strives to bring to term, as a midwife, true selfhood from the chimeras of false births. I see this as a neo-pragmatism opposed to prejudged truth, and one that tries to reopen reason, power, and truth to the fallible and precarious nature of experience and knowledge. In this debate over political nationality—the freedom to *be* different—Locke seeks to go beyond any correspondence or adequacy of thought and language so as to evoke the dissolution of racial myths. His neo-pragmatism, in sum, the culmination of a move to cut the umbilicus connecting race to its phantoms (black appetites to black sexuality).

And so, on 12 November 1907, Kallen sends a letter to Barrett Wendell, his Harvard mentor, on the Thanksgiving incident. Kallen begins with the claim Locke has on him as a Harvard man: "Locke is a Harvard man and as such he has a definite claim on me" (Sollors, "A Critique," 271). The claim, or debt, Kallen owes to Locke implies obligation rather than friendship. It certainly implies that he has an indirect, formal tie to Locke based on a shared corporate identity and not on any intimacy as respective foreigners in Oxford, or indeed strangers internally alienated from American life and institutions. If Kallen announces this "claim" as one of identification rather than empathy or sympathy for Locke's plight, it is thanks to the scholarship of Wernor Sollors that we can now see the limits to that reclamation and its underlying aggressiveness and specular rivalry. On 22 October 1907, Kallen writes to Wendell: "As you know, I have neither respect nor liking for his [Locke's] race" (270). ("Respect," "liking," "enjoyment": the words echo Kallen's 1973 injunctions to Locke concerning the pleasures and duties of difference.) "So he [Locke] is come to tea again tho' it is personally repugnant to me to eat with him. Shylock's disclaimer [*Merchant of Venice* I.iii.35ff] expresses my feeling exactly" (271). (Wendell, in a letter dated 3 November 1907, had expressed a similar repugnance: "My own sentiments concerning negroes are such that I have always declined to meet the best of them . . . at table." He also takes pleasure in admitting, "Professionally, I do my best to treat negroes with absolute courtesy" [270, 271]).[43]

How does one weigh the contrast here between good manners, class gentility, public duty, private distaste? Or the image of Kallen holding fast his repugnance when faced with the appetites and bodily satisfactions of a very sensitive, very easily hurt, black student? The contrast makes repugnance also part of the claim Locke has on Kallen as a Harvard man. Just as inviting a black to dine forms a social bond of like and unlike, so eating, if only at tea, amounts to an ambiguous act of social and moral duty—more, if Wendell's racist gentility is the model for Kallen's imitation, why does he allude to an anti-Semitic comparison for that understanding? Why this appeal to Shylock to register his own indebtedness to the claim Wendell has on him as a Jew at Harvard? Is Shylock—to ask once again—the metamorphosis of Wendell; the enigmatic unity of the two the point at where Kallen's public, American self, is bonded with his private identity as a Jew? In any event, Kallen absorbs Wendell's ideal of public courtesy and private distaste. He identifies himself with them, and them with himself, he incorporates and digests them; he shares the idea of blacks as private objects of loathing, he appropriates the idea of blacks as an alterity that cannot be consumed but that must be guarded against. It's a reciprocal disgust that unites him and Wendell in their mutual mistrust of interracial contact with an unlikeness that is alien.

For the sake of simplicity let us define Kallen's pluralism as asking how the refined social body incorporates (that is to say, embodies or digests) the intruding alien. By a radical separation of public virtue from private life (Wendell) or nationality from caste purity (Kallen), two answers designating why the social ritual of taking tea with a Negro is a metonym for the maintenance of social order. Kallen, of course, caught up as he was in mimetic rivalry with Locke, could not or would not say this, so he said it without saying it, by playing the role of the oppressed Jew, Shylock. "I will buy with you, sell with you, talk with you, walk with you, and so following; but I will not eat with you, drink with you, nor pray with you," so says Shylock, so says Kallen. The truth of desire is expressed through citation; the limits of pluralism are revealed by the tale of disgust when the unwelcome black guest appears at the feast of white ethnocentrism.

It is worth noting that Kallen's reference to Shylock contains other compressed scenes of seduction and conversion countersigned, so to speak, by his correspondence with Wendell. For example, it was while he was a Harvard philosophy student, under the tutelage of Wendell, that Kallen converted to pluralism and Zionism after a time spent as an assimilated Jew. "I was an alienated intellectual," he recalls, "being suddenly challenged in his alienation." "And the challenge turned not on anything in the Hebraic tradition" but "on what Americanism came to mean to me" at Harvard. "The [Zionist] meanings," he continues, "came to me rather in terms of the American Idea [symbolized, here, by the work of William James and Barrett Wendell] than in terms of what I had learned of *Torah* at home or in *Cheder*" (264–265). As a pluralist and Zionist, Kallen's identificatory affection for the American idea, the withdrawal that is also an appearing, suggests that what is at stake is an inscription that can only trace itself as withdrawing the very incision that inscribes it—to become an American Jew one must withdraw from being an assimilated Jew, but only by identifying with the racist mentor-father who presents himself as such before he too disappears in the image of Shylock, a symbolization without a symbol. In the wake of Wendell's tutelage, the American idea is Zionism, and Zionism the American idea. In other words, Kallen feels repulsion for Locke because symbolically his metamorphosis into pluralism has already incorporated Wendell's expulsion of blacks from the American idea.

Alienated and estranged as an American Jew, Kallen begins to see, through his studies with James and Wendell, the essential *sameness* of Zionism and the American Idea; it's a change that allows him to repossess his identity *as* a Jew: "Zionism," he writes, "became a replacement and reevaluation of Judaism which enabled me to respect it . . . which allowed me to see an ongoing pattern, a group personality, called Jew" (265). In the light cast by difference, then, some part of the self reawakens, rediscovered after its painful surrender to assimilation; revalued as the self's indefeasible quality and life. The inseparability of this "maturing" vision from Kallen's own genealogy of pluralism means that his memorial takes us back to 1905, when he briefly taught Locke at Harvard and discussed with him the meanings of pluralism (Kallen, "Alain Locke," 125). Back to 1907, too, when the American-Zionist ideal he shares with Wendell-Shylock returns as Kallen's reluctance to dine with a Negro homosexual. If homosocial gentility prevents Kallen from "digesting" Locke's difference, the refusal to dine, or to go near, is a way of preventing the unfathomable aggressivity toward Negroes from which he and Wendell both flee, that they keep in check, that they turn against themselves in the form of public courtesy, and which prevents them from crossing a certain frontier at the limits of white ethnocentrism. Locke's presence in Kallen's Oxford rooms recalls Banquo's at the feast, it challenges and arrests Kallen's genealogy of himself as a "plural" American Jew. Locke's presence, as we shall see, also challenges the idea of pluralism as a *naturalized* category of difference, with its deeply racist attributes of "taste" and "breeding." Rather than the harmony of differences, taking tea with Locke does not lead Kallen to a melting of individual reserve and a new bondedness of *communitas*, but the reaffirmation of disgust at precisely the difference that Locke's difference makes.

To repeat: the rephrasing of pluralism in terms of dining and *The Merchant of Venice* is neither arbitrary nor incidental. What is the price of entry into American life according to Kallen? The "exchange" of differences which also amounts to an advance payment on what it means to be an American and, as such, is to be preferred to the socially leveling consumption of sameness. In sameness, writes Kallen, in his memorial essay, "you must offer up your own different being to be digested into identification with mine"; here the self appears as indistinct, totally absorbed inside an other's identification (Kallen, "Alain Locke," 120). That is, one's difference is swallowed up and eaten (the irony of turning difference into indigestion, pluralism into nausea, once again turns on the revolting idea of having the other enter one's mouth; the dispute falls on the stomach: do we suffer indigestion or do we make our disgust known?).

In his polemical writings on the "melting pot," Kallen condemns what he sees as the devouring "imitation . . . of the higher by the lower," a "process of leveling" in which the "standardization of externals" has come about because of mass manufacture and the mass media.[44] Against this mediatized, trashy, mass, bogus "attainment of similarity," he opposes "the stuff and essence of [ethnic] nationality," or "likemindedness" (Kallen, "Democracy," 63, 93). "Likemindedness" is what binds us to our kind; it is a kind of "intrinsic similarity" "root[ed] in ethnic and cultural unity"; it is also what reminds us of our shared ancestry, heritage, origin (Kallen, "Democracy," 84). It forms our birth as racial subjects and, over time, our identifications; as such, it gives rise to our consciousness of difference and our experience of kind in that we emulate only those who are like us, whose resemblance to ourselves we recognize. It also, in its permanence, acts as our refuge from the foreignness of the unlike, which is to be feared and resisted because identified with mass culture, whose forms can neither secure like-mindedness nor act as a formative part of the subject's racial past. In Kallen's strictly ethnic terms, mass imitation like miscegenation comes down to an improperly contagious desire; it represents the wish to be by analogy what one is not, the wish to be assimilated. As such, it threatens to dissociate birth from social inheritance, ancestry from *natio,* difference from like-mindedness. By contrast, mimesis properly understood results from the transmission of what is irreducibly innermost—one's spiritual inheritance of ethnic kind.[45] Only a self already *self-*possessed can, it seems, represent itself as different in kind via the doubling of like-mindedness. Sameness, by contrast, denotes a form of mass consumption; it arouses a sympathy (and an appetite) that levels and kills.

This may look similar to Locke's belief in the power of art for the Negro struggling to become who he is, but a wished-for impregnation (by the other's typicality or spirit) is not the same thing as a fear of being consumed (by the masses or blacks). For Kallen, to sit at table with a Negro is to undergo the leveling of hierarchical difference (and is there not something awful in the idea that what one eats has the same *value* for a Negro; that the orifices, intestines, and bowels of the social body produce the same shitty product?). But why, then, should the black have to carry *that* difference as the badge of circumstance; why should he respect, enjoy, or reconcile himself to this offensive idea for what it was? Crucially, in his memorial to Locke, Kallen reuses the metaphors of digestion and recycling to frame that acceptance: "Let him [the black] absorb and *digest* the condition [of his imposed inequality], turning it from a limiting handicap into a releasing endowment, and he frees himself" (Kallen, "Alain Locke," 124;

emphasis added). The terror of racial digestion can thus be overcome when blacks learn to reincorporate (i.e., eat) themselves. This, then, is the pluralist demand to blacks: consume the byproduct of our racism, eat shit and be thankful for it. Difference maybe a silver tureen and not a melting pot, but to imagine either as satisfaction the black has to wear a badge that entitles him to become the heap of smoking food. When blacks are unwilling to eat themselves, do they still have the duties and obligations that come with a right to be different?

I think it is no surprise that Kallen and Locke quarreled over the difference that racial difference makes. What seems to be at stake is who has the last word on pluralism in America: Negro or Jew?[46] Excluding for a moment the matter of personal history—that is to say, Kallen's anxiety about the origins of pluralism, his shared parentage with Locke—can one reconcile Locke's doubting, "not too orthodox response" to the American way of life, with Kallen's belief in America as a place where one has an "unalienable right" to "difference"? (Kallen, "Alain Locke," 123). In asking this, I do not wish to dismiss Kallen's memorial. At least, not yet. When the Jewish boy whispers to the black boy—*you, too?*—in America such sympathy has called forth many complex responses. For many Afro-Americans Jewish sympathy has always been skin deep. Or, in less furious moments, compromised by what is seen to be its strategic whiteness, a minoritarian identification with the dominant same. From this point of view, Kallen's emphasis on equal parity of difference derives from an assimilated Americanness presumed to be representative. It is precisely because he has a self already self-possessed that Kallen represents to himself a difference—that is, a self free of all bonds, self-standing. Hence his anxiety about being affected by an otherness outside the self. For Locke, the black ego is, from the first, dispossessed; difference is what annihilates, consumes, incorporates him, which is why he cannot type, or form himself, as a self-creator of difference. And so, why should blacks be reassured that equality of difference is such an easy path to follow when, in America, they are annihilated and consumed precisely because of their difference? Why should ethnic differences be seen as what is unique, innermost, enduring, when those differences are precisely what is unendurable to the blacks otherwise incarcerated behind the veil? The quarrel between Locke and Kallen are encased by these disputes. The undertow of this politics of representation can be seen in their exchanges and recollections. It is almost as if the note struck in Kallen's memorial—the disavowals and repetitions—is that kind of second blow Freud describes as *nachträglich*; but one acting out a politics of difference as if it were a politics of remembrance and reconciliation. For Locke, black emulation represents a form of cultural recollection, a way of realizing and so rediscovering black self-culture—that "rare opportunity to choose deliberately to be what I was born." The identification with types outside the self is thus seen as secondary to what allows the black to be reborn as a self-conscious *historical* subject. Culture, and not race, emerges as the most permanent of things.

Moreover, in the psychograph, the paradoxes of race are marked, or re-marked, by the peculiar value Locke assigns to homosexuality. This phenomenon is twofold, doubly marked. First of all, homosexuality (or paganism) is a consequence of racial inheritance: "racial inheritance making me more of a pagan than a Puritan." The suggestion is that the sexual desire for sameness emerges from the experience of being black. Homosexual desire, in other words, comes into being when I am other than myself, when I no longer, let us say, resemble myself, when my object-oriented desire can no longer love itself as the same (i.e., narcissistically like-minded or white), but is also unable to hate the other in me, the other self that resembles me, and that I see in the mirror is also black. To be more precise, we may say that homosexuality—love of self as a desire for the other within the same—represents the paradoxes of racial identity in general. This logic—I must be other than myself in order to love (desire) myself—goes missing in Kallen's reading. Since pluralism can only digest the other of the ego insofar as the other is ultimately an enjoyment of myself, what it seems unable to swallow is any homoracial relation to the other (myself) that asks the ego to sacrifice its narcissistic desire *to* another (myself). But most of all, the likeminded ego can only become like (and therefore homoracially loved) insofar as the ego is commensurate with the anger and hostility I feel in my relation to that other *of* myself. It's not so much to be grateful for, really, the fact that the pluralist loves himself more than he does you, or that he really hates that other in himself he suspects you of being.

Such is the scene at the origins of pluralism. Such is the fleshed out implications of Kallen's memorial to Locke, his "notable friend" (Kallen, "Alain Locke," 121). The rhetoric of a right to difference once again absorbs the black into a negative symbolism of the plural. That right contains a truth about which differences are sidelined and which are seen as the rightful property of nation, ethnicity, and selfhood. In the next section I want to go back to the "psychograph," and the letters surrounding it, so as to explore what is most visible and recognizable in the language of pluralism. It seems, reading across from Kallen to Locke, that racial unlikeness deals a serious blow to the fatedness of like repeating like in the organic concert of ethnic similarity. In the letters that follow we see another tension emerge between philosophical writing and progeniture, letters that proceed from the implicit question of how Locke chose to write, philosophically, about race, or how his race came to be intimately reproduced by his philosophical writing. What also makes these letters interesting, caught up as they are in decisions about textual authority and the proper ways of writing about "American" philosophy, are their consequences for the understanding of Locke's critique of pluralism.

Mothers, Midwives, and Ghosts

On 6 June 1935, Locke sent Kallen a brief outline of his planned essay "Values and Imperatives." After taking receipt of the paper sometime after 21 June (Locke sent his draft to Kallen on that day), Kallen's response, in an undated letter, is provocative: "In substance, it fills the bill, and it would in form, if you were a more professional philosopher. But you are a man of letters and you have let your professionalism, and I suspect your anxiety over producing the paper, swamp your sense of English form."[47] Kallen advises Locke to make the following changes: excise philosophical diction, replace long sentences with short ones, include more concise references into the body of the text. "At present," he writes, "it is too conceptual, too Austrian (if you please), and too implicit." In another letter, dated 8 July 1935, Kallen writes: "I have read your paper and think it much improved. I wish you could have tackled the problem of cultural pluralism in terms of the specific Negro contribution to the United States, etc., but I am afraid it is too late for anything like that."[48]

Too conceptual, too Austrian, too professional (but not professional enough), too general (but not black enough): Kallen's list presents a classical series of value-oppositions between literature and philosophy linked to national (and by implication racial) philosophical styles. The litany makes style into a metaphor for both philosophic nationality and racial culture, or what Kallen, in his 1930 essay on "Style and Meaning," presents as the natural proprieties of philosophical style.[49] This essay, written in response to the charge of using obscure "hard technical words" (the ironies abound), starts out from a pragmatic insistence on style as what reveals the phenomenal multiplicities of the inner life. As such, "Style and Meaning" allows us to reconceive Kallen's critique of Locke's style in terms of wider priorities. "The fundamental in every style," Kallen writes, "is the rhythmic idiosyncrasy of its movement."

> Without that we could not possibly perceive the intent of thought, or get to the total significance of expression. It is to speech exactly what it is to music. It generates and deposits words; *which* words is determined by the thought's own pulse and cadences, that orders them as a magnetic flow orders iron filings or a stream carries leaves. . . . The written word is even more dependent upon the transmission of the inward pulse for its effect, for it is not carried by a voice. Rhythm is characteristic, individual, the essence of personality in style. (Kallen, "Style and Meaning," 141–142)

And on diction:

> A man can be separated from his company, even if it be that Freudful
> haunt, his mother. His vocabularly, however, is his very soul; when
> that changes, his nature alters; the words he spontaneously and habit-
> ually uses are the lasting core of his thoughts, the furniture of his
> mind, the framework and order of the world he lives in. (144)

How are we to understand the dominance of these mimetic and homoi-
otic figures whose movement coincides, on the one hand, with an innate,
natural, "essence of personality," the means whereby "the lasting core" of
thought always refinds itself, its own proper analogy, its own resemblance
to itself through the musical figurality of rhythm and of nature; and, on
the other hand, the dependence of these figures on a movement of self-
identity whose rhythm and essence are, in turn, only conceivable through
the music and soul of metaphor—that is, figures that by analogy properly
belong to the masculine ego even more than that "Freudful haunt," the
mother? To think of the essence of style as a *lexis* more intimate than
mothering is already, then, to refer the question of style and propriety to a
genos whose birth, procreation, and family are all somehow less haunting
than one's mother (i.e., she is less integral to the self than the flow of
pulse, cadence, river, voice, etc., animating logos and lexis). Does this
mean that, for Kallen, the least haunted style is the most natural—that is,
the most spontaneous and habitual—in its claims to greatest propriety?

Let me pursue this question through a reading of Kallen's 1915 essay on
"Democracy versus the Melting Pot," with its famous analogy between
music and *natio*:

> Thus "American civilization" may come to mean the perfection of the
> coöperative harmonies of "European civilization"—the waste, the
> squalor and the distress of Europe being eliminated—a multiplicity in
> a unity, an orchestration of mankind. As in an orchestra every type of
> instrument has its specific *timbre* and *tonality*, founded in its substance

and form; as every type has its appropriate theme and melody in the whole symphony, so in society, each ethnic group may be the natural instrument, its temper and culture may be its theme and melody and the harmony and dissonances and discords of them all may make the symphony of civilization. With this difference: a musical symphony is written before it is played; in the symphony of civilization the playing is the writing, so that there is nothing so fixed and inevitable about its progressions as in music, so that within the limits set by nature and luck they may vary at will, and the range and variety of the harmonies may become wider and richer and more beautiful—or the reverse. (Kallen, "Democracy," 116–117)

What is it about music that lends itself more properly than another metaphor to expressing the timbre and tonality of *natio*? What is it about the metaphorical possibilities of *natio* that lends itself to being orchestrated in this way—that is, symbolically? And what is conceptually involved in this self-conscious use of orchestral metaphor to articulate the concept of democratic nationality as philosophical idea? Aside from being open to the charge of lyrical evasion, Kallen's analogy between the spirit of music and the spirit of nations is not a systematic philosophy of history but an aesthetic ideal. (As it turns out, this harmonizing of difference has everything to do with Kallen's difference from Locke.) Kallen's representation of "American civilization" as a symphony of nationalities amounts to a deeply romantic, even racialist, aesthetic vision. The transformation of America into musical metaphor is made possible by an analogy between musical performance and America's "realization of the distinctive individuality of each *natio* that composes it," a "self-realization [working] through the perfection of men according to their kind" (Kallen, "Democracy," 116). This musical analogy already assumes a close and intimate relation between *natio* and kind, a claim that relies in fact on the harmonizing power of metaphor. Or, again, if music is the mother of metaphor under whose aegis the labor of democracy goes on, is rhetoric then its perpetual midwife? For if the "playing is the writing," ethnic groups can never be realized as the source or end of the symphonic movement, they all become part of a performance that they can neither contain nor reflect, but of which they are a tropic moment. Alternatively, Kallen's concerns with the "emotional and involuntary life" of each nationality, with the "esthetic and intellectual forms" through which that life is expressed, proceeds by an articulation of that life as metaphor, symbolized by a "natural instrument" in a symphony. In this metaphorical play with music the natural limits of *natio* can only be known through the abstract and mediated nature of metaphor. That is, the "limits set by nature" can only be represented as they appear in metaphor by analogy; through metaphor *natio* refinds its own ancestral propriety and kind and discovers the "fixed" meaning of its realized perfection, but only through the loss of what properly belongs to nature, since what is inborn can only be known via the detour of analogy. Nature's score, to push the point, can only be heard as writing, which is why there can be any metaphorical music at all.

Further, the origin of these *nationes*, though presented as historical, remains implicit in a pseudo-dialectical movement of time and ethnicity. It follows that democracy's musical score is written in nature, a score engraved in cultural memory and matched in race: "Race, in its setting," Kallen writes, "is at best what individualizes the common [cultural] heritage, imparting to it presence, personality, and force" (Kallen, "Democracy," 77). In the end, it is the sounding of race which allows ethnic nationalities to be able to hear and perform with one another. Race, in other words, not only composes musical metaphors of itself, but also makes rhetorical music out of democratic nationality. The history of America is, then, the harmony that ensues when race outperforms *natio*. But how should ethnic nationality be performed—is it a cultural voicing or the "psycho-physical" marking of a genetic score?

This question, I believe, recalls Kallen's theory of metaphor, a theory in which the truth of race, the unveiling of nature by mimesis, emerges through the imitation of kind via like-mindedness. This theory gives race a permanence that would be strange and incomprehensible to Locke: Kallen's spiritualization and reification of racial kinds permeates his history of pluralism (and in a significant sense actually constitutes it); it makes conflict over values not so much unthinkable as irrelevant to his moralization of American history and culture. The will to resemblance, or like-mindedness, is no less than a totalizing will for the same. It is a truth that assigns the risk of mimetic impropriety to the massed, industrial, and the inferior. Mimesis properly understood, then, results from the transmission of what is irreducibly innermost *and* similar; indeed, the very conception of harmonious difference distinguishes, in figural terms, the proper from the impure.

In contrast, Locke's thought appears as a chiasmic series of substitutions and reversals pitted against Kallen's harmonious metaphors and their ontological analogies between racial being and human kind. In "Values and Imperatives," for example, Locke suggests that race is itself a metaphor condensing several senses: projection, fiction, idolatry, dogma, symbol, will to power, genera and species (all terms that occur in "Values and Imperatives"). As such, the concept of metaphor no longer refers to proper meaning but is always already an interpretation; a fictioning driven by a desire for the imaginary simultaneity of sameness reaffirming itself. Whereas for Kallen race is more originary than metaphor, for Locke the engendering of meaning is never identical to itself but is always mediated by values whose history has been forgotten and repressed. Locke's interest in the imperative nature of values stresses the psychical and political history of all claims to representational truth. In this sense, his writing on the value that is art and the art, by analogy, of valuation works to free values from the realm of fixed ideas so as to make them reimaginable both culturally and historically. It is a procedure by which, to recall Kallen, values are freed from the idea of *genos* as origin and reconceived as the demands of affect and desire on social existence. This is why, in his 1910 Oxford thesis, "The Concept of Value," Locke argues that valuations are feelings, affective attitudes that can be disclaimed or acknowledged, but are neither simply logical nor veridical.[50] Values are, if nothing else, categorical feelings whose sense of obligation is habitually reinforced by our actions. And so, "ethical distinctions . . . present themselves in aesthetic contrasts, and actual motives of ethical action may often be purely aesthetic or mixed aesthetic as conveyed by terms 'noble' or 'ignoble' action."[51] Locke knows that the language of distinction cannot finally distinguish temperament from metaphor, for, just as metaphors end up invading the realm of ethics and aesthetics, the distinction between "real psychological linkage" and "figurative transfer" in whose name noble and ignoble moods are also aesthetic acts or judgments, can only be stated and recognized due to the differing metaphorical values of those temperamental acts in the first place. Better put, because values are devoid of any logical or semantic consistency, mastery over their affects whether in art or, what amounts to the same thing, philosophy, can only ever be arbitrary.

In a later essay on "Value," Locke adds to his argument: to the extent that values are conflictual, never absolute, any belief in their perdurability is a "dangerous illusion":

> Unless it is discounted, it will hardly be recognized that stable values are exceptions rather than the rule. They bulk large because they are attended to and selected. Their stability is always more or less a construction for methodological purposes, like the exception of stable objects out of the flux of happenings. It is always to some extent a fiction, because it is never absolute, and because there are no eternal values, none that endure unchanged and untransformed by new valuations forever, unless it be life itself, so long as that lasts. It may even become a dangerous illusion, if its character is not understood, and it is made an obstacle to salutary and necessary changes. In such changes the old values always condemn the new, and *vice versa*, often with tragic results. Transvaluations are the stuff out of which heroes and martyrs of "reform" or "loyalty" are made, at every step in human progress. The question of what is the right value is unanswerable for

the time being, because it is precisely the question which is being fought out. But we can predict that such changes will always be opposed, for there is always a conservative and a progressive party with respect to any change. These party attitudes are essentially valuations, as any one can discover for himself, if he is open-minded, and also distracted enough to have a "cross-bench mind" and to feel the force of both the opposite contentions. Nor are these the only conflicts which may lead to a change of values. Every society, and nearly every soul, is full of conflicts between opposing valuations, and any variation in their relative strengths may entail a change in values. *The chief agency which blinds us to these transvaluations is the stability of words;* for these change their form much less rapidly than their meaning.[52]

If there is no "right" value that is because each claim to value is a legitimizing claim whose meaning and history have been obscured by the "stability" of meaning—identified, here, with a sublimation of the affects through which values are realized. Only by being open to value differences, to the antithetical meanings of words, can the fall into metaphysical absolutes and their dour literalisms be avoided. Words and values are deluding *fictions* whose contingencies of meaning have been disavowed; hence the violent and abusive repressions of antithetical valuations. Moreover, Locke traces the power of value imperatives to what, via Jung, he terms the self's "directional drives," which are categorical in nature, primal, and noncognitive; these are "primary processes" that transcend every genre, every predicate, all form (Locke, Values and Imperatives, 327). These "wild" imperatives must be kept "within bounds" but freed from dogma and arbitrary power if we are to thrive rather than mirror the irrationalities we identify with, our obsessional wish to re-create the self-same viciously opposed to the competing relevance of "opposite contentions" (329). In brief, Locke's work on value is concerned with what drives us, the seemingly familiar accidents and improprieties of being human, and one engaged with the imperative force of thought itself—not just because of the urgings of desire, but because of a need to understand something of the pleasure, the unconscious pleasure, we derive from attacking "opposing valuations." We value what we do because we love and desire what we value; and so he can say: what endears us to certain values is the narcissistic process of valuation through which we represent ourselves, and in relation to which we identify our egoic core (that internal unity that is also a point of otherness).

And this too is an insistence that can be seen in Locke's Socratic style. The letters to Langston Hughes, the "psychograph," and "To the Young Friend on Reading *Jean Christophe*" all evoke, at the level of ethos and trope, the delicate ministries of the midwife as what brings to term thought and desire, male wisdom and homoerotic truth. As nursemaid to homoerotic genius, Locke does not perform the self-presencing of the self-same, rather he manages the encounter between the self and the otherness that infinitely haunts it, the specter which interrupts all racial genealogies, including that of harmonized plurality. The ethical birth of valuation here emerges as a simultaneous movement of severing and rejoining, release and confinement, reservedness and a self delivered from restraint: in the double and interacting implication of such self-states, Locke's philosophical midwifery is part of a much larger double movement interspersed now with a distrust of absolutist faiths, now with a refusal of sexual and racial repression. The work of midwifery, in short, is part of his wish to preserve an individual cosmopolitan ideal against the racial hegemony of American values. Hence the emphasis, respectively, on the "blind practicality" of these values as imperatives realized in the inner sentiments of the feeling self; in contrast, Locke wants to assist our awareness of "valuation" as cultural meaning, to bring forth the proximate nature of valuing as it relates to passion, feeling, and judgment. Locke's thought on the legitimated violence of validation thus accounts for his presentation of himself as a midwife to culture. In a certain sense, Locke's belief that "values create these imperatives . . . and . . . norms control our behavior as well as guide our reasoning" is always balanced by the idea that, historically speaking, "there is no fixity of content to values," an awareness that is also attuned to the fact that we give birth to the impera- tives to which we are bound—that is, just as values are the "sole tyrant[s] of the whole human *ethos*," their strength and their power relies on the fact that we also crave imperative modes of assent (328).[53] Imperatives, in short, are not categorical but motivated by desire, by our wish to master the uneasiness of who we are, a wish that feeds the tyranny of political communities and their holistic pursuit of metaphysical truth.

In conclusion, for Locke values are ghosts, disqualified and deadened illusions that are misrecognized as living, substantial things. Even the nature of political nationality rests on spectral illusions whose origin has been mystified and forgotten. And so Locke looks to art, philosophy, him- self to demystify the metaphysics of race, and, like a ghost, unveil its claims to cultural legitimacy. For example, his libertarianism and ironism, often misread as resignation or elitism, signifies an attempt to preserve competing valuations based on contingent and unstable identities. Far from melancholia and cynicism, Locke's avocation of midwifery leads to a different symbolics and semiotics of black homosexual desire. Rather than Kallen's harmonious syntheses of racial being and human kind, Locke's key trope is paradox: his life in America is proof enough that blacks were visibly excluded from the cultures of like-mindedness. Looking for a black historical rebirth, Locke had to untie, almost unwinding himself, the theo- retical web that linked blacks to the existence of an inferior kind. In Kallen's essentially white symphonic world, blacks are restricted (by nature?) to the role of passive spectators; they are never foregrounded as performers of American national life. As such, pluralism could never be fully linked with Locke's own experience of race in America. It could never quite assess the extreme, *unnatural*, series of relationships separating whites from blacks. No, to rediscover and affirm what it meant to be black in America Locke had to turn to the figure of the midwife for his avocation of a new black cultural movement; for his transvaluation of the Negro through art and culture. That *turn* helped to explain and to justify what, in 1923, he confessed to Langston Hughes: the affirmation of a new black *communitas* dedicated to the birth of "beautiful things."

It was a queer birth. Locke's passion for black art and men, a way of answering the damaged and scarred lives of black Americans. It's a view of art as a mirror to culture. Art and homoeroticism identified, here, as the future "manhood and expression" of Afro-America. Or, as he writes in "To the Young Friend on Reading *Jean Christophe*," "the quickening, galvanizing effect" of a frankly pagan life in which "the only lesson . . . is for the future."

6 The Love of Neither-Either

RACIAL INTEGRATION IN
PRESSURE POINT

A white man can't know the depths of a black's
suffering. I search for truth but it's never there
for me in its totality. All I ever seem to find is
part of it.
　　　　—Stanley Kramer, *Stanley Kramer Filmmaker*
　　　　　　　　　　　　　　　　　　　　(1978)

As I talked out these things, I started to "see"
me. . . . I was seeing for the first time a kind of
whole Sidney.
　　　　　　　　—Sidney Poitier, *This Life* (1980)[1]

This chapter, my second attempt at reading a film produced by Stanley
Kramer (*Pressure Point* to be exact, a 1962 film starring Sidney Poitier and
Bobby Darin), is also my second attempt at understanding why Kramer's
portrayals of black masculinity seem so problematic. If my writing
appears littered with question marks, that's because I haven't yet attained
anything like a satisfactory answer to my concerns. I confess that Poitier's
role troubles me deeply. He appears to be both metaphor and metonym,
cipher and symbol—as if there is something about him that the film can
neither face nor address, something that cannot be spoken, and yet, just as
revealingly, something "strangling, alive, struggling to get out" via a curiously male, interracial anguish. In a film that sees a bewildering chain of
symptoms and afflictions (the film stages, via flashback, Poitier's wartime
psychoanalysis of Darin's fascist) my essay is, if anything, a rumination on

the failures of symbolization, thoughts on the intrusiveness of what is absent or what remains as a trace in the unsaid. Poitier's role is crucial here. Why is he such a displaced-condensed figure, both enigma and mask, in *Pressure Point*? What role does his "race" play in the film's consideration of his image, his representability? For what, and how, is his portrayal necessarily limited to something *seen* and simultaneously *barred* in his image? And again: why does he leave me feeling such sullen, silent discontent? Why is the image of Poitier in *Pressure Point* so maddening?

As a way into the unpleasures of *Pressure Point*, the spectacle and representation of racial sympathy is my starting point. Can a white man (as Kramer describes himself) ever know the depths of black suffering—that is, experience the afflicted, interior life of being black, in all of its totality—from *within*? What does it feel like to see oneself as spectacle, looking on from inside the acceptable mask of integration, seeing oneself taken over—disintegrated—by a deeper and more desperate hope? These questions—adapted from my opening citations—speak to both the promise and failures of the movies Kramer and Poitier made together during the 1960s. As leading witnesses for the truths this cinema professed, both men confess a certain failure, or blindness, exposed by their struggle to represent (in Kramer's words) "the black man's search for justice." You might say that, for Kramer, Poitier symbolized that hope and belief central to his quest for the truth of black suffering. For Poitier, his role as symbol within that cinema evokes, instead, an inward-turning vision that allows him to retake possession of a self that had been obscured by the many delusions and snares informing Kramer's search for truth. This may be a difference between knowing and talking out in analysis, but it is also, in part, a feeling of sudden release from having been possessed by someone's fantasy. Indeed, it is psychoanalysis—with Viola Bernard—which draws Poitier into a series of reflections on the hold of the image as spectacle, the clash between image of self and self as image in Kramer's cinema, and, finally, the integration, the promise of a whole Sidney, as he starts to see himself as if for the first time. "Psychoanalysis," Poitier notes in *This Life*, "started spotlighting the fact that the images one holds of people are quite often far from the reality of those people's lives" (Poitier, *This Life*, 273).

This chapter is an attempt to explore the strained effects of sympathy as revealed by integrationist cinema. If white compassion has often been represented by blacks as a provocation that binds as well as blinds (I return to this point), the question remains open as to why Kramer and Poitier's search for the truth of black male suffering, black male identity, should end up revealing the different truths that blacks and whites have to live by in America. How is it that the attempt to know, to analyze, and not to forget fascism and racism should end up unwittingly repeating the logics of both in its plea for antiracist tolerance? Is this because the wish to know the depths of black suffering can often blind itself to the reality beyond the spectacle of suffering by mistaking what it projects for the thing itself? That blindness has a long history in American racial typology and can even be seen in liberal sympathy for blacks. This chapter is concerned with the drama or scene of this blind vision (which I call neither-either) as it appears, contentiously, in *Pressure Point*'s substitution of black for Jew. Neither-either because in this odd, deforming vision, what is visualized or represented is not a black truth, but the white imagining of blackness. Stranger still, that imagining is obsessive, dream-filled, unwitting, absorbed into an imaginary of race that gives voice to longings and fears deeply embedded in America's social and psychological character. American cinema has been central to this symbolic complication of race and nation and is more than comprehensible as a projection of that imagining. *Pressure Point*, in bringing black and Jewish responses to this neither-either, also highlights their significant differences concerning the promise of American democracy and the psychopathology of race.

"The Jew," writes Leslie Fiedler, "is struggling with the vestigial sense of being a third thing, neither-either, however one says it; and he therefore thinks of himself (his kind of awareness driving him compulsively from feeling to thinking) as being free to 'pass' in either direction," neither white nor black but somehow both.[2] Whereas for blacks, to be caught up in the fantasy of neither-either is to be paralyzed and dispossessed by an inwardly alienating vision; for the American Jew, as Fiedler argues, neither-either offers its own protective sanctuary from the negative and deluded dream life of whites and blacks. There is, to be sure, an inevitable pursuit of inclusion in this thought of neither-either, but here the passing self differs in its attitude toward enforced concession to the segregated social world.

For American Jews, passing is not necessarily conceived as a theatrical role, a mask behind which one conceals mental disobedience, but a necessary ritual for taking one's place in the melting pot of American democracy without losing the sense of oneself as a Jew. For blacks, coping with the unseeing and always vengeful eye of white imagining, passing has always offered scope for feigning, disobedience, or hidden judgment; for seizing directly, as it were rapaciously, upon the truth that race is only a mask, literally a white lie and a ritual performance of race power in a tale of subjugation and unfreedom always intimate, always unwilled. If blackness remains the countermark of a victimized-wishfulness in American culture, can it ever be freely neither-either in Fiedler's sense? Can blacks ever be, in America, free to pass? My sense is that this opposed echoing of freedom and assimilation also appears to anchor and destructure the idealism and wishfulness that informs the coded struggle for black civil rights glimpsed in integrationist film. So this chapter turns out, in the end, to be about the destructive element informing the masks and scenes—the masked scene—of a cinema moved by racial sympathy, a cinema moved by the simultaneously revealing and misleading spectacle of a black man wholly failing to bear witness to himself as black.

"I cannot go to the cinema," writes Frantz Fanon, resignedly, in 1952, "without seeing myself. I wait for me. In the interval, just before the film starts, I wait for me."[3] It's a silent, and anguished, waiting—"My heart makes my head swim," Fanon recalls—for the image of self about to be sprawled on screen (Fanon, *Black Skin*, 140). Who will "I" be? *Where* will "I" be? What self will be thrown back to me from the spectacle, at once real and imaginary, about to unfold?

Working at the juncture between psychoanalysis, philosophy, and politics, Fanon pursues, and is pursued by, these questions throughout *Black Skin, White Masks*—a book that is central to the study of racial identification and visual culture. Over and over again, Fanon returns to the dialectic of image and inwardness, to the image of the black man in cinema—the image of the black *on* screen, certainly, but also the black man *before* the screen, the black spectator about to be confronted with the racist imago identified by Fanon as part of the dream and nightmare of European and American culture. The black man, Fanon, *lives* and sometimes dies that imago; the phantasmatic image of the black that is (once again) both real and imaginary, inside and outside, on and off screen. His picture of himself—psychiatrist, black man—recast as the pressure of the social world on cinema reinscribes the pressures of self-fashioning. Moreover, the formation and undermining of identity *within* cinema remains a salient feature of his rendering of black identity. It is as if, for the black spectator, desire and seeing can only ever coincide in a moment of acute alienation, shattering, grievous, and dream filled. Here, cinema is conjured up as both trial and arrest for the black spectator; it is a specular violence in which the innermost life is taken and handed over to the murderous vengeance of public fantasy.

This experience enables us to pursue why cinema, particularly U.S. cinema, became so identified with a sadistic and shattering shaping of black existence for Fanon and other black commentators. "One of the irreducible dangers to which the moviegoer is exposed," writes James Baldwin in 1976, is "the danger of surrendering to the corroboration of one's fantasies as they are thrown back from the screen."[4] It's a danger—surrender, corroboration—which Baldwin will write in terms of race and dream, emulation and disavowal which recall Fanon. *"No one,"* Baldwin notes, quickly, *"makes his escape personality black,"* and yet, as he concludes "Congo Square" (in 1967), "the camera sees what you want it to see. The language of the camera is the language of our dreams" (Baldwin, *Devil*, 34).

The questions are inevitable: Who is the dreamer here? Who, or what, is his desire? Baldwin's response is stark: "White Americans have been encouraged to continue dreaming, [. . .] black Americans have been alerted to the necessity of waking up" (56–57). The danger of cinema to the spectator, in other words, is marked by race, by racism. For its white spectators, cinema *can* be a type of waking dream—a common theme in psychoanalytic film theory—or false illusion; by contrast, the black spectator finds himself struggling to wake from a reverie, at once terror and pleasure, which works itself through his projected image. Rather than dream-filled refuge, cinema becomes a form of racial entrapment, a lure by which blackness is conjured up as negative or void. No escape from this one-way self-fashioning; cinema takes up its place in a visual history of the black as cowed, mutilated, dead (think, for example, of the spectacle of the black body in the photographs of lynch mobs from the early decades of the twentieth century). Part of a visual nightmare, then, cinema stakes its claim to the black body, to what, in his remarkable commentary on the consistency with which cinema threatens that body, Baldwin describes as its "unlucky posture" (54).

We know that posture, its staging of the black man, poised to attack; the white woman, frail, unconscious, dead; the arrival of the murderous mob (or, for some, the gallant and furious Klan). Across five decades of cinema, from *The Birth of a Nation* to *In the Heat of the Night*, that scene is agitating, worked and reworked to support both the most virulent phantasms of race on film. It is there, too, in the cinematic imaginary of race reconciliation: the dream of cinema as a form of cultural politics; cinema as therapeutic intervention; cinema as, in Stanley Kramer's words, a player in "the black man's struggle for justice," resisting, by replaying, America's negrophobic dreams (Kramer, *Stanley Kramer*, 16). In fact, what first struck me on reading Baldwin's *The Devil Finds Work* was his attention—uneasy, embarrassed, even anguished—to *that* cinema: more precisely, to the considerations of representability (to borrow Freud's phrase) of the black man in a cinema driven by a desire for race integration. On the cusp between dream and nightmare, that desire finds expression through a figure who, in Albert Johnson's words, was to become *"the* symbolic Negro actor of his generation"*: Sidney Poitier.[5] Symbol of Negro-Jewish integration—or sometimes "showcase nigger," in Clifford Mason's well-known slur—Poitier *carries* something for both cinema and politics, cinema as politics.[6] He is, in Baldwin's terms, at once virile and "choked," a figure cleft in two by something that remains unreadable, "not quite in focus" and yet exposed, virtually fetishistic, as Baldwin concludes (56). At issue is Poitier's beauty: political, moral, and aesthetic. Baldwin's analysis of the desire—homoerotic, interracial—screened (in both senses) by *The Defiant Ones,* for example, uncovers the demand on black male love, black selflessness, in a telling construction of the bonds between black and white men, bonds which only allow the black man to win honor insofar as he sacrifices himself.[7] Recall, for example, the final scene of this film in which Poitier, cast as the black fugitive bound but no longer chained to his white "partner" (Tony Curtis), jumps off the train, refusing the promise of freedom because he refuses to abandon his friend. *Get back on the train you fool!* was the resentful response of one Harlem audience, greeting the wish for integration with enraged, self-mocking laughter. *But . . .* says Baldwin. *But.* What about black hatred? What about black rage? What about the fact that black men *hate* white men, that "the root of that hatred is rage"? (61–62).

The omission of that hatred in *The Defiant Ones* leads Baldwin to condemn Poitier's role as one that allows admiration but prohibits (black) anger. "There is no way to believe," he concludes, "both Noah Cullen [Poitier] *and* the story" (61).[8] Black anger. What to do with it? Why does it go missing? What does that liberal, and political, cinema do with a force that threatens to drive it toward *dis*integration? Choke it, perhaps? There is, in Baldwin's reading of Poitier's cinema, something "strangling, alive, struggling to get out" (56). Words, affect, are stuck in the throat, choked,

but always compelling, source of a disguised, but all-pervasive embarrassment that might be called ethical. As symbol, as cinematic projection of
integration, the black man—Poitier, the actor, his image—displaces the
fetid history of relations between black and white men, displaces the anger
which belongs to that history—and so, as one contemporary reviewer of
The Defiant Ones complained in 1958, supports the film's refusal to analyze
"any of the real psychological forces behind race hatred."[9] The film's deep
equivocation concerning that hatred expresses itself through an "impas-
sioned, if slightly strangled, plea for humanity and tolerance" (61). No
anger, no psychology, no *analysis* of the racial politics of projection: the
dreamwork of cinema, you might say—the lure of the image, the imago of
the black—has displaced the work of interpretation. Cinema goes back to
dream.

"Tit Tat Toe, Here I go, Three jolly butcher boys all in a row."

I want to pursue this confabulation between cinema and dream, race
hatred and analysis—and, in particular, the filmic evasions of black
anger—through what remains, for me, one of Poitier's most troubling
appearances on screen: his role as a black psychiatrist in Stanley Kramer
and (Hubert) Cornfield's *Pressure Point*, released in 1962. (I wonder what
Fanon, waiting for his image to erupt on screen, could say about this film.)
Part of the cinema forged between Poitier and Kramer, *Pressure Point* was
quickly condemned as a failure by both men. Poitier, speaking at the
Berlin Film Festival in 1962, identified its commercialism—"the overall
intent of the film was to make money"—as a symbolic vacuum: "The kind
of character I played in *Pressure Point*," he insisted, "was not important."[10]
(Not important? Let's just note Edward Mapp's description of Poitier in
Pressure Point as "the only Negro characterization in a leading role in
American motion pictures in 1962" [Keyser and Ruszkowski, *Cinema*,70].)
For Poitier the success of *The Defiant Ones*, his earlier collaboration with

Kramer, was based on of their shared vision as Negro-Jewish outsiders "on the margins of American social reality," a perspective which allowed them to create a film that "reveal[ed] to us the selves we cannot see," selves otherwise invisible to that social reality but whose depiction was nevertheless necessary to the nation's moral and psychic health.[11] By contrast, *Pressure Point* fails, in Poitier's view, to "illuminate, to educate, to enlighten" (Keyser and Ruszkowski, *Cinema*, 71). *Pressure Point*, both in purpose and execution, was vacuous because it was mythic, and so it was unable to critique the legitimating fictions of race. Similarly, Kramer concedes that, after an initial enthusiasm, he lost interest in the film. "I liked the idea when they brought it to me," he recalls, "but as the screenplay developed I became less enthusiastic. I thought the organization of the book made it difficult to develop unity in the film."[12]

It's an admission that puts us on the track of the various origins, and destinations, of *Pressure Point*, a film that is part of the ongoing exchange between psychoanalysis and cinema, black and Jewish America. On Kramer's reading, *Pressure Point* is under pressure from its origins in a strange and compelling book: Robert Lindner's popular account of psychoanalysis in *The Fifty-Minute Hour: A Collection of True Psychoanalytic Tales*, first published in 1955.[13] The penultimate chapter of that book, "Destiny's Tot," describes Lindner's work with a young man, Anton, imprisoned for sedition in 1942. Anton is a fascist member of Fritz Kuhn's German-American Bund; Lindner is a "Jew psychologist" (to borrow Anton's phrase). Apart from his politics, Anton's symptoms are various: hallucination, amnesia, loss of consciousness, nightmares. "You have the mentality of a stormtrooper," Lindner tells him, opening the sexuality and violence of his patient's family romance onto the scene of political hatred (Lindner, *Fifty-Minute Hour*, 207). Like his symptoms, Anton's fascism— more precisely, fascism as symptom—is derived, Lindner tells us, from the "murderous impulses [he] had been charged with from the earliest days of his life, as well as punishment for the fantasized carrying out of his vicious intent" (203). Wanted too much (by a seductive mother) and not enough (his father is vengeful, brutal, sadistic), the story of Anton's childhood slides easily into Freudian fables of incest and murder. As an adult, it seems, Anton is doomed to repeat, and transfer, the loves and hatreds of his family into the realm of political life. Fascism allows Anton to project, displace, and so perform his aggression, to fashion and so shape an identity with the world as his theater. Aggressed and aggressing, victim and executioner, Anton settles scores in play, in fantasy, in politics. Take, for example, the startling daydream in which, disguised as an Eastern potentate, he orders the execution of the world. This, Lindner concludes, is the ur-fantasy: it "sets the pattern" of his patient's psychic and political life; the death of the world—a fiction forged through an Oedipal drama—comes to found the phantasm of race subtending political hatred: the fascist drama of "life unworthy of life."[14] This ur-fantasy divides itself between a voluptuous show of love and the acutely felt pleasures of violence in a tension that not only transforms erotic sadism into murderous hatred but, as play and as fiction, suggests how Anton's unconscious fantasy reproduces the hatreds of culture. Retributive daydreaming because Anton can only take hold of and so master himself, in fantasy, through the sadistic destruction of others. The pleasure of killing the world, then, is also a kind of self-execution, a way of sentencing and allaying the murderous incestuous impulses that "demanded this payment in kind"; but it is also a way of following the path of least resistance in a mind at war with itself, a mind conflicted and ever eager to perform the superegoic pleasures of hatred defining American culture (203). It is this ambivalence that allows Lindner to see in fascism both a resistance and disguise: fascism not only performs the hateful pleasures of resistance—if I may put it this way—it also tries to block alterity and difference from the internal horizons of the mind. Fascism possesses, in short, because Anton is already possessed—driven by a ruthless, murderous love "from the earliest days of his life."

As a psychoanalysis of fascism and the pleasures of fantasy, "Destiny's Tot" remains a remarkable and suggestive text (one that could be read alongside the critical theory of authoritarianism being developed through the 1950s).[15] In the context of racial self-fashioning, however, it is Lindner's preoccupation with sadism and, in particular, with the hostility between analyst and patient, which demands attention. Anton's hatred for Lindner, the "Jew psychologist" (as he puts it), may be taken for granted as an attempt to abolish all that threatens his identity. But Lindner is also careful to locate his own "little piece of sadism" in the work of this therapy: his hope, for example, that the "process of psychotherapy would be painful to Anton." "I was aware of my own hostility toward him," Lindner concludes, "aware of the secret satisfaction I took in having him, an avowed fascist and anti-Semite, in this kind of authority-subject relationship with me, a Jew" (174). No surprise, perhaps. The direction of persecutory desire, expressed in terms of mutual risk and threats to identity, is by no means one way. Indeed, it is the mutual experience of hatred and distrust that comes to embody their elaborate transferences. Nevertheless, it is Lindner who is running psychoanalysis into sadism, the work of interpretation into the pleasures of vengeance and mastery—an identification which begins to disperse sadism across the text, to become part of its "organization" that, in Kramer's terms, is going to put pressure on the unity of the film by becoming part of the difficulty of transferring case history to the screen (more specifically, in sustaining interest in that transfer).

It's a difficulty which goes beyond that of knowing how to figure—to give "plastic representation," to borrow Freud's phrase—to the pressures of unconscious life.[16] How do you represent the time and place of the analytic hour in cinema? How do you screen psychoanalysis? The question has a long, and complicated, history to which *Pressure Point* gives a further twist. For Hubert Cornfield, who collaborated on the screenplay with S. Lee Pogostin, the film had to give expression to Lindner's struggle to bring about, in the words of one reviewer, "the righting of a disordered mind"; but it simultaneously had to *show* that disorder via the unconscious, recollected scenes of humiliation, revenge, and anger informing Anton's "obsessive hatred for Negroes and Jews" (*Product Digest*, Oct. 3, 1962, 665). Fascism operates here as a clinical and cinematic metaphor for

Anton's sufferings as a boy, and what the film recounts is the Oedipal relation that links them. The memories that fascism authorizes Anton to forget or deny are thus shown to be constitutive of his political dreams and
fantasy. I want to track the transfer from text to screen, the transfer of
Lindner's response to Anton onto Poitier, via another scene that emerges
between "Destiny's Tot" and *Pressure Point*, one discernable as a fantasy of
displacement onto the black man. That overlay will not only restrict
Poitier's role in relation to that recollected background, it will redefine
him as the figure of displacement connecting text to film. It's a move that
will complicate the film's political wish for integration, the wish to transcend the psychic games and patterns of white-black conflict by reimagin-
ing white racism as psychotic fantasy.

On the one hand, Lindner—"Jew psychologist"—is displaced by
Poitier—black psychiatrist. On the other hand, that "little piece of
sadism," the hostility expressed by the *object* of hatred toward his persecutor, goes missing, neither witnessed nor entertained. (The persecutor—
white, male, fascist—remains constant.) What appears for a moment as a
simple transfer, or substitution, at the level of narrative, gives way to a
complex and intricate game of appearance and disappearance, a game of
neither-either that will reflect *Pressure Point*'s illusory and symbolic resolution of American racism. Driven by a liberal sense of responsibility, the
film's showing of white sickness, black pain, can only secure black alle-
giance, on screen, by locating the psychiatrist's anger elsewhere, replacing
it with the racist hostility of a white fascist angered by the diverting pressures of fantasy. (Pressure in the sense of affliction, oppression, trouble,
embarrassment—unremitting and consuming.)

Negro for Jew; Negro *as* Jew—this displacement recurs, obsessively, in
the film via a kind of vicarious and disorienting gaming. I want to pursue
that gaming through a reading of two scenes from the film and the discourse surrounding its release. On the one hand, the narrative is structured by a series of oppositions. Doctor/patient; black/white; therapy/
hatred; freedom/prison; democracy/fascism. These themes hold the

narrative in place, underscoring the link between theme and historical circumstance, war and psychoanalysis, the embattled nature of race pass- ing alongside the therapeutic and democratic assurances offered by the talking cure.[17] On the other hand, there is a *pressure* brought to bear from the very beginning of the film; the invasive force of the patient's race fan- tasy, simultaneously attacked and imitated by the analysis in Lindner's account, means that the cure already contains within itself a version of that which the film is politically trying to transcend. Pressure point: a sensitive part of the body, a point susceptible to pain; the title pressing in upon us the fact that those pressures are at once deeply complicit in the projective identifications of racism, linked as they are to a fascistic concep- tion of pleasure-unpleasure. That complicity is scored into the opening credits: white lines—diagonals, verticals—are inscribed, crisscross, on a black ground. Letters, lines, movement: the stars' names only become leg- ible across the two halves of a split, or segregated, screen (see fig. 5).

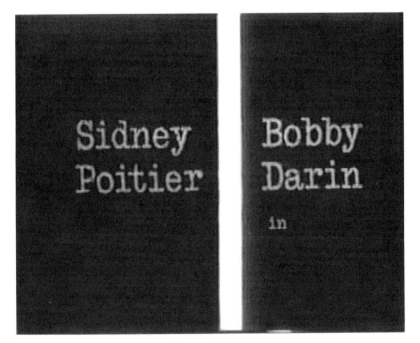

Figure 5 Opening credits for Pressure Point.

It is tempting to read this image as anticipation of the relations between violence and inscription that are going to preoccupy the film, the persecutory anxieties about boundaries and borders that will structure some of its crucial scenes, paranoid scenes told in flashback where the patient's identity is given over to assault and seizure by projected images. And it is this possibility that is suggested by Ernest Gold's jarring, atonal, jazzy score, for the music invokes conflict, rage, and anxiety in just those terms that the two protagonists will reserve for their violent, transferential encounter. Certainly, as we move from the bar to the opening scenes, the frame narrative contains but also begins to destructure the film. These images also call attention to the deep anxieties facing Negro-liberal projection in 1960s America concerning the limits and excesses of black rage, black aspirations. In a crucial and no doubt highly symbolic opening exchange, the doctor (Poitier) is confronted by a white colleague (Peter Falk) at his wit's end about how to treat a black teenager in his care. The boy is thirteen years old, his mother is a prostitute to white men, his father has been hanged for the murder of one of her clients. Falk is insisting that he be taken off the case. The treatment is going nowhere, one of the "Negro" psychiatrists on the staff should take the case. The boy's anger, it seems, threatens to drive him mad:

> FALK: The boy hates me. I just can't handle it.
> POITIER: I understand. That's his problem.
> FALK: Oh, I know that's his problem. Believe me, I know that. You
>   don't know how deeply he hates.

For a moment the film hovers on a white failure to cope with black hatred, but that hatred is immediately revealed to be a sign of personal pathology. As a pathology it need not be associated with liberal ideology—the idea that blacks hating whites has no ontological or political validity other than as a symptom restricted to blacks. Nameless, hating, the young black boy mobilizes the liberal ideology of the film. "I understand, I understand," the doctor assures Falk, a sympathetic identification which his face, barred by lines of shadow, underlines Poitier's symbolic appearance-disappearance, while it works to secure his reminiscence and the film's extended flashback to his treatment of the white fascist. Here *Pressure Point* announces its status as liberal apology through the rhetorical displacement of black hatred by Poitier. For the assurances he offers makes explicit the real political pressures which the struggle for black civil rights exerted on white liberal-Jewish America and on the film. To put this another way: a young black boy's story—the specificity of the hatreds between white and black—is at once binding the narrative and excised from it. At the same time, "I understand, I understand": Poitier's reassurance—calm, professional, part of the "job"—stages one of the film's most equivocal integrations ("I had the same thing once," he will insist later). How do we interpret this (the doctor's, the film's) association between the black boy's anger at the white man—a therapist who, it seems, symbolizes the law that kills his father, the sex that used his mother—and the virulent racism directed at a black psychiatrist by the fascist? What is the principle of mediation that threatens to collapse black anger into fascism? And why do those assurances immediately give way to a case history of fascism rather than, say, America's long history of anti-black racism? For me, the decision to present Anton's obsessed Oedipal memories as proof that whites and blacks undergo similar resistances to the pressures of race hatred—I'll say this again—ends up reducing the irreducibly singular pressures of American anti-Semitism and anti-black racism.

It's a substitution which takes us to the heart of the film's analysis of race hatred—the analysis that, for some critics, *Pressure Point* simply fails to deliver—in its figuring of the black man/psychiatrist suspended between idealization and hatred. For me, the key scene in this context is the one in which a game of tic-tac-toe comes to stand for a sexualized violence massified as the metaphor for fascism. (Although this scene does not occur in "Destiny's Tot," the pattern of Anton's sexual life is described as cruelly sadomasochistic, in which he "rarely hesitated to behave brutally with others to pay for his earlier submission and shame. His contacts with women,

too, were fleeting, savage, and lacking even the pretense of tenderness"
[Lindner, *Fifty-Minute Hour*, 214].) Scene. Doctor and patient are talking
across the doctor's desk, the patient drawing lines on a pad. Voiceover—
the patient's voice—describes how he has joined a traveling construction
crew, how, despite his youth, he has become their "leader"; the crew, he
says, started "listening to me and, eventually, they even obeyed me." What
does he ask them to do? Lots of "funny things":

PATIENT: You know what tic-tac-toe is?
DOCTOR: It's a game, isn't it?
PATIENT: You ever play it?
DOCTOR: Once, when I was a kid.
PATIENT: We played it once. I mean really played it.

As the camera pans slowly from right to left, the scene dissolves into
memory, into what the patient's voice describes as "a nothing place," in
the "middle of nowhere," full of "nothing people." A bar, a bartender, his
wife. Nothingness, void, vacuum, that, it seems, licenses the child's game
to become "real" (we "really played it"). The patient is drunk, chalking
tic-tac-toe onto the bar. The bartender intervenes, tells him not to, hands
him some paper. The patient throws the paper away and smiles. A close
up on the face of the woman signals a fear that she attempts to assuage
by inviting the patient to "play" with her: "Come on, play with me."

And so play he does, drawing his crew into the game, mobilizing them:
"I'm going to give everyone some exercises." The patient is pedagogue,
leader. He and his crew cover the bar with tic-tac-toe—white lines criss-
crossing on a dark background, echoing the credits to the film. The denser
the lines the less they reveal, effacing all signs of the bar's nothingness by
an inscription, a game whose most visible and repeated effect is that of
concealment. (That is, their most significant aspect is to make legible, paradoxically, what can only be seen from *the inside*, from the patient's own
point of view as he reminisces: the repeated drawing makes reappear
what the analysis reveals has had to be abolished internally, the lines of

tic-tac-toe symbolize that abolition externally from without, on the semi-otic surface of the world.) As the crew disperses outside, the patient is left with the bartender, his wife, and one remaining member of the gang. Ordering the bartender behind the bar, the patient tells him to lie down and go to sleep: "Don't make a sound." He and the crew member then open the woman's bag, remove her lipstick, and begin to draw down her exposed back after unzipping her dress. Her body, unlike the bar, perfectly reveals the horizontal and vertical alignments and configurations of the game as if the body of the woman makes the meaning of the game per-fectly clear. Indeed, it is as if her body allows discovery precisely because it refuses to give way to the rigors of the game, warding off the symbolic abolition of self and identity by a refusal to appear. (After all, is she being included or excluded from the game?) She closes her eyes as they continue to draw—and the camera cuts back to the doctor's office and the patient's laughter.

The doctor's voice comes over the patient's laughter: "In all those many months, there had been many times when I was uneasy, times when I was repelled, but that was the point at which I became frightened. And the really frightening thing was that I wasn't sure just what I was fright-ened of." Fright? It is as if binding fails at this point as sadistic gaming exposes the doctor to radical self-questioning. The doctor does not *know*, does not know his patient: What he is, why he is, what he might do. In fact, the doctor's fright in this sequence can become the fright of the film. It is his voice that has guided us through what Donald Spoto has described as the unsettling "grotesquerie" of hallucination on display in *Pressure Point*, conveyed through abrupt shifts in point of view and a whimsical gaming with sound and image (Spoto, *Stanley Kramer*, 241). Driven by memory—the doctor's, the patient's—the film is forged through flashback and voiceover, constructing scenes within scenes, drawing us closer to the childhood traumas that on this reading (Lindner's reading: the terms are those of "Destiny's Tot") generate the fascist character. A slab of bloody meat hurtling toward the spectator, for example, catches us up into a child's terror at a father who "butchers" the mother, while the juxtaposition of shots equates the maternal body, the child's desire to kill his mother, with the father's bloody trade. Describing, interpreting, making knowable the origins of racism in (individual, family) sickness, the doctor's voiceover has been part of the film's defense against its traffic in delusion, against the fascism to which its strange and hallucinatory images are supposed to be the key. Indeed, far from producing a sense of boundary and closure, these voiceovers occasionally produce the opposite effect, reinforcing the film's arresting "subjective-hallucinatory quality" at the expense of any realist aesthetic (Spoto, *Stanley Kramer*, 241). Moreover, the film's intensely complex and varied use of sound and image sometimes works to suppress any distance between point of view and identification. At such moments, the audience has no defense, compelled, as Spoto puts it, to inhabit an "unjustified identification *with the* [patient's] *hallucination*," his curious fusion of persecutory and persecuted (241).

On the other hand, if voiceover fails, defense fails. *Pressure Point* does not so much analyze fascism as inscribe it, disperse it across its text. Fear enters the black man as he listens to the patient describe how he, as leader of the group, can use the pleasures of a child's game to unleash the drive to persecute—to play, cruelly, with those others cast as "nothing." Fright? Is the doctor an object of this game, another "nothing," aligned with the woman: symbol of the cut, cut into? I think so. But there, too, is the patient's manipulation of and connivance with an imaginary that would catch the black man up into this sexual gaming as both persecutor and persecuted. "You ever play it?" the patient asks him, half mockingly, half menacingly. Play what? Play a game of tic-tac-toe in which the body of a white woman is violated? Where is the black man in *that* scenario of sadistic defilement? A man who also finds himself stripped of his certitudes by that scenario, dispossessed of his authority by the patient's menace and cunning?

The fright that the patient arouses in the doctor, the fright that resists interpretation, the fright that displaces the repulsion that he feels, is bound to that image of white femininity—and, though it is displaced to another scene in the film, to the vindictive word of a white man—"Who did they believe? Me or you?"—is the patient's taunt to the doctor, who loses the case for delaying his parole. While the narrative of the film authorizes the doctor's anxiety (at the very end of the film we learn that the patient was hanged, ten years later, for the murder of an old man), this scene makes us feel the social and juridical power of the white man's word. We are back with the rich and disturbing pathos of Baldwin's "unlucky posture," now visible as the point of pressure at which a black man fails. That is, we glimpse in this brief exchange the boundary or bar of racism, its arbitrary ability to reconfigure the hopes, desires, and ambitions of a black man (tails I win, heads you lose).

In this context, it is important to note that the tic-tac-toe sequence, conjoined with the threat of sexual violence, played a key role in the commodification of the film (commodification that, on Poitier's view, cast him into the symbolic vacuum of racial myth). Consider, for example, the imagery and rhetoric of the poster campaign which accompanied *Pressure Point* on its release (see fig. 6). Cast up on the margins of the poster, the

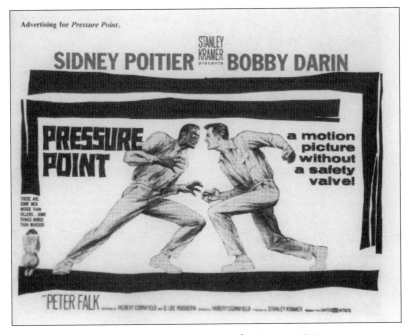

Figure 6   Poster advertisement for Pressure Point.

image of a woman, kneeling, her back exposed and scrawled with tic-tac-toe, secures the rhetoric of rage in its caption: "There are some men worse than killers . . . Some things worse than murder!" Black and white, Poitier and Darin, are enraged antagonists, locked in combat over that violated body of the white woman—privileged signifier of the carefully fashioned fury between the two. But who has violated whom? Who is defending whom here? Given the archetypal symmetry established between Poitier and Darin, the grammar of the poster remains ambiguous. Against this backdrop of neither-either, is it possible to read the figure of the black man as defender of white womanhood rather than its presumed violator? What are the conditions for such a reading? "Whoever says rape says Negro," writes Fanon in 1952. What would it take for the figure of the black man *not* to collapse—predictably, wearily—into that alienating yet constitutive spectacle of sex and violence courted, so flagrantly, by these images and by the persistent and obsessive obliquity of the black man as symbol?

You might say that it is precisely this version of black manhood as symptom and projection that *Pressure Point* resists, protests against. Rage and sexuality are barred by, and from, Poitier's image on screen (he is, as one critic puts it, "hypnotically wholesome").[18] More myth than substance, desperately nurturing and worthy, Poitier's character carries the film's *wish*, its politics of democratic integration and erstwhile celebration of liberal hegemony. It should not surprise us that he can only tolerate, never retaliate, that his role is there to perform the marriage of blackness and reason, rather than excess or passion. "Yes, I wanted to kill you with my bare hands," the doctor acknowledges to his patient, "but more than that I wanted to help you." Black anger gives way to the white wish for black therapeutics, the wish to *help* as well as forgive those who hate you. To reproduce in oneself—one's innermost being—that narcissistic identification with whiteness, with all its projective, alienating elements: repressed desire, repulsed wish, and subsequent projection into the outer world of black denigration. To take on and so to bind the torments of white racist hostility again and again. Is this a version of Baldwin's choked virility, as the submissive duties of Poitier's persona in cinema suggest: stricture, discipline, self-alienation (all the burdens of the cure, the wish to heal the racist's psyche pain)? Object of the film's political idealism, then, the black man speaks its commitment to democracy, the remarkable paean which draws the narrative toward its conclusion, and which leaves us with an image of Poitier literally choked by anger, an image that also conceals, by displacing, the film's symbolic center:

> POITIER: This is my country. This is where I've done what I have done. And if there were a million people like you—all sick like you are sick, all shouting down destroy, degrade—and if there were twenty million more sick enough to listen to them, you are still gonna lose. You're gonna lose, Mister, because there's something in this country, something so big and strong that you don't even know. Something big enough to take it from people like you and come back and nail you into the ground. You're walking out of here? You are going nowhere! Now get out!

Here, suddenly, the black man is angry, angry on behalf of "his country," on behalf of a nation bigger than the sickness of xenophobia and hatred of the foreigner, a nation, let it be said, still wedded to the pernicious pleasures and dominations of race segregation. It is as if *Pressure Point* can only found its confidence in cultural, if not racial, assimilation by reaffirming the disappearance of black selfhood through a still deeper submission to liberal versions of assimilation, that bizarrely opaque "something" to which fascism will invariably give way. Poitier's vision, and the political vision of the film, thus end up with a befuddled and staggeringly ambiguous exchange of dominations—the "sickness" of race, the black experience of racism-as-sickness, can only be cured by dissociating American democracy from the anti-black racism that perpetuates it. At a time when the campaign for black civil rights was strongly insisting on the ties between the two, as well as trying to counter the psychic and social refusal—by whites—of black assimilation, the ending of the film again insists on placing Poitier into a startling vacuum. Not only must he forget his race, forget that he is a black man, if he is to stand for and symbolize that democracy; he must also be visibly punished by losing his job as a black psychiatrist—"the best job I'd ever had," he says at one point— mainly because he is unable to successfully contest the racist assumptions of both his psychiatric colleagues and the parole board. The latter willingly set free the sick fascist against Poitier's wishes, liberating him to hate once more, to wage war on behalf of a racist vision of nationhood (the institutionalized culture of which was already meting out violence to those who dared to contest it).

Certainly, that institutionalization would allow us to situate the profoundly raced difference in audience response. To the contemporary black reviewer Albert Johnson, *Pressure Point* seemed to reproduce the segregated relations of power that the filmmakers had hoped to displace and absorb. After all, the white audience, "dazed and moved by the unusual image of the symbolic Negro as a modern Patrick Henry, roars its spontaneous approval with deafening applause [to Poitier's final speech in praise of America's democratic kingdom of ends]," while the black audience "is contemplative, tensely moved, and silent."[19] Tensely moved—or moved to tension? Quite simply, the message of reconciliation at the film's close is, for these two audiences, different. It's a question, to recall Baldwin, of who is dreaming whom here. If, for white audiences, Poitier's vision is what allows the escape into the dream that is felt as—is only conceivable as—the dream of reconciliation, for blacks, by contrast, that escape from the truth, that escape into race fantasy, remains deeply in thrall to a representation of American democracy from which they are *inclusively* barred—thus, in a very real and imaginary way, a vision of neither-either.[20] *Pressure Point*, in any case, is not a film where black men can freely go, or escape to dream. How could it be otherwise? The ending of the film is still imagining the black man as a kind of cover, or metaphor—a way of referring to and discussing white liberal torment and anguish without addressing the growing refusal by blacks, to take—again and again—white hate. The film cannot legitimately address this tension because that would involve the liberal dream of integration, its sadistic fantasy, being called into question—left behind and revealed, as it were, in black and white.

Finally, we may ask, is it here that the film's ideal also becomes the object of its violence (a violence repeatedly figured in the film as a sadistic game of exposure and concealment)? It's a violence which demands that Poitier speak white anguish and forget that he is a black man. The demand that he disappear *as* Negro, reappear *as* Jew? In the transfer of psychoanalysis from case history to cinema, *Pressure Point* becomes a symptom of that displacement and that pressure. Negro for Jew; Negro *as* Jew. Reading Lindner's case study as the latent text of the film, the relation—at once hateful and therapeutic, sadistic and political—between fascist and Jew becomes its repressed representation: the representation screened (again, in both senses) through the projected image of a black man. As such, that image (again, articulated through an unspoken but powerful male bond) must *suffer*. It substitutes for, and so attempts to bind, the sadism uncovered in Lindner's study; it forms the screen onto which all the most compelling integrationist fantasies of Negro-Jewish relations are projected, fantasies that begin by limiting black identity to the role of sacrifice and moral stricture. At the same time, black is integrated into Jew, an integration—by no means unique to this film—that identifies anti-Semitism with the hatred directed at black people in American life.[21] It's an identification that may begin to choke the political promise of this cinema, an identification that, in so far as it refuses to lend the authority of a Jewish sadism to the black man, can only reinforce the persecution—the active disappearance—of his image. "As analyst," one critic notes in response to *Pressure Point*, "Poitier has assumed the white man's burden" (Keyser and Ruszkowski, *Cinema*, 69). Or, as the patient taunts the doctor in the course of the film: "You must be a masochist" for playing the role of psychiatrist in a racially segregated, anti-black world; for trying to become "white and respectable"; for imitating those would-be imitators, the Jews. (At one point in the film, the patient describes Jews as more dangerous than blacks because they can "pass for white"). And in a sense it is masochism, disturbingly confused with compassion and clinical empathy, that encapsulates Poitier's racialized stricture. Denied Lindner's secret sadistic pleasure as a Jew, in the eye and mind of the movie Poitier's masculinity can only ever be self-blinding, crossed and recrossed by a sadistic fantasy of integration, in which, over his wishes as a victim of racism, there is superimposed, in close-up, the power of a sadistic, victimizing wish. This is a cinema, then, in which, painstakingly organized and framed, a black man is repeatedly rewarded and condemned for playing the game of neither-either, offstage, onscreen, again and again.

The eyes were the guilty organs.

—Robert Lindner, *Rebel without a Cause* (1945)

Sadism is part of the story, I think, of Kramer's failed search for a true spectacle of black suffering. It also forms part of the pressures driving Poitier, angrily, guiltily, into analysis of the entrapments and lures of images.[22] For both Kramer and Poitier, black hostility and anger forces them to rethink the spectacle of cinema's integrated image. How could touching scenes of interracial sympathy be mistaken for cruel defilement? How could a film about black affliction and redemption, white compassion and affirmation be accused of displacing racist punishment onto the black? In a sense, this problem of *dis*integrating identifications went way beyond integrationist cinema—becoming both obsessive metaphor and primal scene for the embittered divisions of white and black America during the 1960s.

In March 1964, in a roundtable discussion on "Liberalism and the Negro," organized by *Commentary*, James Baldwin explained why, historically, white liberalism had been experienced as an "affliction" by many blacks.[23] Asked to clarify that remark by Charles Silberman, Baldwin

The Love of Neither-Either

replies by defining what he means by a liberal: "What I mean by a liberal is someone . . . who has a set of attitudes so deep that they're almost unconscious and which blind him to the fact that in talking to a black man, he is talking to another man like himself" (Baldwin et al., "Liberalism and the Negro," 38). In his growing isolation on a roundtable which included a number of prominent Jewish intellectuals—for example, Nathan Glazer, Sidney Hook, and Norman Podhoretz—Baldwin's sense of the different cultural experience of Negroes, Jews, and whites in America, leads him to doubt the panel's persistently held faith in America's pluralistic society. Toward the end of the discussion, Baldwin speaks of a collective history at once ignored, unrecognized, unaccounted for: "What happened to the Negro in this country is not simply a matter of my memory or my history; it's a matter of American history and American memory. As a Negro, I cannot afford to deny or overlook it, but the white American necessity is precisely to deny, ignore, and overlook it" (41). The assumptions of liberalism, in short, rather than resisting white disavowal have participated in it; if anything, those assumptions have been held in the face of a drastic and manifestly illiberal history. "My complaint here," Baldwin notes in a reply to Shlomo Katz, "is that you have the power to enforce your doctrine; your vision of me you have the power to make real" (41).

It is difficult not to see in this miniature scene an uncanny doubling or echo, as Baldwin's arguments are displaced, in turn, by a repeated misreading of what he's trying to represent. Indeed, it is as if the other participants are compelled to deny, or counteract, the disavowal he evokes. This misunderstanding sets up a parallel between a liberalism blinded by its own racial attitudes, and the spectacle—analyzed in *The Devil Finds Work*—of blacks propelled, by cinema, into the vacuum of a racial dreaming made real. In appearing before whites, then, in this entirely alien but still somehow recognizable role, Baldwin manages to expose the politics of evasion informing both. White liberalism and film, from this standpoint, both stand accused of using a language of race to screen out, more or less unconsciously, the inner life of blacks. It is a way of seeing, Baldwin suggests, that substitutes for that inner life a racial imago upon which to project. A way of seeing that allows the self-generating imagination of white liberalism to substitute for the realities of black demands, to pass itself off as and so to define the representative desire of what it means to be an American. And with that imagining comes a whole raft of inadmissible fantasies and symbols disseminated in the culture and increasingly projected onto blacks. Baldwin's complaint that the history of American liberalism participates in, rather than resists, this national imaginary of race is secured by his analysis of its visual culture—and, in particular, the fantasy of integration at the heart of liberal American cinema.

It is a complaint which, as we have seen, reveals how the guilty pleasures of that cinema depends on blacks appearing via the spectacle of neither-either—screened-out and exposed by a love that is self-blinding, molded in conformity to the wish that they suffer to appear, afflicted and flawed, displaced by that obsessive love.

7   *Bonding over Phobia*

I think I have sufficiently emphasized that the unconscious is the unknown subject of the ego, that it is misrecognized [meconnu] by the ego, which is der Kern unseres Wesens [the core of our being] . . . The core of our being does not coincide with the ego.

—Jacques Lacan, *Seminar II* (1954–1955)

But I too am guilty . . . There is no help for it: I am a white man. For unconsciously I distrust what is black in me, that is, the whole of my being.

—Frantz Fanon, *Black Skin, White Masks* (1967)

I know I am black. Even so, I occasionally fantasize and dream about being colorless, or at least invisible. Often I allow myself the comfort of placing this confused identification in my experience of everyday life, as if racial visibility and violence existed solely in the public domain, or only inside the heads of some hate-filled white people rather than in the minds and fantasies of black people. This is not, however, simply a case of displaced desire or social persecution. An unoccupied seat next to me on a full train sharply reminds me not only of white racial fears and anxieties about somatic contagion, but of how my life has been shaped by an introjected and anxiety-producing fear of being attacked—both within and without—by phobic intrusions. This evacuated space represents a place where whites care to—or dare—not go, a space that a type of X-ray might reveal as black alienation and psychic dispossession. On these occasions, an unoccupied seat can help one recognize an apparently immutable cycle of white projected fear and black social invisibility. One also recognizes in oneself a violent desire to fend off this intrusion, either by glaring at one's frightened aggressors or by putting an end to this sickening charade by looking at oneself *as if one were in their place.*

I don't think I am overstating my case. Nor am I trying to articulate a black existential fear of nothingness. Instead, I am trying to outline the interstices of cultural fantasy and racial anxiety, abjection and desire; in the above example, these interstices pair or bond racially segregated social surveillance with black obsessional neurosis. Taking as its primary theme racial misrecognition, this chapter asks how we can understand black identity when, through an act of mimetic desire, this identity already gets constructed as white. If the act of identification produces a fractured doubling of self, how can we distinguish what is interposed from what is properly desired?

To engage these questions, imagine the following scenario: a black analysand is in session with his white psychoanalyst—an encounter with multiple connotations, of course, and one rife with racial anxiety—discussing his traumatic experience of seeing himself, and being seen, as black in a series of racist encounters. As the analysand is talking, giving no thought to the pain or disruption which his talk of racial fear may be giving to his analyst, he suddenly realizes—inexplicably, uncritically—that the experiences he's describing don't concern him at all, but rather someone else lying in his place. Lying there enthralled by this double, who appears to be white, he is completely surprised by the analyst's announcement that it is the end of the session. He leaves the room in a daze, promising to himself not to return. A week later, he does.

The experience of being taken over by a racial *imago*—of being intruded upon, displaced, and fixated by an imaginary double—recurs in many accounts of black identity and identification.[1] The disorientation and trauma this displacement produces suggest that an unconscious that seems to be "white" has displaced a conscious black identity. A number of difficulties arise from this too hasty account of racial intrusion, however, though the most crucial is also the most banal: the commonplace but no less intractable phenomenon of having a phantom unconscious which appears to hate you, because it undermines your psychic well-being. In light of this imaginary bonding between racial self and intrusive imago, it is difficult to say where the phobia in this scenario actually resides— whether in transference, incorporation, introjective, or projective identification. Yet the sense of having an internal screen—of presenting an internal frontier where ego and imago can meet—is irreducible here.

I shall introduce two further examples of this encounter, the first a four-year-old girl fixated by her image in a mirror, the second a famous Martinican psychiatrist reflecting, in more or less analytical discourse, on an encounter with a French boy. In both examples, the sense of being hated from within also seems inseparable from the condition of being hated from without:

> A four-year-old Negro girl in the Arsenal Nursery School in Pittsburgh used to stand in front of the mirror and scrub her skin with soap. When gently diverted from this she began to scrub the mirror. Finally, when induced to paint instead, she first angrily filled sheets of paper with the colors brown and black. But then she brought to the teacher what she called "a really *good* picture." The teacher first could see only a white sheet, until she looked closer and saw that the little girl had covered every inch of the white sheet with white paint.[2]

> "Look at the nigger! . . . Mama, a Negro!" . . . Hell, he's getting mad . . . My body was given back to me sprawled out, distorted, recolored, clad in mourning in that white winter day. The Negro is an animal, the Negro is bad, the Negro is mean, the Negro is ugly; look a nigger, it's cold, the nigger is shivering, the nigger is shivering because he is cold, the little boy is trembling because he is afraid of the nigger, the nigger is shivering with cold, that cold that goes through your bones, the handsome little boy is trembling because he thinks that the

nigger is quivering with rage, the little boy throws himself into his
mother's arms: "Mama, the nigger's going to eat me up."[3]

In these two scenes a suppressed but noticeable anger and confusion
arises in response to the intruding other, a response partly to do with
the realization that the other, as racial imago, has already occupied and
split the subject's ego. Reading these two passages makes us aware of
how intrusion may be experienced as an irreparable psychic separation
of the ego, and that this intrusion produces an internal splitting of the
subject between what Melanie Klein has termed "good" and "bad" internal
objects, in which the sense of displacement is all the more acute. Both
accounts suggest that the pain or anger which intrusion provokes derives
not from something missing, but rather from the addition of something
undesirable and dirty that fragments the body by destroying all positive
semblances of self. The aggressivity this intrusion unleashes introduces a
new dynamic into the structure of the personality as described above,
for the symptom involves the self's desire to hurt the imago of the body
in a passionate bid to escape it.

Fanon's example in *Black Skin, White Masks* recollects an actual
event as it occurred—there is no doubt that the black psychiatrist traipsing
round the streets of Lyon is Fanon himself. It is he who experiences the
child's look of racial fear as a painful inner splitting and anguished self-
obliteration. On the other hand, this sense of intruding violence shattering
the ego seems to be happening to someone else, damaging someone else,
as if, for a moment, Fanon was merely an actor in a mise-en-scène and not
the terrifying nigger he sees reflected in the boy's eyes. He sees but does
not recognize this imago as himself—as if a counterpart were performing
in his place in this "racial drama" (Fanon, *Black Skin,* 150). Fanon's public
humiliation and loss of prestige derive not from the discomfort of provoking fear in a child, but rather from how that child's words and look strip
him of whatever imaginary coherence or identity he may have had, leaving him in a crumpled, traumatized and amputated heap of fragmented

parts; he "hemorrhages" a deplorable quantity of black blood. Other spectators of this scene, including the child's mother, seem to confirm, rather than dispel, Fanon's shame—shame because despite Fanon's (and others') high opinion of himself, he is reduced here to the imago of a cannibal, and there is something genuinely frightening about cannibals, something primordial and unreconstructed but frightening nonetheless, and something projected onto him. Fanon realizes that he performs the role of intrusive racial imago for the white child, yet he cannot easily unburden himself from this scene without indulging in a pitiful denial of his blackness. Fanon's inability to escape this look of fear that imprisons, overwhelms, and designates him—combined as this inability is, say, with an awareness that the boy's persecutory assault is prompted by genuine fear rather than a desire to abuse—produces a state of confusion as to what exactly he has lost. After all, the strange paradox of seeing someone presumably looking directly at you but enthralled by an image of someone else seems to typify the sense of unreality dominating this exchange, of everything being out of place here. As if all the spectators to the scene were acting out predetermined roles in a racial phantasmagoria whilst discovering, for the first time, their interchangeability as counterparts with no beginning and no end. Consequently, Fanon gives the child a "tight smile" as he passes, steeling himself against the brutal intrusion of the other's perspective. Fanon's loss of the wherewithal to express hurt in this situation being arguably the cruelest deprivation of all.

Symbolically, Fanon knows that any black man could have triggered the child's fantasy of being devoured that attaches itself to a fear of blackness, for this fear signifies the "racial epidermal schema" of Western culture—the unconscious fear of being intruded upon and literally consumed by the black other (Fanon, *Black Skin*, 112). Neither the boy nor Fanon seem able to avoid this schema, moreover, for culture determines and maintains the imago associated with blackness; it is cultural fantasy that allows Fanon and the boy to form a bond through racial antagonism. Mournfully seeing himself trapped and reflected in the eyes of the little

French boy, Fanon describes himself as "arriving too late," as being displaced by and intruded upon by racial hatred and phobia that fixes him as an imago. The picture of the black psyche that emerges from Fanon's description of this and related incidents is one always late, never on time, violently presented and fractured by these moments of specular intrusion. The child's combined fear and anxiety—at the level of identification—acts as a stain upon Fanon which may never go away. The scene's overwhelming alienation—the literal fear and trembling it engenders, the foul language that despoils—remains traumatic for Fanon. He retains in memory the boy's fear of being eaten, of literally being turned into shit by an organic communion with the black body. Generally, this absorption of the black body into a fecal object is one of the most depressing and melancholic fantasies ensuing from the psychodynamics of intrusion.

The question of unconscious belatedness, discussed earlier, is also relevant in my first example—the girl's obsessive concern with her mirror image. From Erik Erikson's description above, we learn that the girl has tried many times to remove physically what we can call a stain from both her body and its mirror image, as though her specular alienation were indeed not only ritual but also a compulsion. And how did her teachers respond? By a series of diversions and inducements, we are told, as if the expression of the girl's phobia through paint were somehow less troubling—for her teachers—than her obvious physical alienation before the mirror. Such inducements may have been therapeutically designed to offset the girl's more isolated sense of alienation in front of the mirror. Yet the girl also seems enraged by something continuing to cover her image despite all her efforts to remove it.

Curiously, in the description above it is not clear whether the girl's partial search for something hidden, in part at least, "beneath" her body and mirror image—something her scrubbing away might reveal—is a consequence of what these mirror images effectively screen out or what they fail so desperately to reveal. It is also unclear whether her reluctance to turn away from the mirror image of her body (she has to be distracted and then induced) is a refusal to give up on something this image seems to hide, or, more complexly, something this image fails to reveal and symbolize. The trace of this failure seems to remain with that white sheet covered over with white paint, the outcome of a loss involving pain and destitution. So it is not all clear whether the girl offers us the fantasy of a screen or secret, or even a combination of both. Whenever she scrubs the image it seems to remain the same, and she eventually gets angrier and transfers her need for solace onto the teacher, implying "isn't this a really good picture of myself, isn't it a truer representation of myself than those dirty black images and what they reveal?" (Erikson, "A Memorandum," 648).

According to Erikson, in whose 1964 essay "A Memorandum on Identity and Negro Youth," the above scenario appears, this girl is punishing and denying her black body precisely because she unconsciously believes herself to be white. The girl's fantasy is not simply an imaginary or delusionary identification with whiteness: it represents the intrusion, into her unconscious, of phobias which racist cultures project onto the bodies of black people. The clash between seeing oneself—and being seen—as black manifests itself in the form of an "aggravated identity-confusion," whose symptom is a disabling hypochondria that the girl's attempt to scrub herself white fully illustrates.

In its recapitulation of themes previously announced in Erikson's *Childhood and Society* (1950), the "Memorandum" suggests a link between black unconscious fantasies and racial imagoes. However, while the girl's racial identity seems to conflict with how she is represented culturally—whether at the level of a racial self and imago or of unconscious and cultural fantasy—Erikson suspends this conflict by advancing a historical articulation of black identity and hypochondria. He reads the girl's confused racial identity, which produces a "hypochondriac invalidism" and "total self-eradication" of the ego, as an example of how "infantile drive control (cleanliness) and social self-esteem (color) are associated in childhood" (Erikson, "A Memorandum," 648). Initially, the link between black infantile drive control and social esteem is not clear. Yet Erikson considers this association traumatic for the black child, for blacks allegedly have been asked historically to assume the burden of white racist representation:

> Negro babies often receive sensual satisfactions which provide them with enough oral and sensory surplus for a lifetime, as clearly betrayed in the way they move, laugh, talk, sing. Their forced symbiosis with the feudal South capitalized on this oral-sensory treasure and helped to build a slave's identity: mild, submissive, dependent, somewhat querulous, but always ready to serve, with occasional empathy and childlike wisdom. But underneath a dangerous split occurred. The Negro's unavoidable identification with the dominant race, and the need of the master race to protect its own identity against the very sensual and oral temptations emanating from the race held to be inferior (whence came their mammies), established in both groups an association: light—clean—clever—white, and dark—dirty—dumb—nigger. The result, especially in those Negroes who left the poor haven of their Southern homes, was often a violently sudden and cruel cleanliness training, as attested to in the autobiographies of Negro writers. It is as if by cleansing, a whiter identity could be achieved . . . Three identities are formed: (1) mammy's oral-sensual "honey-child"—tender, expressive, rhythmical; (2) the evil identity of the dirty, anal-sadistic, phallic-rapist "nigger"; and (3) the clean, anal-compulsive, restrained, friendly, but always sad "white man's Negro." (Erikson, "A Memorandum," 645–646)

This "forced symbiosis" between U.S. plantation slavery and black orality leads to a "dangerous split" in black (and white) identities, resulting in a series of bizarre liturgies around which black, especially migrant, identities have formed. Black identity experiences the trauma and despair of racist rejection because of its "unavoidable identification" with white culture—an identification against which whites must defend themselves owing to the dangerous temptations of black oral-sensuality. Underlying this psychohistory of racial hatred is a conflict, the legacy of which blacks will never ever be able to throw off: they cannot love themselves as black but are made to hate themselves as white. The dangerous split in black identity between black abjection and white superegoic ideal thus registers as a failure of the black ego to accept the reality of its abjection. This failure of adaptation, in which the ego does not synthesize the historical splitting of black identities, condemns blacks to neurotic regression in hypochondria. The ensuing division between identity and identification manifests itself as one between bodily ego and unconscious fantasy.

However, Erikson's reading of American racial history goes much further than a straightforward psychoanalytic account of racial intrusion: It manages to equate the campaigns for civil rights, racial equality, and desegregation (remember the "Memorandum" was published in 1964) with black hypochondriac neuroses, thus explaining the latter as the inevitable outcome of black civic attempts to acquire forms of white social authority. Are we meant to assume—against Erikson—that the aberrant forms of the girl's ego—expressed in traumatic aggression—are complicit with a narcissistic injury and loss whose appearance stems from the combined history of racial enslavement and black demands for racial equality? Are we also meant to assume that a fantasy of dirt underlies the girl's neurosis—as signaled by the wider culture's association of blackness with uncleanliness, a racial fantasy in which the experience of having a black body is tantamount (at the level of both unconscious and cultural fantasy) to being smeared over with shit?

If so, then the choice for blacks, according to Erikson's reading, is as follows: for black instinctual demands to be recognized and valued, rather than condemned, they must be compromised by the black ego's successful adaptation to the realities of American society. The question is whether blacks, undergoing this "long and painful inner reidentification," could unburden themselves of the image of the black body in fantasy—as shit, for example—when this adaptation takes place (Erikson, "A Memorandum," 648). Could such adaptation to social demands, given the bleak, frenzied, and ghostly presence of racial imagoes that afflict these demands, really absolve blacks of intrusion given what these demands reveal—the sick bonds of phobia whose trauma remains with the black subject? But what could the full liberation of black libidinal adaptation have meant in the 1960s (the decade of black civil rights), when a mass outbreak of white racial (and sexual) fears in extreme forms of racial violence effectively tried to deny such liberation, at least as equated with the fulfillment of social wants and aspirations?

There are immense complications here, so it is hardly surprising that Erikson's reading sounds like a reductive—if not a naive—psychohistory of racial conflict. An interesting point of comparison nonetheless emerges in the work of Kenneth and Mamie Clark. Working in Chicago during the 1940s, these two black social psychologists conducted on black children a series of tests primarily using dolls. Their research was to prove instrumental in the 1954 case of *Brown v. The Board of Education*—a case brought by the NAACP in their campaign for the legal desegregation of schools.[4]

The Clarks' doll tests aimed to measure how racism and segregation damaged the self-esteem of black children aged three to seven. These tests involved showing the children four identical dolls—two brown and two white. The children were asked eight questions: the first four—"Give me the doll that you like to play with," "Give me the doll that is a nice doll," "Give me the doll that looks bad," and "Give me the doll that is a nice color"—were designed to test preferences. Requests five ("Give me the doll that looks like a white child"), six ("Give me the doll that looks like a colored child"), and seven ("Give me the doll that looks like a Negro child") were meant to test the children's knowledge of racial differences. The final request, "Give me the doll that looks like you," was meant to show racial self-identification. The Clarks' tests revealed that by the ages of three or four, the children could correctly select the dolls that "looked like a white and like a colored child." However, when requested to "Give me the nice doll," half of the children chose the white doll; and half chose the brown doll in response to the request "Give me the doll that looks bad." A cause of particular concern was that a third of the children effectively

"misidentified" themselves as white when demonstrating a marked preference for the white doll—a preference decidedly more noticeable in children aged three and four years rather than at a later age (remember the girl
at the Arsenal Nursery School is also four).

To the Clarks, this preference signified a confusion, even a loss of
racial identity; for the narcissistic choice of the white doll necessarily
involved "a concomitant negative attitude toward the brown doll" (Clark
and Clark, "Racial Identification," 608). Obviously, we simply do not
know who or what these children imagined themselves to be; when asked
why they preferred the white doll, however, some of the children
replied "'cause he's white" or "pretty." Conversely, the brown doll was
rejected with the words "cause him black" or "ugly," or, more revealingly,
because he "got black on him." If the former suggests a form of psychic
tautology (and I'm not sure what could solicit such identification if not
racial fear and white superegoic authority), the latter suggests a look
marked by both positive and negative desire.

Observing the trauma provoked by these eight requests, some of
which left the children inconsolable and convulsed in tears, Kenneth Clark
wrote: "some of these children, particularly in the North, were reduced to
crying when presented with the dolls and asked to identify with them.
They looked at me as if I were the devil for putting them in this predicament. Let me tell you, it was a traumatic experience for me as well."[5]
Again, the symbols of racial intrusion on display here ensure that the
children cannot defend themselves in their identifications from the affects
of reactional neuroses. These tests, prefaced as they were by the children's
exposure to their phobic representation in the wider culture, unleashed
feelings of rejection, psychic splitting, negativity, and trauma. Given these
children's profound ambivalence, it is not surprising that a mixture of disavowal and fixation, of concealment and revelation, should seep into the
spectacle they present of black alterity. Having had their demands for
love denied at the level of their own visual image, these children (rather
like the girl at the Arsenal Nursery School) seem to carry a burden of

representation that they perceive but do not understand. Such examples of cultural alienation and psychic dereliction complicate Erikson's earlier reading of black childhood self-eradication in terms of an tension between libidinal adaptation and social life —unable to develop black self-love these children are forced to hate themselves as white.

It is no coincidence that the girl in Erikson's "Memorandum," whom he presents as an example of ego disintegration, came from a deseg-regated school located in the North where racial tensions in the 1950s and 1960s were particularly acute. Despite its intention to explain why the girl's confused racial identity hinges on an "unavoidable identification" with racist cultural fantasy, Erikson's reading utilizes the same stereotypical racial fantasies. The intrinsic fault of black drives, he implies, is that they are oral-sensual or sadistic anal-compulsive *before* that traumatic (although unavoidable and necessary) identification with culture. The appeal of this opposition prevails throughout Erikson's account of black identity's alleged difficulties with ego synthesis. Proceeding from this account's implicit assumptions, he issues a warning: a crisis in this identity will emerge if black mothers, in their search for "Anglo-Saxon ideals," "cre-ate violent discontinuities" in their children—or, if black children, in their pursuit of ego autonomy, learn to "disavow their sensual and overprotec-tive mothers" (Erikson, "A Memorandum," 648). Paradoxically, this warn-ing entails concern for the black ego's possible alienation from the libidinal, unconscious structures that apparently help produce culture racism in the first place. Erikson can thus view the phobic effects of black misidentification as secondary to internal psychic factors, or else reappro-priate these effects as illustrating an intrinsic fault in black libidinal devel-opment. An explanation of what it means to be seen as black, or to see oneself as black, apparently requires nothing more than this developmen-tal schema of the dangers of black orality. And the phobic aberrations of this schema derive from elements in black child care and the passing on—to the child—of a pathological racial unconscious.

Erikson seems to forget that black people experience racial fantasies as intrusive because such fantasies are felt to be inescapably and all-pervasively *there*; the black unconscious is always belated, always late. There is nothing spectacular or mystifying about this sense of belatedness; in racial dramas the pain of displacement effectively eradicates a sense of self preceding the traumas of intrusion. But this pain, in turn, can manifest itself as a melancholic reaction to being taken over by someone else's anxiety or phobia, an intrusion that violently evacuates the subject. The trauma resulting from this abduction hurts all the more. I'm thinking in particular of Fanon because the form it takes (via a kind of nominal indicator or racial deictics—"look, a Negro!") is so impersonal, leaving an empty space where before there was arguably a self, or, at least a proper name. This derelict and evacuated psychical space, governed by a subject reduced to a nervous and miserable silence (Fanon remarks, "I could no longer laugh"), attests to a loss for which the black subject has no witnesses: "I was denied the slightest recognition" (Fanon, *Black Skin*, 112, 115).

It may not be too fanciful to suggest that the black ego, far from being too immature or weak to integrate, is an absence haunted by its and others' negativity. In this respect, the memory of a loss is its only possible communication. Yet if there are no witnesses to offer atonement for, or deny, or prevent, the internal and external injury of intruding phobias, could such mourning ever console those black mourners left to mourn? In these circumstances, having a white unconscious may be the only way to connect with—or even contain—the overwhelming and irreparable sense of loss. The intruding fantasy offers the medium to connect with the lost internal object, the ego, but there is also no "outside" to this "real fantasy," and the effects of intrusion are irreparable.[6] Here we can return to Fanon's own account of racial intrusion and how it effects both white and black psyches.

As I discussed earlier, the intruding double is experienced in fantasy as the subject's internal displacement—a turning of the subject inside out through the breaching of an internal enclosure or screen. The irreducible uncertainty between what is outside and what is inside constitutes the frontier where ego and imago meet. In an extensive footnote to *Black Skin*,

White Masks, in which he questions the separation of unconscious and cultural fantasy to clarify racial identification, Fanon tries to analyze this aporia in light of clinical observations on black Antilleans' self-representation in dreams and color neuroses: "In the Antilles perception always occurs on the level of the imaginary. It is in white terms that one perceives one's fellows" (Fanon, *Black Skin*, 163). This confusion of self and other, which Fanon considers a "normal" consequence of alienation caused in racial intrusion, relegates skin color to the status of an empirical accident, a neurotic maneuver designed to keep the outside out and the inside in. That is why these Antilleans, as fantasists, are particularly germane to Fanon's diagnoses of racial neuroses. Beginning with a notion of the specular counterpart—"*l'imago du semblable*," derived not from Freud but from Lacan's theory of the mirror stage and the imaginary—Fanon speculates whether the aggressivity directed at the racial imago of the other derives from the subject's own internal aggressivity:[7]

> It would certainly be interesting, using the Lacanian notion of the *mirror stage*, to ask to what extent the *imago* of his kind/counterpart [*semblable*] built up in the white youngster at the usual age would be subjected to undergo an imaginary aggression with the apparition [*apparition*] of the Black Man [*du Noir*]. When the process described by Lacan is understood, there can be no more doubt that the true Other of the White Man [*Autrui du Blanc*] is and remains the Black man [*le Noir*]. And vice versa. (Fanon, *Black Skin*, 131)

It is worth noting immediately, although I do no more than note, that Fanon's understanding of *le stade du miroir* derives from Lacan's 1938 *Encyclopedie Française* article, "Les complexes familiaux," where he discusses "*l'imago du semblable*" regarding narcissistic, specular identification and the "intrusion complex"; and the Oedipal identification proper to the parental (i.e. paternal imago) (Lacan, *Les Complexes*, 88–112). Lacan's account of the ego's *imaginary* genesis, in which it fantasizes unity from observing the body's reflected image, interested Fanon because it binds the ego to primitive libidinal drives. Since for Lacan, "everything pertaining to the ego is inscribed in imaginary tensions, like all the other libidinal tensions. Libido and ego are on the same side," Fanon explores this equivalence via the symbolics of racial intrusion or "breaching."[8] The ego's constitution and the subject's ensuing process of identification can explain racial aggressivity, for the ego is initiated into representation by the specular image of the other, the rival "other" whom it loves and hates, and with whom it ambivalently identifies. Claiming that "the true Other of the White Man is and remains the Black man," Fanon suggests that the imago of the black other is an instinctual component of the white psyche, linked inextricably to the psychic processes in which aggressive drives associated with phobic anxiety and fear become psychically effective in and through a racial substitute object or delegate.

Fanon's "sociodiagnostic" of the racial neuroses and their "anomalies of affect [*les anomalies affectives*]" locates these neuroses at a point where aggressive cultural and psychic fantasies seem to converge (Fanon, *Black Skin*, 12). If we follow through the logic of this convergence, recalling the traumatic aggressivity of the girl before the mirror, aggressivity itself represents a kind of constitutive fantasy. Fanon's analyses of interracial trauma pronounce this fantasy as the irruption of the "unidentifiable, the unassimilable" in the rival other, an irruption receiving significant attention in *Black Skin, White Masks*. The metaphors of breaching, staining, and contamination that Fanon invokes to conceptualize the ego's imaginary and racial capture suggest that the ego experiences racial difference as a violent rupture of bodily ego. Additionally, these metaphors relate to a phantasmatic intrusion of the black (or white) imago. As part of the ego's origins, this imaginary intrusion receives its stimulus from the sight of the black other, a sometimes unbearable vision signifying a dangerous violation of white bodily integrity.

This sense of violation is crucial to understanding white racial violence, in which the ego represents the imago through phobia. Fanon refers to this imaginary identification as follows: "A few years ago, I remarked to some friends during a discussion that in a general sense the white man behaves towards the Negro as an elder brother reacts to the birth of a younger. I have since learned that Richard Sterba arrived at the same conclusion in America" (Fanon, *Black Skin*, 157). Sterba's article "Some Psychological Factors in Negro Race Hatred and Anti-Negro Riots," first published in 1947, analyzes the unconscious motives of white analysands who participated in, or who were affected by, Detroit's race riots of June 1943.[9] In his discussion of these analysands' dreams, Sterba suggested that racial phobias derive from repressed sibling rivalry. Playing the role of an imaginary younger sibling in these unconscious fantasies, Negroes are represented as "unwelcome intruders."[10]

To be sure, the turning outward of aggressivity in real racial violence did allow these analysands to satisfy their destructive drives through a substitute object—the Negroes who happened to be on the streets during the actual riots. Sterba discerned in the analysands' dreams attempts to offset their Oedipal anxieties: Apparently, they could satisfy their repressed hatred of the white father only by the real and symbolic murder of black men. This allowed positive feelings for the father to remain intact, while ambivalent emotional ties to the father were allowed to appear—as a cultural and unconscious fantasy of racial intrusion—through substitute objects. The question nonetheless remains, what did the black men suffering real injury because of these ties make of this desire, which sacrificed them to protect the prestige of the white father? Put slightly differently, did the role these black imagoes performed allow the desire for real racial murder on the outside to intrude on these dreams of paternal hatred, and in a way that is not simply described as an example of fantasy becoming real?

We can demonstrate this issue by focusing on what I earlier called the proximity between a failed mourning and the role of aggressivity in racial intrusion. If black men must die so that the aggressive structure of white repression and sublimation of libidinal drives can remain in place, why aren't these deaths mourned as a loss in the dreams of Sterba's analysands?

If they can't mourn the resonance of such a loss, is it because the loss as such for them did not occur? Far from being a form of disavowal, could not these dreams—in becoming real—reveal the fixations where culture and unconscious fantasy become inseparable? Rather than concealing a secret, unavowable loss, this example of an unconscious failure to mourn surely points to a more general truth concerning the place of the black imago in the white unconscious—a place marked by murderous aggression and a phobic transferal of feelings of loss onto the black other.

This place is also marked by the eruption of unconscious hatred into the real and, conversely, by the breaking in of a murderous real into the white (and black) unconscious. Such bonding in real fantasy allows the subject to negotiate aggression and loss while ensuring that the imago of blacks carry the imaginary "work" of this dreaming. This may explain why, finally, the shadow of white racial phobia continues to fall across the black unconscious via the sick horror of a double intrusion: fixation and aggressivity. It may also explain why the etiology of racial prejudice must be located elsewhere—not solely in the public domain. To fathom the mechanism and structures of racially violent fixations and obsessional neuroses, it is not enough to point out the oppressive experience of the social and its myriad forms of institutional violence against black people. One must also explain the effects of unconscious and identification on racial identity. Insofar as cultural and unconscious fantasies are experienced as real, exclusively psychoanalytic or culturalist readings must be abandoned for us to appreciate the authority and persistence of these racial imagoes in white and black identifications.

So imagine the following scenario: a white analysand is free-associating on the word "black" before his black analyst.[11] He is embarrassed because he can only think of negative words and mental associations; for some unknown reason, the word doesn't seem to conjure up any positive quality. Despite his attempts at repressing it, the word "nigger" urges itself to the forefront of his mind, refusing to go away. He utters it, conscious of his own spiteful fury, and with as much venom as he can muster—he has never, to his knowledge, used this word before. The analyst shows no response. Now even more embarrassingly conscious of his own stupid, blind, and violently impotent rage, the analysand thinks of another phrase: "black nigger." The association seems right; it seems to fit (despite himself), and, what is more, it seems to mean something, but it is not a phrase the analysand wants to utter here. He utters the word "death" instead—a classic association, so banal in its obviousness, but reassuring nonetheless. The analyst nods with obvious enthusiasm and urges him to continue.

Afterword

ICE COLD

Politics is therefore death that lives a human life.
—Achille Mbembe, "Necropolitics" (2003)

A gaze that is petrified and that petrifies itself: all of the foregoing is contained here—that is, the dark enemy that one sees, whom you half believe will rape and murder you if you look his way, mirrors the endless abjection that is your own fear in being seen seeing. In this final text on the difficulties of assuming all too readily that what one sees in the mirror is what one (b)lacks, I want to know what it means to have been facing in the wrong direction all along. That is, the question is no longer what is seen but how one is consumed by the unseen with eyes closed, lying in the dust. That is, seen by a glance that must remain hidden even from the dead who enclose it. An orphic glance that signifies survival and impotence, and yet one that survives death by becoming death's advent and commandment.

The man who inspires this afterword is Louis Rutaganira, who survived the Kibuye massacres during the Rwandan genocide by hiding beneath the dead and dying scattered amid the pews of Kibuye's Catholic church. One of those dying was his wife, whom he watches helplessly: "I saw my wife, who was still alive. They had cut off her arms and legs and left her to bleed to death" (*Guardian*, 29 March 2004, 4). As for his children, he simply doesn't know how they died. Louis Rutaganira still lives in Rwanda and believes in forgiveness. "The nation is learning," he suggests. "Even the prisoners are confessing saying what they did and asking for forgiveness. If you have someone who comes to you and pleads and says 'I've done something wrong,' even writes letters, there's something that it shows. It shows that someone wants to change. Someone is not bad forever. People change," he says (9). I confess that I admire this wish to go beyond *lex talionis* by distinguishing sincere confession from juridical guilt from a concealed wish for amnesty. Having borne witness to the unforgivable, it seems that Rutaganira has made death his hope and task; has made death that is, rather than endless dying, the affirmation of his existence. But I needs must ask what does confession show and how does this showing relate to that butchered image of a wife annihilated because judged and decided by some to be less than life, less than a cockroach?[1] Confession after the fact, after all, may put contrition on display, but how does one tell the difference between he who looks sincere and he who is awaiting the benefits of sincerity? And how does one forgive and preserve one's trust in the world when knowing all the while that forgiveness is unavailing for the destroyed being of the black whose blood is always guilty?

Haunted Life has perhaps been too earnest and fervent in its insistence that blackness has become a right to death that sees in death its most essential property.[2] The essence of blackness, its origin or its possibility, would be this right to death; but a death denuded of that Hegelian sovereignty that gains from death its own sacrificial mastery (*Herrschaft*) and maintains itself in it. This is life as the work of death, a work born of fidelity to death, but death without transcendence. For better or worse, the "total war" that Fanon spoke of to describe colonial state terror during the 1950s is no longer.[3] Instead, and unexpectedly, we now see the emergence of a black sacrificial sovereignty; that is, a language of power indissociable from the fabulous and ecstatically cruel deaths blacks now inflict on themselves via an onslaught against spectral "enemies." In this new "semiosis of killing," writes Achille Mbembe, the dead are not even corpses, but "simple relics of an unburied pain, empty, meaningless corporealities, strange deposits plunged into cruel stupor."[4] That is, stupefied, petrified, maculate bones lost to all meaning. But how then do we read this cold, implacable indifference to death, black death? And how can we continue to look when, lying on the cold floors, we are unable to retrieve the beloved from the shadows? Louis Rutaganira never got up during the day.

He only got up from his bed of death at night, walking down to the lake to drink water and eat bananas. What kind of dreams did he dream when he slept amid the slain and the dying? Blackness, I repeat, is a right to death in which dying has no value and is no longer sovereign. It is a death in which sovereignty is marked by unreal cruelty and night makes visible a room full of wounds one can no longer look on.

In brief, I need to be looking rearward; only then will I be able to sense the light about to break somewhere above the ruins of incomprehension. But this is not the sun about to rise in "the sky of history," more the intermittent flashes from an underworld of images that happen and keep on happening.[5] The Angel who appears here, eyes staring, mouth open, looking on, bored as images of catastrophe appear on the TV monitor, creates another monument to history. As the eye of the camera endlessly photographs him there is no roar that descends, just tedious tabloid stories about black deaths and suffering; no sound of beating wings, just the odd whirring sound of police helicopters. "A historical materialist must [also] be aware of this most inconspicuous of all transformations" (Benjamin, "Theses," 257). Yes, but what connects the "time of the now" to the cold sun rising is a gaze petrified, a gaze relishing the time of disaster; and one that wants, at the same time, the infinite deferral of that pleasure (265). This moment is not so much the "presence of a now" as the tension and vulnerability of being surreally open, both within and without, to the imagoes of culture (263). And so I close with this fable. It shows an Angel chilled before the blue-black thing gliding toward him, like a latticework of ice flashing in the cold morning air. The closer he gets to it the colder and more relentless it becomes. It sucks the air right out of his chest, but he goes to meet it anyway.

The logic of this fable, then, is about a certain ethics of decision when one feels both fallible and precarious but compelled. It is a call haunted by the dear departed, a summons in which we can no longer see the world clearly: a fear, a judgment, worth defending to the death. The point is not to affirm redoubt nor despair, but to release, and set free, the life lived as

the acknowledgment of risk, and to learn a little bit about, well, the negation that affirms and holds itself out as a life lived in a spirit of affirmation.
Or, better put: "Man is a *yes* that vibrates to cosmic harmonies," but it is
the yes that compels him.[6]

Dying in a hospital bed in Bethesda, Maryland, Frantz Fanon writes the
following letter to his friend, Roger Tayeb:

> Roger, what I wanted to tell you is that death is always with us and
> that what matters is not to know whether we can escape it but
> whether we have achieved the maximum for the ideas we have made
> our own. What shocked me here in my bed when I felt my strength
> ebbing away along with my blood was not the fact of dying as such,
> but to die of leukemia, in Washington, when three months ago I could
> have died facing the enemy since I was already aware that I had this
> disease. We are nothing on earth if we are not in the first place the
> slaves of a cause, the cause of the peoples, the cause of justice and lib-
> erty. I want you to know that even when the doctors had given me up,
> in the gathering dusk I was still thinking of the Algerian people, of the
> peoples of the Third World, and when I have persevered, it was for
> their sake.[7]

"Death is always with us": in Fanon's oeuvre death and dying are potentially interminable; what matters is neither the working through nor the
acceptance of the inevitable ending of life, but how one's ideas have been
secured against an unjust and illiberal world. For Fanon, the letting go of
life is framed by the endless death that is always with us, which our work-
ful beginnings in thought can only, and must always, overcome and renew
through our actions and the causes we believe in. Death will come, this is
certainty: more, it is precisely this possibility which makes possible all
other possibilities, but, and this is an important but, only insofar as this
possibility is never grasped as possibility does it free our knowability, only
insofar as death remains absolutely unforeseeable can we grasp this life as

our own and so become free as political, ethical subjects. And yet, in another sense, the pathos of this letter comes not from mortality but from the fear that one may well die before one's time, that the time in which one will be no longer will arrive too soon, before one has had the chance to achieve the maximum for the ideas we have made our own, dead in a "nation of lynchers" rather than on a battlefield facing the enemies of the Algerian people (Geismer, *Fanon*, 183).

Death at a proper time and place: it's a wish to make death accountable to what has been desired and what achieved in life, an adding up of life that makes leave-taking possible and so consolable for those whom one leaves behind. Four weeks after writing this letter Fanon did indeed die from double pneumonia on 6 December 1961. He was thirty-six years old. According to Peter Geismar, before he died, Fanon envisaged writing a book on "a psychological analysis of the death process" called *Le Leucémique et son double* (Geismer, *Fanon*, 186). The project was never begun. Fanon's body was flown back to Algeria and buried in the border town of Ghardimaou. The funeral ceremony was reported in the FLN's official newspaper, *El Moudjahid*, as follows: "In a valley, further to the north, there was the thunder of artillery. Two airplanes passed over at a very high altitude. The war continued—very near. At the same time, a calm enveloped the brothers who had come to fulfill the last wish of one of their own" (Geismer, *Fanon*, 187).

Fanon's last wish to die on a battlefield was finally honored by the people (and the cause) for whom he had fought and ultimately died for. But there is something about his final letter to Tayeb which, I believe, can never be honored as such: the wish that the life of the mind, the life of reason, be answerable to death insofar as it is incommensurable and nonfoundational; that the only ethical responsibility of political thought is to the nonrepresentable working of death as such. Only by bearing witness to this impossibility can life come to terms with that unredeemable death identified here with the political failure to bear witness and assume responsibility for the cause of justice and liberty. In an interview conducted between Hussein Bulhan and Fanon's oldest brother, Félix, Fanon is described as one who believed that "life did not deserve to be lived unless one jumped into it and took it by the horns."[8] And in a memoir to Fanon, published in 1982, his younger brother Joby cites Fanon as saying: "One must constantly, Joby, put one's life in line with one's ideas" (Bulhan, *Frantz Fanon*, 21). The deserving life, a life lived according to one's ideas is, then, intricately linked to the inner integrity of that life as experience and praxis. It is precisely that integrity and that responsibility that makes death and time redeemable and livable. But this redemption can only be imagined as what will have been achieved; its an integrity that sets the life of the mind against a mind endlessly dying, the perseverance and struggle of life against a death seen to be a transcendental fact but without transcendence. In brief, how do we distinguish, in Fanon's work, the thought that comes from the anticipation of one's own death, from the thought that derives its strength from an endless proximity to death? The thought, that is, whose inner meaning is its willing divestiture by death?

Put slightly differently, the power and frailty of the letter to Tayeb is not so much about dying before one's time, but about having lived without ever being truly alive; dead because never ever alive: as such, Fanon's letter raises, for me, a question. The life of the mind is both what potentially redeems us from the death we carry within us, but also what potentially sacrifices us to that endless dying. On the one hand, the assumption of death affirms resolution and certitude as we grasp life by the horns. On the other hand, to assume this death is also to tarry in negation, to step blindly into what, via Fanon's many allusions to Kierkegaard, is defined as a teleological suspension of the ethical, where one walks without surcease, or return, and all certainty is reversed.[9] Fanon's views on ethical political life are complex but read schematically can be put as follows: one must work through the death within us if the life of reason is to be reborn within the polis, secured against the tyranny of an endless dying. The obligation is to live with death as an impossible possibility—why? Because of the legacy bequeathed to blacks by colonial racism—that black life is meaningless and so black death is meaningless—a legacy in which death is nothing.

That is, neither a passage nor a journey, but simply the arbitrary visitation of a catastrophic violence. My belief is that what is being witnessed here—the scene recalls Louis Rutaganira in Kibuye—is a death that cannot ever die because it depends on the total degradation and disavowal of black life. Ipso facto: death emerges as a transcendental fact of black existence but without transcendence (similarly, black existence is one condemned to live without the possibility of being). This is no longer death but a deathliness that cannot be spiritualized or brought into meaning. This is death as nothing, less than nothing; as such, this death is never assumable as possibility or decision, but remains the interminable time of meaningless, impersonal dying. And this is why, throughout his work, Fanon is concerned with how this death, which testifies to a lawless violence almost beyond representation, can be redeemed, in turn, by black revolutionary violence.

It's a point of view that will see him critique all black eschatologies, whether they be geared to the future or the past, as incapable of this radical transfiguration. Because blacks have, historically, come to view their redemption in terms of either a return to a mythic, precolonial past or in terms of a radical futurity where salvation rather than the redemption of time is of the utmost importance, black political ethics has, ironically, resulted in a disavowal of death as the horizon of historical existence. This is a politics of an endlessly deferred commencing and the endless reality of an ending; it cannot let go of mourning for the time that was or the future to come as one of appeasement and repetition. But if the time of salvation is evoked as a return from death this is also a time in which it is impossible to rejoin or reaffirm the opposition of actuality and possibility. Because that which has happened remains irredeemable it becomes necessary to wait for the future as an overturning or to turn to the past as an elegy for the all but coming, the all but that will finally allow us to wipe the slate clean and begin again our destined lives as saints or black queens and kings. But what is to deliver us from death as lawless violence when life is designated and magnified as absolute loss rather than possibility or power?

It's a question that defines Fanon's oeuvre, from *Black Skin, White Masks* to his last theoretical work, *The Wretched of the Earth*. From beginning to last, nihilism and affirmation emerge as the two parallel dialectics defining Fanon's approach to ethics and political judgment and the reactive limits of black life. Crucially, Fanon conceives of black reactive life as a psychological attitude toward time.

"The problem considered here is one of time," Fanon writes in *Black Skin, White Masks*.[10] "The architecture of this work is rooted in the temporal. Every human problem must be considered from the standpoint of time. . . . I belong irreducibly to my time. And it is for my own time that I should live" (Fanon, *Black Skin*, 12–13). Why time? In European thought blacks have tended to be excluded from the historical and from futurity as such. There are a host of examples. Hegel's conclusion to *The Lectures on World History* is a case in point. Africa, he argues, "lies out of the pale of History. . . . What we properly understand by Africa, is the Unhistorical, Undeveloped Spirit, still involved in the condition of mere nature."[11] Or consider Levy-Bruhl's remarks on time and the primitive mind: "We know, however, that the primitives' minds do not represent time as exactly as ours do. . . . To the primitive mind time is not, as it is to us, a kind of intellectualized intuition, an 'order of succession.' "[12] As unhistorical peoples, Africans lack the ability to know and express time, and as such they remain the children of world history. As primitives, their identity and language makes the future unthinkable and therefore impossible. This is not life but the phantasm of life, the supernatural emptiness of a natural life without history, without commencement, without possibility. Fanon makes this exclusion from history the basis for his critique of black "reactive" modes of temporality which, he argues, preserve racist ideas of time in their notions of the future as advent, or notions of the past as the recommencement of a black imaginary. In contrast to these views, Fanon writes that for history to be realized black existence must learn to grasp itself as a dialectical work in and through time, rather than a spiritual transformation which dispenses with both time and work. Or, as he goes on to

say: "Man's behaviour is not only reactional. And there is always ressentiment in a *reaction*" (226).

Fanon borrows this formulation from Nietzsche, in particular *The
Genealogy of Morals* and *The Will to Power*. Nietzsche defines "ressentiment"
as developing in those "natures who are denied true reactions, those of
deeds."[13] Ressentiment psychology—and this point is crucial both for Nietzsche and for Fanon's appropriation—is distinguished by a consciousness
of loss, by a failure to integrate experiences of powerlessness, leaving this
experience to remain in the memory as a traumatic kernel, leading to an
obsession with past racial injuries that poison the ability of the self to
function in the present or project an active future. In *The Genealogy of
Morals*, Nietzsche defines "Slave ethics [as what] begins by saying *no* to an
"outsider," an "other," a non-self, and that no is its creative act. This reversal of direction of the evaluating look, this invariable looking outward
instead of inward, is a fundamental feature of rancor. Slave ethics requires
for its inception a sphere different from and hostile to its own. Physiologi-
cally speaking, it requires an outside stimulus in order to act at all; all
action is reaction" (Nietzsche, *The Birth*, 170–171). The slave blames the
other, or outsider, for his suffering, makes him or her the symbol of evil
and a phobic object. This response remains reactive. The slave does not act
on the basis of his or her sovereignty, but in opposition to the other's domination. Nietzsche argues that ressentiment indicates a failure, not so
much to accept responsibility for one's existence (Sartrean "bad faith"), but
a failure to affirm life as a spirit of becoming. Fanon terms it a slavish, reactive attitude toward the future and the past. In this "pessimism of indigna-
tion" one assumes that one can do nothing because one is wretched, and
one blames someone else for one's wretchedness. This is why, in *Wretched
of the Earth*, Fanon argues that the first stages of spontaneous anticolonial
violence are always reactive: "racism, hatred, resentment," "the legitimate
desire for vengeance," cannot sustain a war of liberation.[14] Such reactive
moments are linked to questions of time but in a negative sense, as
examples of a reactive affirmation of history.

It is precisely because he recognizes racist historicity in these attitudes that Fanon's work is taken up with the problem of time and death. If the limit set to black life is the significance conferred on presence by racism which voids all black life of value as life, with the result that one cannot live it, racism also robs the black of his or her ability to live and so to die as a free subject. Spurned by history, the attempts by blacks to reimmerse themselves in time, have resulted in a turn toward allegory and myth. These attempts are condemned because they restrict the life as lived to one held in abeyance, in suspension, a life ossified either by its slavish reverence for the precolonial past or by its abject sacrificing of itself to the future to come, the freedom always to come in eternity. Both attitudes are positings of finite being that refuse to tarry with death as the true scandal of black historical experience and so become even less capable of resolving it. This is not to say that Fanon has lost faith in a redemptive future, or that he wants to routinize and categorize such temporal ecstasies by representing death as life's categorical commandment. Rather that, as in the letter to Tayeb, what matters is the life earned when it plunges into the inexplicable and emerges from it; what matters is how we, like Orpheus, take up the cunning and creativity of ressentiment as a culture on the edge of nothingness. Only by negotiating power and violence can we engage and reconfigure virtue for the modern polity (the "new humanism" that emerges from the "tabula rasa" opened up by the colonized on the path toward revolution—a possibility which is neither an end nor a beginning but an endless "tension of opening" between the two).[15] That is, death as lawless violence is the predicament and possibility of who we are and might become, here, now, the tenses through which we belong irreducibly to this time.

This is also why Fanon rejects Sartrean, Hegelian, and other forms of determinate historicism, the logic according to which everything that happens *had* to happen. Against dialectical logic—and its view that out of experience, no matter how negative, something emerges—Fanon posits a black existential time in which what happened happens and keeps on happening in ways that remain unforeseeable and unknowable but which nonetheless forces us to be responsible at the level of ethics, politics, and will. Throughout Fanon's oeuvre, antihistoricism turns on the difficulty of naming and situating a black orphism beyond identity and alterity, beyond loss and the annihilation of being. True anticolonial violence, if it is to go beyond such Manichaeism, must arrive at a teleological suspension of the ethical and so go beyond the spurious opposition between murder and illegitimate right, or murder dressed up as political vengeance. Manichean violence is ressentiment, for liberation is not a higher ethical law than murder and can only be justified in the pursuit of freedom, which is incommensurable with domination but nevertheless implicated in its violence. Hence Fanon is not trying to ethically justify the violence of anticolonial war (as he is often accused of doing), but trying to account for the use of violence in the revolutionary pursuit of freedom.[16] Liberatory violence, in brief, as one possible memory of the future; as one possible pathway through the unjust violences of the political world.

Both the conclusions to *Black Skin, White Masks* and *Wretched of the Earth* define that memory as the horizon of revolutionary hope and politics, as a rupture of time without end but within time's workings. For this reason, I cannot accept Patrick Taylor's diremptive opposition between *Black Skin, White Masks* as a work that ends with ethics over history, and *Wretched of the Earth* as a work that moves from ethics to revolutionary history (Taylor, *Narratives*, 74–76). Such opposition misreads the conclusion to *Black Skin, White Masks*, where Fanon writes, "I am not the slave of the Slavery that dehumanized my ancestors" (230). Antillean culture is a slave culture for Fanon, following Nietzsche, because its ressentiment represents a cultural-historico paralysis which has not yet become creative and so achieve that active forgetfulness of the past that accompanies successful repression and defines a noble memory of the will. This peculiar anamnesis, which is the result of historically distinct configurations of power, domination, and race war, reveals how, for Fanon, the traumas of cultural assimilation for the colonial subject is already marked by historical forces and decisive events whose trauma cannot simply be dispelled by the time of analysis or the methods of genealogy.[17] Slave ethics, insofar as it is reactive and denies responsibility and its ability to act, cannot achieve this cultural-historico transmutation. Through decolonization and violence the colonized can break through the impasse of ressentiment and enter into history. The task for the colonized, Fanon implies, is to risk the orphic "leap" into the "black hole" while also moving out to the universal (199). One must move beyond the "absurd drama" of colonialism dialectically. One must move to ethics from history because ethics is the affirmation of the radical transformation of time, a decision to change both the meaning of the deathliness of black life and its sign of ressentiment.

In the essay "West Indians and Africans," Fanon writes, "The task consists of removing the problem, putting the contingent in its place, and leaving the Martinican the choice of supreme values. One sees everything that could be said by envisaging this situation in accordance with the Kierkegaardian stages."[18] These stages are the aesthetic, the ethical and the religious. Fanon's turn to Kierkegaard is not, as Patrick Taylor presents it, a move from ethics to history or, more accurately, inner morality to objective or ethical freedom, but a recognition of how violence and law pervade each other, and of how ethics is an encounter with the violence of power and its legitimation. The task is to move, not from values based on race to human values understood as transcending the old humanisms of Europe, which formed the foundations of colonial racism, but to address the phantasmatic and racist underpinnings of value as such. Fanon explicitly mentions Kierkegaard when discussing how law and violence remain implicated in the movement from ethics to freedom in history. The slave's struggle for freedom cannot only be defined in ethical terms. On the other hand, it is naive to assume that the decolonial world will exist beyond law and coercion. In *Black Skin, White Masks* Fanon writes, "The former slave, who can find in his memory no trace of the struggle for liberty or of that anguish of liberty of which Kierkegaard speaks, sits unmoved before the young white man singing and dancing on the tightrope of existence" (221).

Because the slave has no memory of that "anguish of liberty," the ethical and the historical condition of freedom remains unavowable. The slave remains a dumb witness to his own violated singularity which he can neither comprehend, renounce nor test. Fanon says that "the real *leap* consists in introducing invention into existence" (229). One shows how the ethical is mediated by the promise and actuality of such "invention" by becoming actively creative at the level of history. Acceptance of this coexistence does not "eliminate . . . the ethical in oneself," but forces one to return to the ethical as the always potential encounter with the violence of the world as a test of one's faith (Taylor, *Narratives*, 76).

Kierkegaard contrasts the knight of faith, the person who experiences the discrepant relation of violence and law, commandment and coercion, with the tragic hero, or knight of infinite resignation. The knight of faith is the person who, in fear and trembling, calls the law into question and assumes responsibility for it. In the Abraham and Isaac story, God asks Abraham to sacrifice his only son. According to Johannes de Silentio (Kierkegaard's pseudonym), Abraham finds himself outside of the ethical because God's command contradicts his other commandments "Thou shalt not kill" and the duty of the father to the son. His options are as follows: he can retreat into the ethical via understanding God's commandment as a higher ethical law; or by denying this request. Because Abraham believes—has faith—neither option is acceptable. Ethics becomes aporetic: God's commandment denies the validity of his commandments. In fear and trembling, Abraham could confront the abyss of his freedom and despair. But what makes him great is that he confronts the anguish of his freedom and acts on the basis of faith. In *Fear and Trembling*, the ethical is bracketed for the sake of the test of faith, the test of the risk: only by taking on the risk does one return to the ethical rather than remain the victim of the infinite pain and resignation of the suffering soul.

In Fanon it may be that the imperative of decolonization becomes an ethical law—hence his ambiguous references to Kant—a law justifying risk and ruin rather than sacrifice and resignation. Hence, the move from colonialism to decolonization represents a move, not from the ethical into history, but involves a radical leap into a way of life based on indeterminate negation, a negation without end but always at work in the depths of history. On the other hand, Fanon also states, "My black skin is not the wrapping of specific values. It is a long time since the starry sky that took away Kant's breath revealed the last of its secrets to us. And the moral law is not certain of itself" (Fanon, *Black Skin*, 227). This statement follows another explicit reference to Kant: "One duty alone: That of not renouncing my freedom through my choices" (229). The text referred to here is Kant's *Critique of Practical Reason*, which concludes as follows: "Two things fill the mind with ever new and increasing admiration and awe, the oftener and more steadily we reflect on them: the starry heavens above me and the moral law within me."[19] It is important to note that Fanon is not denying Kant's confidence in the sublime presentation of moral ideas, which, in the *Critique of Judgment*, Kant argues discloses the whole power (*Macht*) of the mind. Rather he is stating that Kant's enthusiasm for the infinitude of the starry heavens—the infinitude of which allows us to recognize, in turn, the infinite destiny of our own moral nature—cannot happen in the Antilles. It cannot happen there precisely because of the racial distribution of guilt and its paralysis at the level of the imaginary.

Fanon's critique of Kant echoes that of Nietzsche's. For Nietzsche, the sacrificial exercise of morality in Kantian ethics results in impotence when the will to obey the law against natural desire and out of no interested motive—not even fear—overwhelms the individual and produces the resort to ressentiment, the culture of reaction. Nietzsche is not condemning the disciplining of natural desire, on the contrary, he commends it, but what he objects to is its moralized accountability when it is justified as disinterested submission to categorical law. For Nietzsche (and Fanon), the law is interested, which is not to deny it is sovereign or universal, but to imply that the meaning of sovereignty depends on a principle of calculability, which, in his view, is to suspend the law itself and the opposition of disinterested reverence and natural desire. For the genealogist, the moral law in the universality of its form constitutes the misrecognized form, not of law, but of will to power. Its cruelty—from Kant's perspective its indifference to heteronomous interests—is the displaced symptom of its affective truth. For Fanon, it is this cruelty and this impotence which is deeply racialized both in terms of its psychology and historical sociology. In considering the uncertainty of moral law, of racism and of time, Fanon holds fast to a notion of the colonial subject as always divided and never fully present to itself. The aporias between blackness and history, for example, illustrated this in the form of blacks as reactive or nihilistic. *Black Skin, White Masks* explores this aporia in terms of a question: namely, what is it about colonial authority that allows it to generate forms of nihilistic passivity rather than Kant's inner freedom of moral law? What is it about the autonomous imposition of duty that turns the black subject into a reactive affect, thematized here as a submission to racialized time and history?

Colonial power reveals the limits of Kant's categorical law here understood as the autonomous imposition of duty. The moral law is uncertain of itself in the Antilles because colonial racism makes that law, in terms of duty, an impossible demand which is aporetic: be like me and do not be like me, be white but not quite. As such, colonialism transforms the moral law into a will to power based on racial exclusion. In order to grasp why Fanon thinks this is the case, I have explored the relation between the loss that racial forgetting represents and the negative sublimity of moral law in the Antilles. A negativity that exposes, almost inevitably, the extent to which the will to power in the colonial nation-state is one defined by its perpetual readiness to wage war against the colonized at the level of both ideological fantasy and psyche. For Fanon, colonialism operates a pure power politics completely divested of ethical and universalistic considerations. A war in which blackness is understood as a source of historic failure in need of cathartic cure and/or annihilation. A war in which the death of blacks, as utter abjection, is a nothingness without history and so indistinguishable from the unhistorical nothingness of a people without time.

In conclusion, given that Fanon's last work—*The Wretched of the Earth*—was an attempt to work out the idea of an ethical state in the context of decolonization, many commentators have tended to lose sight of how the political question of social justice and revolutionary struggle was, for Fanon, invariably tangled up with questions of responsibility and risk.[20] In other words, the difficult task Fanon set himself was how to resolve the problem of power and justice in cultures distinguished by Manichaeism. What could the idea of an ethical state mean in nations divided according to whether blacks are the remnants of an unhistorical, unethical substance, neither life nor being, but the unhappy existence of spectral life? Notions which were not only inscribed in economic and social relations but, more often than not, in judicial procedures and constitutional and parliamentary practices of executive governance. Fanon's idea of revolution should therefore not be restricted to the political but must also be seen as an attempt to describe how national desires come to be bound by somatic fantasies. Fanon's error, according to many, may have been in conceiving imperialism too psychologically, but his ideal of the decolonized cultural nation and political state cannot be understood without taking into account his ideas on the heteronomy of political demands and unconscious desires. If Fanon's political vision of the world was essentially Nietzschean—divided between sovereign life and slavish abjection—his call for national liberation and unity in the developing nations went hand in hand with a call to look at death in the face, to make death as such possible for blacks otherwise condemned to the nothingness of death, death as the representation of lawless violence. In Fanon's oeuvre the politics of black experience calls for the endurance of such negation and hence its movement, but only in the knowledge that the death within us cannot be determined, and this is the price we pay for life lived at the limits of both political virtue and political violence.

In Fanon's work this constant risk and sojourn is conceived in orphic terms. We too must descend into the icy depths like Orpheus if we are to experience that endless death that pierces us and that we preserve inside ourselves like a lump of ice. Only by turning toward absence or loss can we grasp the gaze that petrifies and arrests at the very point of experiencing it, the essential deathliness of black experience: the irony and perversity of a haunted life.

Notes

PREFACE

1. See C. Norris and G. Armstrong, *The Maximum Surveillance Society: The Rise of CCTV* (Oxford: Berg, 1999).

2. See *The Damilola Taylor Murder Investigation Review: The Report of the Oversight Panel* (London: HMSO, 2002); and *Torso in the Thames: Adam's Story*, 3BM Television Limited, 2003.

3. "Capital is dead labour that vivifies itself only by sucking up living labour like a vampire" (Karl Marx, *Capital* [New York: International Publishers, 1970], 1:233).

4. Marx, *Capital*, 1:47.

5. See Michael G. Schatzburg, "Power, Legitimacy and 'Democratisation' in Africa," *Africa: Journal of the International African Institute* 63, no. 4 (1993): "First, power and politics in African society often have more to do with consumption than with transformation. They concern the capacity to consume, or the ability to 'eat,' as expressed both literally and figuratively in many indigenous languages" (446). See also J. Fabian's discussion of the axiom "le pouvoir se mange entier" ("power is eaten whole") in *Power and Performance: Ethnographic Explorations through Proverbial Wisdom and Theater in Shaba, Zaire* (Madison: University of Wisconsin Press, 1990).

6. See Otto Fenichel, "The Scoptophilic Instinct and Identification," in *The Collected Papers of Otto Fenichel*, 1st ser. (New York: W. W. Norton, 1953), 378.

7. Jean and John Comaroff, "Occult Economies and the Violence of Abstraction: Notes from the South African Postcolony," *American Ethnologist* 26 (1999): "Imagine, also, the magical drama of an African postcolony 'screenroom' where one pays to watch a white cloth mounted on the wall, a room in which you sit and watch ethereal pictures appear on the screen, images revealing your most obscure, intimate objects of desire, or the secret evil eye that kills you" (287). "Contrary to what Max Weber would later assert, the modern world is not 'disenchanted,' but *enchanted*, precisely insofar as it is the world of objects and objectified values" (Etienne Balibar, *The Philosophy of Marx*, trans. Chris Turner [London and New York: Verso, 1995], 60).

8. Stephen Heath and Gillian Skirrow, "Television: A World in Action," *Screen* 18 (Summer 1977), 7–61.

9. See Martin Heidegger, *The Question Concerning Technology and Other Essays*, trans. William Lovitt (New York: Harper and Row, 1977), 3–36.

10. For Freud's analysis of "fort-da," see *Beyond the Pleasure Principle*, vol. 11, Pelican Freud Library Series (Harmondsworth: Penguin Books, 1986).

11. Stephen Heath, "Representing Television," in *Logics of Television: Essays in Cultural Criticism*, ed. Patricia Mellencamp (Bloomington: Indiana University Press, 1990), 268. As Mary Ann Doane also notes, "Television does not so much *represent* as it *informs*." See "Information, Crisis, Catastrophe," also in *Logics of Television*, 225.

12. See Slavoj Zizek, *The Sublime Object of Ideology* (London: Verso, 1989): "[Ideological fantasy] consists in overlooking the [unconscious] illusion which is structuring our real, effective relationship to reality" (30–31).

13. Walter Benjamin, "Central Park," trans. Lloyd Spencer, *New German Critique* 34 (Winter 1985): 50.

CHAPTER 1 — SPOOKS: WIDEMAN'S CATASTROPHE

1. On the notion of "creaturely life," see Eric Santner, *The Psychotheology of Everyday Life: Reflections on Freud and Rosenzweig* (Chicago: University of Chicago Press, 2001).

2. Frantz Fanon, *Black Skin, White Masks*, trans. C. L. Markmann (New York: Grove Press, 1967), 112.

3. This phrase, "I occupied space," recalls Roger Callois's observations on how schizophrenics experience space as a depersonalizing, "devouring force": "*I know where I am, but I do not feel as though I'm at the spot where I find myself.*" See "Mimicry and Legendary Psychasthenia," trans. John Shepley, *October*, no. 31 (Winter 1984): 72.

4. Hannah Arendt, *The Origins of Totalitarianism* (New York: Harcourt, Brace & Co., 1979), 192.

5. See Jacques Derrida, *Specters of Marx: The State of the Debt, the Work of Mourning, and the New International* (1993), trans. Peggy Kamuf (New York: Routledge, 1994), 126 and 137–138, where he offers an intriguing interpretation of Marx's "obscure" comments on the representative generality of the "Negroid form" of pseudo-concepts.

6. John Edgar Wideman, *The Island: Martinique* (Washington, DC: National Geographic Society, 2003), 121.

7. Ibid. If writing and photography act here as a technical supplement to memory, the means for composing, recording, and even reproducing the past, the time taken for recognition suggests that one is never simply touched by the gaze, or by memory, without the technical process of archivization.

8. Roland Barthes, *Camera Lucida*, trans. Richard Howard (New York: Hill and Wang, 1981), 3.

9. The word "colossal" retains the idea of something being erected, something that has been set up as a double, or *psuché*, to act as a substitute for the dead in between the worlds of the dead and the living. As a double, the colossos is a "peculiar and ambiguous presence that is, at the same time, a sign of absence," writes Pierre Vernant; and, like a dream-image, shade (*psuché*), or supernatural apparition (ghost), the colossos is neither an image nor a natural object, nor an imitation of a real object, nor an illusion of thought or a creation of the mind, but something of the effect of a trick, a deception, a snare. See Jean-Pierre Vernant, "The Representation of the Invisible and the Psychological Category of the Double: The Colossos," *Myth and Thought among the Greeks* (London: Routledge & Kegan Paul, 1983), 307. See also Jacques Derrida, *The Truth in Painting*, trans. Geoff Bennington and Ian McLeod (Chicago and London: University of Chicago Press, 1987), 119–149. The structure of the colossos is also related to that of fetishism, as described by Freud: In response to "the conflict between the *dead weight* of the unwelcome perception [the absence of the woman's penis] and the force of the opposite wish [its presence]," the fetish emerges as an unconscious "compromise"; it emerges "because the horror of castration sets up a sort of *permanent memorial* to itself by creating this substitute [the fetish]" (Sigmund Freud, "Fetishism," *On Sexuality*, Pelican Freud Library [Harmondsworth: Penguin Books, 1986], 7:353; translation modified, emphases added). Of course, I'm interested in the racial dynamics of disavowal and displacement described here.

10. John Edgar Wideman, "Whose War? The Color of Terror," *Harper's Magazine*, March 2002, 34, 36.

11. Wideman, *The Island*, 86–87. Curiously, Wideman compares the delusory freedom of commodified choice and our entrapment by "technology producing the spectacle" to enslavement—"Like slaves on the sugarcane plantations . . . my [French] neighbours and I are caught up in an administered existence" (86–87). The analogy between slavery and global consumer culture—how "choice [is] preempted" for both worker and slave—suggests that slavery and commodified labor are both "ghostly" forms of unfree life. Part of Wideman's concern with the price of life, this analogy leads him to speculate on what freedom meant to the slave: "It's not difficult to empathize with slaves who visualized freedom not as a metaphysical burden and privilege, but as the instant when body-consuming, soul-crushing labor ceases" (94). But does "labor" mean the same thing for a wage laborer and for a slave? The conflation of the two leads Wideman to equate freedom for the slave with the worker's right to "withhold labor, to rebel, to organize, to disrupt the imaginary holding us in place" (95). At this point, the analogy

between the distractions and lures of consumer culture and the constraints of slave life becomes oddly ahistorical and confused. To assume that slaves and workers occupy a similar place in civil society, or that they share similar forms of unfreedom, represents a failure to think through the diremptions between them, especially the difference between slavery and capital consumer culture, economic exploitation and enslavement.

12. John Edgar Wideman, "The American Dilemma Revisited: Psychoanalysis, Social Policy, and the Socio-Cultural Meaning of Race," *Black Renaissance* (Spring 2003): 33–45.

13. Wideman draws on Fanon, Baldwin, and Freud to underscore these points. All sorts of interpretations come into play when he cites Freud on the "misere psychologique" of groups, sentences taken from *Civilization and Its Discontents*, in which America is evoked as a prime example of the "damage" done to civilization when "the bonds of a society are chiefly constituted by the identification of its members with one another" (Sigmund Freud, *Civilization and Its Discontents*, trans. James Strachey, Pelican Freud Library [Harmondsworth: Penguin Books, 1987], 12:307). But here we run into trouble. As soon as Freud mentions the "present cultural state of America" in *Civilization and Its Discontents*, he immediately withdraws from "the temptation of entering upon a critique of American civilization," precisely because such a critique would itself involve "American methods" (307). To find that critique we must look elsewhere—that is, to Freud's correspondences. "The Americans are really too bad," he writes to Ernest Jones in 1921. "Competition is much more pungent with them, not succeeding means civil death to every one, and they have no private resources apart from their profession, no hobby, games, love or other interests of a cultured person. And success means money. Can an American live in opposition to the public opinion, as we are prepared to do?" Freud, cited in Peter Gay, *Freud: A Life for Our Time* (London: J. M. Dent, 1988), 567. "Nowhere is one so overwhelmed by the senselessness of human doings as there," he adds, "where even the pleasurable gratification of natural animal needs is no longer recognized as a life's goal. It is a crazy anal *Adlerei*" (568). America, then, presupposes the subordination of pleasure to conformity, culture to anal-sadistic retentiveness, but also the crazy, aggressive pursuit of material wealth and money as the only proof of public success and affirmation. To this list of the damages done by America to its citizens, Wideman adds another: the reinforcement of libidinal ties when the ultimate grounds of success are synonymous with the civil death of others, when the pleasures of conformity are sustained by the pleasures of social denigration.

14. See Vicky Lebeau, "Psycho-Politics: Frantz Fanon's *Black Skin, White Masks*," in *Psycho-politics and Cultural Desires*, ed. Jan Campbell and Janet Harbord (London: UCL Press, 1998), 121; Frantz Fanon, *Black Skin, White Masks*, trans.

C. L. Markmann (London: Pluto Press, 1986), 106; Frantz Fanon, *Peau noire, masques blancs* (Paris: Editions du Seuil, 1952), 86.

15. While for most commentators the events of 9/11 soon became a metaphor for how trauma seizes us—as images of catastrophe would seize us, that is—it brings us to a standstill, keeps us transfixed, sends us back to a world where we no longer recognize ourselves; such earnestly rehearsed sympathies tended to ignore the other news item: the destroyed towers also expose a legacy of looking that has never been able to see what happened in Africa and elsewhere as a loss.

16. John Edgar Wideman, "Whose War: The Color of Terror," *Harper's Magazine*, March 2002, 33–38.

17. W.E.B. Du Bois, *The Souls of Black Folk* (1903) (New York: Penguin, 1989), 5.

CHAPTER 2 — THAT WITHIN

1. See Jacques Lacan, *The Four Fundamental Concepts of Psycho-Analysis*, ed. Jacques-Alain Miller, trans. Alan Sheridan (New York: W. W. Norton, 1978), 212, 218. Here "aphanisis" refers to a "fading" away of the subject when it substitutes meaning for "Being."

2. Frantz Fanon, *Black Skin, White Masks*, trans. C. L. Markmann (New York, Grove Press, 1967), 63; idem, *Peau noire, masques blancs* (Paris: Editions du Seuil, 1952), 51. The evocation of the "royal road" and "black soul" opens onto two further scenes derived from Jean-Paul Sartre's *Orphée Noir*.

3. Harold Rosenberg, "The Stages: A Geography of Human Action," *Possibilities* 1 (Winter 1947–1948): 47–65.

4. In 1970, Rosenberg writes that Guyonnet's "inspired" title was "appreciatively re-echoed" in the title of his review of Jean-Paul Sartre's *Les Mots*: "From Play Acting to Self" (Rosenberg, *Act and the Actor: Making the Self* [New York: World Publishing Co., 1970], 205–206). Rosenberg also claims, again in 1970, that Guyonnet's existential (read Sartrean) reading was anticipated by a 1932 essay of his called "Character Change and the Drama," first collected in *Tradition of the New* in 1959 (206).

5. See Ernest Jones, *Hamlet and Oedipus* (New York: W. W. Norton, 1976), 57.

6. It's a view echoed by Hannah Arendt. See "Personal Responsibility under Dictatorship," first published in 1964, where she writes: "Whoever takes upon himself political responsibility will always come to the point where he says with Hamlet: 'The time is out of joint: O cursed spite / That I was ever born to set it right!'" (Hannah Arendt, *Responsibility and Judgment*, ed. Jerome Kohn [New York: Schocken Books, 2003], 27–28).

7. On "phantoms" as fantasized personalities, see F. Wittels, "Unconscious Phantoms in Neurotics," *Psychoanalytic Quarterly* 8 (1939): 141–163. See also Otto Fenichel's essay "On Acting," where he writes: "If an actor's 'phantom' fits his part, we say: 'The part suits him.' The good actor is characterized by the high multiplicity of his 'phantoms,'" (Fenichel, *Collected Papers* [New York: W. W. Norton, 1954], 354).

8. Gide translates the lines "But I have that within which passeth show;/These but the trappings and the suits of woe" as "Mais j'ai ceci en moi qui passe la parade;/le reste n'est que faste et parture de la douleur" (*Hamlet*, trans. André Gide [Paris: Gallimard, 1946], cited in R. Guyonnet, "Du Jeu au Je, Esquisse d'une géographie de l'action," *Les Temps Modernes* [April 1948]: 1732). It is not until the republication of "The Stages" in *Act and the Actor* that Rosenberg encloses the phrase by italics. An act that raises an intriguing issue of precedence, suspense, and haunting to which I'll return.

9. See Vicky Lebeau, "Another Child of Violence," *New Formations* 42 (Winter 2001): 24.

10. Maran, *Hommage a René Maran* (Paris: Présence Africaine, 1965), 33. My translation.

11. "Repetition *and* first time," notes Jacques Derrida, "this is perhaps the question of the event as question of the ghost" (Derrida, *Specters of Marx: The State of the Debt, the Work of Mourning, and the New International*, trans. Peggy Kamuf [New York: Routledge, 1994], 10). Or, more accurately perhaps, the structure of the "that within" is already one of repetition and first time, and one that is embedded in the relations between writing and the eventuality of the ghost.

12. We know, for example, that a version of *Un homme pareil aux autres* first appeared as "Journal sans date," in *Les Œuvres libres* 72 (1927): 105–236, and that it forms part of an autobiographical sequence beginning with *Le Coeur serré*, first published in 1931 but actually started in 1928 (Paris: A. Michel).

13. René Maran, *Un homme pareil aux autres* (Paris: Arc-en-Ciel, 1947), 38, translated by Femi Ojo-Ade, *René Maran: The Black Frenchman* (Washington, DC: Three Continents Press, 1984), 92.

14. "René Maran," *Opportunity* 1, no. 1 (January 1923): 31.

15. Jacques Lacan, "Desire and the Interpretation of Desire in *Hamlet*," trans. James Hulbert, in *Literature and Psychoanalysis: The Question of Reading Otherwise*, ed. Shoshana Felman (Baltimore and London: John Hopkins University Press, 1982), 44.

16. The Swiss analyst Germaine Guex uses the word "décalage"—gap or rupture—to describe the affects of abandonment. She refers to "le décalage entre

leur *apparence* dans la vie présente" ("the gap between their [abandonics] *appearance* and their present life"); and "le décalage entre le stade œdipien et le stade adulte" ("the gap between the oedipal stage and the adult stage") in their "profound infantilism" (Guex, "Les conditions intellectuelles et affectives de l'œdipe," *Revue Française de Psychanalyse* 13 [1949]: 273, 274, my emphases and translation). As we will see, her clinical observations on "le spectre" of isolation and object loss also have a role to play in Fanon's reading of Maran (273).

17. Sigmund Freud, *The Origins of Psychoanalysis: Letters to Wilhelm Fliess, Drafts and Notes, 1887–1902*, trans. Eric Mosbacher and James Strachey (New York: Basic Books, 1954), 224.

18. Fanon's reading of Guex also casts a new light on the enigmatic sentence: "the Oedipus complex is far from coming into being among Negroes [in Martinique]" (Fanon, *Black Skin*, 151–152). I cannot pursue this complex matter here, but there is evidence to suggest that Fanon linked racist affects to preoedipal forms of attachment and rivalry. Prior to his famous footnote on Lacan's mirror stage, for example, Fanon describes a "destructuration" of the ego produced by the "appearance of the body of the [racial] other" ["l'irruption d'un autre corps"] (160, 161).

19. See "Frantz Fanon's War," in *On Black Men* (New York: Columbia University Press, 2000).

20. René Maran, "Manière de Blanc," *Présence Africaine* (Summer 1948), no. 2:344: "There are no barriers, no race, no birth, for courageous hearts. Bias and prejudice can do nothing against them. The passion that animates them brings them closer and unites them. It is their sole *motherland*. Everything gives way before its power. They sacrifice everything for their passion, forever, and, first of all, they sacrifice themselves."

21. This partly explains why Veneuse's anxieties and doubts do not even merit a comparison with that fantasizing, sadomasochistic wish for a whiter child defined as intrinsic to Martinican culture and psychopathology in Fanon's chapter on Mayotte Capecia's *Je Suis Martiniquaise*. "Whiten the race, save the race": "lactification," according to Fanon, is the black woman's fear of "niggerhood" ["la négraille"], a fear which drives her to "select the least black of the men" (Fanon, *Black Skin*, 47). But why restrict this symptom and fear to her alone? If men and women are both "feminized" by "the pathology of desire and recognition in the colonial context"—a positioning which continues to identify the feminine with submission—why does Fanon insist on keeping black men and women apart as negrophobic subjects of desire? (Ato Sekyi-Otu, *Fanon's Dialectic of Experience* [Cambridge, MA: Harvard University Press, 1996], 214). Why, given that both are

driven by the compensations and impoverishments of narcissism, is the desire to lactify in the woman invariably a metonym for cultural betrayal, while in the man it remains a metaphor for self-alienation? And why, no doubt for the same reason, is the desire to lactify—to be recognized and loved as white—presented as the black women's degraded *gift*? Is not the desire to be recognized as a white *man* also encased in an economy of gift and debt, and one which freely appropriates the *white* man as the object to be envied, hated, but also loved? Fanon here opens, and closes very quickly, the door that might lead to such a possibility.

22. Fanon, *The Wretched of the Earth*, trans. Constance Farrington (New York: Grove Press, 1965), 203. The politics of misrecognition has a radically different status in Fanon's late work on decolonization. In the collision between the Algerian revolutionary and pro-French members of the settler community, the struggle for recognition produces a desire for substitution that escapes the closed circuit of narcissistic dependence and the hypertrophy of ethical substance (objective freedom) found in Martinique. Fanon's focus, during the Algerian War, on the institutional politics of psychoanalysis and psychiatry was equally invested in the reverses of misrecognition as in the question of what arises when one's self-relation is mediated by the self-relation of the racial other. In "Colonial War and Mental Disorders," for example, Fanon refers to the "nationaliz[ation of] all affective or emotional movements" as the conflict over colonial authority and the systematic use of torture results in various psychoses (247). In *Black Skin, White Masks* and the early case studies of black psychoneuroses, Fanon offers a genealogy of why, in Martinique, the body of the colonized, disciplined by pain and the threat of abandonment, has learned to inhibit the affective residues of rebellion and mistrust and so "cannalize" anger.

23. Compare Rosenberg's response to Sartre's *Réflexions sur la Question Juive* in the essay "Does the Jew Exist? Sartre's Morality Play About Anti-Semitism," in *Commentary: A Jewish Review* 7 (1949): 8–18. Rosenberg's reading appears a year after the publication of the English translation of *Réflexions sur la Question Juive* in *Commentary: A Jewish Review*. "Does the Jew Exist?" is an acute revocation of Sartre *the* actor. What makes Rosenberg's reflections so acute is the slippage he uncovers in Sartre's replacement of the referential value of the term "Jew" with its autonymical value, *the* Jew. The Jew, writes Sartre in *Réflexions*, is not free to be a Jew: "no matter what he does, he is and will remain a Jew" (Jean-Paul Sartre, *Anti-Semite and Jew*, trans. George J. Becker [New York: Schocken Books, 1995], 76). The Jew, Sartre asserts, assumes a "phantom personality, at once strange and familiar, that haunts him and which is nothing but himself—himself as others see him" (78). Nothing more disquieting, then, than this spectral resemblance to the "impalpable and humiliating image" of *the* Jew, an image that the Jew takes with him everywhere and which, it is

said, ensures that he is "not like other men" (101). The Jew's racialized being is then a being that is lacking, dispossessed—a being in which absence is presence, an absence without address or history; the Jew is someone who is "perpetually over-determined" by the negative meanings of being "Jewish" (95). In Sartre's "imaginary deictic" (to borrow Lyotard's phrase), the history, art, knowledge, and lived experience of the Jew disappear; he no longer has the freedom to be anything other than what his situation and the infinite disgust of the anti-Semite wants absolutely to prevent him from being (Lyotard, foreword to Denis Hollier, *The Politics of Prose: Essay on Sartre*, trans. Jeffrey Mehlman [Minneapolis: University of Minneapolis Press, 1986], xvii). The Jew finds himself in this dialectical condition—of having to flee from himself, of having no "historicity" or nation, and of having to grasp this extremity as his freedom and being. The world, things, and knowledge are for him only reference points across the void of his being. And he himself is already reduced to the imago others see in him. He can only take possession of himself, in other words, by self-annihilation; that is all there is to it; he must will to be "nothing-but-a-Jew," which "as a Jew [is] nothing" (Rosenberg "Does the Jew Exist?" 16). Further, if he "denies with violence and desperation the Jewish character in himself, it is precisely in this that he is a Jew"—a being poisoned by the image others have of him (Sartre, *Anti-Semite and Jew*, 89). "To be a Jew," Sartre concludes, "is to be thrown into—to be *abandoned* to—the situation of a Jew" (89).

I've already indicated why I think *abandonment*—a word that haunts *Black Skin, White Masks*—is a sign of displacement in Sartre. From the moment it appears, so does "that within," that feeling of inner nothingness that writing and politics helped Sartre to pretend was not there, and, arguably, the source of that strange sense of freedom exemplified by Jewish authenticity. The Jew is he who must choose himself as a Jew, even though the outcome is incalculable he must struggle to exist, for the "[anti-Semite] wishes to destroy him as a man and leave nothing in him but the Jew, the pariah, the untouchable" (Sartre, *Anti-Semite and Jew*, 57). What the "authentic" Jew has to achieve— "in pride and humiliation," "in horror and hate"—is what may, at first, seem deeply inappropriate: to make the Anti-Semite into a witness of his refusal to be nothing more nor less than a Jew (Sartre, *Anti-Semite and Jew*, 90). "Jewish authenticity consists in choosing oneself *as Jew*," Sartre writes, "[the authentic Jew] knows that he is one who stands apart, untouchable, scorned, proscribed—and it is *as such* that he asserts his being (136–137). His freedom lies in the affirmation of who he is; it is a kind of freedom in which he consents, says yes to the hate that defines him—and nothing more. There is something incongruous in this freedom, or at least its desire, that resembles an impulse to be the Other in me; this impulse is as nothing compared to what Sartre calls Jewish inauthenticity: the wish to be me in the Other. The inauthentic Jew is always "possessed by the consciousness of being a Jew"; it is his fervent wish that passers-by take him for "only one man among others, and like others," yet he feels himself "compromised by the demeanor of the first passer-by, if that passer-by is a Jew" (106–107). For Sartre, such shame and trauma is the evidence of a betrayal; it is an attempt to run away from himself. But there is an ambiguity here: if Jewishness is, in essence, always mediated by the gaze of the Other, and the Jew can only see himself as others see him, why is the wish to see oneself as only one man among others condemned as masquerade, while the other wish, the wish to become a pariah, is seen as a result of knowledge and conscious choice? (This question anticipates Fanon's reading of René Maran's novel *Un homme pareil aux autres*.) Racial inauthenticity, as far as I am concerned, is no worse a choice if the question is how one lives in a state or culture driven by a wish for racial separation and/or compassionate pity for racial differences (am I alone in seeing the deeper antipathy in the latter?). Or, as Rosenberg puts it, why should we be "willing to lose ourselves as we were for the sake of the men we might become"? (Rosenberg "Does the Jew Exist?" 9). Further, why is the wish to stand apart, to be untouchable and scorned, distinguished as the work of commitment, while the wish to belong is, at best, an irreal and deluded desire for freedom? Why is chosen pain and suffering a sign of more personal responsibility rather than less? And finally, what, after all, does Sartre's Hegelian motif of experience as negation have to say to the ethics of being Jewish?

Part of Rosenberg's dismay at *Anti-Semite and Jew* may be related to the fact that neither Jew—of the two types—has all that much choice when it comes to enjoying freedom. Pain or delusion, resistance or assimilation: the semblance of the choice expressed really concerns how one accepts anti-Semitism. "Sartre *is not offering a choice in action*," Rosenberg adds (15). The Jew, he continues, can no more "choose" his situation than Oedipus: the gaze that defines who one is is always hidden; one approaches it as one approaches absence—it is an emptiness that is both unforeseeable and unknowable (11, 16). The choice to be or not to be a Jew—the words recall *Hamlet*—only delivers one to the interminability of not knowing; the choice itself can never begin or end for it represents "the way of despair" (16). *Anti-Semite and Jew*, Rosenberg concludes, is Sartre's morality play that takes the Jew as the accused and condemned. "Sartre's Jew," he writes, "is a personification of the man in the camp, and it is as a concentration-camp drama that his study of the Jew hangs together." It is the fiction of "the pure human Nobody, an adjective without a [pro]noun" (16).

24. Jean-Paul Sartre, *The Transcendence of the Ego: An Existentialist Theory of Consciousness*, trans. Forrest Williams and Robert Kirkpatrick (New York: Noonday Press, 1957), 49.

25. See Jean-Paul Sartre, *Being and Nothingness* (1943), trans. Hazel E. Barnes (London: Routledge, 1995), 251.

26. Jean-Paul Sartre, *The Words*, trans. Bernard Frechtman (New York: G. Braziller, 1964), 87, 90. Compare Nicolas Abraham, "The Phantom of Hamlet," in Nicolas Abraham and Maria Torok, *The Shell and the Kernel*, edited, translated and with an introduction by Nicholas T. Rand (Chicago and London: Chicago University Press, 1994), 191–205.

27. In a 1964 review of *Les Mots*, "From Play Acting to Self"—a title reprising "The Stages"—Rosenberg refers to "that within" and its opaque doubling of the *I* when trying to understand Sartre's unceasing "spectral struggle" with the "illusory egos that kept forming themselves in the gaps of his being." (See Rosenberg, *Act and the Actor*, 126.) Dwelling on the pathos of Sartre's wish to be weighed down by being, Rosenberg makes the point that Sartre's decision to live "among simulcra" was essential to both his politics and his writing: in the activity of writing, the suspicion of absurdity and nothingness could be driven away as the "classic author-to-be" became a "changeless eidolon" for the boy of ten (129).

28. J.-B. Pontalis, "Preface" to Jean-Paul Sartre, *The Freud Scenario*, trans. Quntin Hoare (Chicago: University of Chicago Press, 1985), xii.

29. The connection here between incorporation and emptiness is oddly echoed in comments by Sartre on anality and racial castration in *Being and Nothingness*. When does the child discover that his anus is a hole? "It is only to another person that the anus appears as an orifice," writes Sartre, it is "through the words which the mother uses to designate the child's body . . . that he learns that his anus is a hole" (612, 613). What these words are is left unsaid, imaginary; the point being that it is through the mother's discourse that the child's anus is revealed to him as an orifice while his being-in-the-world is revealed through the bond linking anality and language, femininity and absence. It is because the hole "presents itself to me as an empty image of myself," writes Sartre, that "[a] good part of our life is passed in plugging up holes" (613). It is because of the child's fundamental anxiety about nothingness that he will come to identify "the obscenity of the feminine sex is that of everything which 'gapes open'"; more than that, it is because the mother is already a hole that she can name the hole that is the anus (613, 614). It seems, then, that both the anus and the mother's mouth are holes that can be filled by discourse and meaning, whereas the gaping vagina has something exorbitant and inadmissible about it. Sartre's imagery may well be shocking, but in the same way that the child's discovery of his anus results in a search for a "plenitude of being," Sartre's identification of the feminine with a terrifying "absence" is also wedded to the notion that her sex is a "voracious mouth that devours the penis" (614). The

feminine hole-mouth that creates, that brings into existence, is also one then that castrates and annihilates: woman is the void that gapes open.

What this passage reveals is, I think, a deeply ambiguous fantasy about anality, meaning, and the obscenity of emptiness. First of all, if masculinity is seized by the desire to fill up holes, Sartre's silence on the ideal penetrability of the anus exposed by the mother emerges as a telling moment. It may happen that "the child can not restrain from putting his finger or his whole arm into the hole" that is himself, but Sartre does not openly address the homoerotic aspect of this desire (613). He remains attached to anality as pleasure—as the child's desire to emerge from its deep inner vacuity is summoned into being by the mother's language; it is her words which form his body image and illuminate his anus as a zone of fascination. "We gladly recognize along with the Freudians," Sartre writes, "the innumerable relations existing between sexuality and certain matter and forms in the child's environment" (612). But for Sartre the situation is not one of sexual instincts charged with a sexual significance. Not only is childhood sexuality mediated by the language of the other; the child recognizes himself in the mother as interlocutor; the psychic affect of his body can only be experienced in the exteriority of her representation. Once again, the anus appears here as something to be filled; the fact that the child's anus is also experienced via the pleasure-unpleasure of flow, of passing, of evacuation, is entirely absent from Sartre's reading. Then, when he does have something to say about "the horror of a pleasure unknown to itself"— Freud's term for anal-sadistic fantasies—it is to the castrated figure of a black man that he turns. Sartre invokes the passage from Faulkner's *Light in August*, in which the castrated and dying Negro, Joe Christmas, looks at his executioners "with his eyes open and empty of everything save consciousness. . . . For a long moment, he looked up at them with peaceful and unfathomable and unbearable eyes." And Sartre concludes: "Here once more we are referred from the being-in-the-act-of-looking to the being-looked-at; we have not got out of the circle"—the narcissistic circle of possession and dispossession occasioned by the look of the Other (406).

The exchange of gazes in this scenario is complex and ambiguous. What does Faulkner want us to see in this fantasy of a look expressed and revealed through racial castration? What do the eyes of Joe Christmas see? The fact that there is something other than consciousness missing from the Negro's gaze makes consciousness itself expressive of absence. For me what is unbearable here is the vision of a castrating, mortifying look—that is to say, a look that disfigures and cuts because it emanates from an unfathomable absence which makes reciprocity unthinkable. (Is this a look emptied of *me*?) In Sartre's commentary, the look of the castrated Negro is what overwhelms the white sadistic look with the knowledge that in the other there is a hole beyond which he cannot be penetrated however strong the wish to incorporate or possess his otherness. "The sadist discovers his error," he writes, "when his victim *looks* at him; that is, when the sadist experiences the absolute alienation of his being in the Other's freedom" (405). In terms of the sadomasochistic contest of gazes here, the sadist can never possess the freedom of his victim. But Sartre has nothing to say on the mirroring between castration and the victim's impenetrability. What is required of the Negro to make him impenetrable? He must be destroyed but via an act that aligns him with the gaping hole of femininity / existence. But if the latter signifies an obscene penetrability, in the eyes of the Negro appears an emptiness that cannot be borne, a vacuity which suggests an equivalence between pure victimhood and a masculinity that cannot be penetrated, but only on the principle that the black man corresponds to the gaping hole. One could elaborate on this identification in a thousand ways—from discussions around racial hegemony and phallic fantasy, to questions around violence and the gaze—nevertheless, what interests me here is the scandalous law of exchange assumed between certain holes and the cultural privilege of impenetrability. To conclude, for Sartre all sexuality is a protest against penetrability and emptiness, and yet the ideal of impenetrability offers no consolation. Just as the child's sexual fecundity begins with the receipt and the possession of a hole which he then strives to fill, the absolute victim's loss of selfhood and manhood stems from a depropriating hole that cannot ever be filled. What retains the power of emptiness in both examples is sexuality itself—we are all plunged into its enigmatic hole without that gap being compensated by any racial or parental fantasy.

30. Jean-Paul Sartre, *Being and Nothingness* (1943), trans. Hazel E. Barnes (London: Routledge, 1995), 251.

31. Jean-Paul Sartre, *The Imaginary: A Phenomenological Psychology of the Imagination*, trans. Jonathan Webber (London, New York: Routledge, 2004), 191.

32. See Jean-Paul Sartre, *Sartre on Theater*, ed. Michel Contat and Michel Rybalka, trans. Frank Jellinek (New York: Pantheon Books, 1976), 60, 163, 167.

33. Jean-Paul Sartre, "Orphée Noir," *Situations III: Lendemains de Guerre* (Paris: Gallimard, 1949), 254–255; idem, "Black Orpheus," trans. John MacCombie in *Race*, ed. Robert Bernasconi (Oxford: Blackwell, 2001), 126.

CHAPTER 3 — "THE DERIVED LIFE OF FICTION"

1. Frederic Wertham, *Dark Legend: A Study in Murder* (London: Victor Gollancz, 1947), 87.

2. Frederic Wertham, *Seduction of the Innocent* (London: Museum Press, 1955), 15.

3. I will be coming back to Wertham's concept of catathymic crisis. For now, in "The Catathymic Crisis: A Clinical Entity," he defines catathymia as a "rutlike

fixation," a disturbance between "logic and affectivity" in which "the patient acquires the idea that he must carry out a violent act against others or against himself." Frederic Wertham, "The Catathymic Crisis: A Clinical Entity," *Archives of Neurology and Psychiatry* 37, no. 4 (1937): 976.

4. In the 1940s, the prevailing stereotype of the "active mother" seen to be "at fault" vis-à-vis her male children dominated discussions of dysfunctional family life. Such narratives of blame, in which the "mom" is the death mask of the mother, as Max Horkheimer writes in his 1949 essay "Authoritarianism and the Family Today," were founded on the supposed pernicious effects of domineering mothers on their male children. See R. Anshen, ed., *The Family: Its Function and Destiny* (New York: Harper & Brothers, 1949), 367. A view echoed by Philip Wylie's *Generation of Vipers*, first published in 1942: "Disguised as good old mom," he writes, the active mother "is the bride at every funeral and the corpse at every wedding" (New York: Rinehart & Co, 1942), 185.

5. Wright, cited in Michel Fabre, *The Unfinished Quest of Richard Wright*, trans. Isabel Barzun (Urbana and Chicago: University of Illinois Press, 1993), 171.

6. Frederic Wertham, "Book Review," *American Journal of Psychiatry* 112, no. 10 (April 1956): 486.

7. Richard Wright, *Black Boy: A Record of Childhood and Youth* (New York and Evanston: Harper & Row, 1945), 111.

8. For a related analysis of Wright's views on paternity, see David Marriott, *On Black Men* (Edinburgh: Edinburgh University Press; New York: Columbia University Press, 2000).

9. Richard Wright, *Native Son* (Harmondsworth: Penguin, 1983), 9, 25.

10. See Richard Wright, *Twelve Million Black Voices: A Folk History of the Negro in the United States of America* (London: Lindsay Drummond, 1947), 44.

11. On the ties binding racism to fiction, compare Theodor Adorno's analysis of anti-Semitism in "Freudian Theory and the Pattern of Fascist Propaganda": "Just as little as people believe in the depth of their hearts that the Jews are the devil, do they completely believe in their leader. They do not really identify themselves with him but act this identification, perform their own enthusiasm, and thus participate in their leader's performance. . . . It is probably the suspicion of this *fictitiousness* of their own 'group psychology' which makes fascist crowds so merciless and unapproachable." See J. M. Bernstein, ed., *The Culture Industry* (London: Routledge, 1991), 131, my emphasis.

12. Wertham, "An Unconscious Determinant in 'Native Son,'" in *Psychoanalysis and Literature*, ed. Hendrik M. Ruitenbeek (New York: E. P. Dutton & Co., 1964), 321, my emphasis.

13. Richard Wright, *The Outsider* (New York: HarperPerennial, 1993), 22.

14. Richard Wright, *Savage Holiday* (Jackson: University Press of Mississippi, 1994), 216.

15. *The House I Enter*, directed by Van Fox, NBC TV Sunday, 27 October 1957.

16. Richard Wright, "Urban Misery in an American City," "A World View of the American Negro," "Psychiatry Goes to Harlem," in *Twice a Year*, no. 14–15 (Fall 1946/Winter 1947), 339–355. See also Sidney M. Katz, "Jim Crow Is Barred from Wertham's Clinic," *Magazine Digest* (September 1946): 27; Norman M. Lobenz, "Human Salvage in Harlem," *Coronet* (March 1948): 133–136; James L. Tuck, "Here's Hope for Harlem," *This Week Magazine, New York Herald Tribune*, 26 January 1947.

17. Frederic Wertham, "Underground," MS, Wright Papers, James Weldon Johnson Collection, Beinecke Rare Book and Manuscript Library, Yale University, box 108.

18. Richard Wright, "The Man Who Lived Underground," *Eight Men* (Cleveland and New York: World Publishing Co., 1969). For a commentary, see Michel Fabre, "From Tabloid to Myth: 'The Man Who Lived Underground,'" in *The World of Richard Wright* (Jackson: University Press of Mississippi, 1985), 93–107.

19. At this point I'd like to highlight a real murder case Wright and Wertham were involved with in 1941. Early in 1941 Wright received an extraordinary letter from an elderly woman requesting that he help secure the release of one Clinton Brewer, a black man serving a life sentence for the murder of Wilhelmina Washington, a mother of two who had refused to marry him. Fascinated—seduced?— by this letter, Wright stirs himself to visit Brewer in prison. Following this visit he writes the governor of New Jersey, Thomas A. Edison Jr., on 30 March 1941, requesting that Brewer be released on parole. In his letter Wright presents Brewer as a sensitive artist who has established an organic social relationship to the world (Fabre, "From Tabloid to Myth," 236). The oddity of this plea, that art cures murder, that art—rather than repressed desires or symptoms—is somehow tied to life (and to law), gives the key to Wright's fascination with Brewer. Writing (or art) can apparently save black men from the iniquity of their desires by forcing them to confront the agon of racist seduction; or, insofar as blackness is marked by the racist fictions of culture, only fiction, it appears, can start to master (and so to resist) racism's effects. Wright's plea seduces Governor Edison. In turn, on 8 July, Edison releases Brewer only to see him stab another young woman three months later in circumstances similar to those of the first crime. For this second crime, Brewer is sentenced to be executed without delay. It is at this point that Wright discovers *Dark Legend*. Wertham's method reveals to him what lies hidden behind Brewer's two crimes; that method allows him to discover a new kind of agon behind Brewer's murderous obsessions: an unconscious intruded upon by the fictions of culture. In the letter of 24 October, Wright asks Wertham whether

Brewer's second crime might, like the first murder, be deeply rooted in his past, buried in some repressed content disguised by the fictions of secondary revision. Fascinated by Wright's presentation of the case, Wertham not only retains a lawyer for Brewer, he also agrees to give expert evidence himself on Brewer's behalf. Indeed, Wertham's testimony not only saves Brewer's life but also reveals a matricidal scene underlying the two crimes. Brewer acts because of a self-deception which he can neither master nor control; he is driven to destroy mother images. From Gino's and Brewer's case, then, Wright and Wertham discover their shared fascination with sons who unwittingly murder their mothers, murderers who are drawn to the enchantments and lures of fiction and whose crimes require the ability of the writer-as-analyst to unveil the hidden meanings of their repetition: the hateful "fictions" of culture that have unwittingly "perverted" their mother love into its murderous opposite.

20. Wertham to Wright, 16 March 1945, Richard Wright Papers, Correspondence with Frederic Wertham, Beinecke Rare Book and Manuscript Library, Yale University, box 108.

21. Wright, *"Wasteland uses Psychoanalysis Deftly,"* P.M. Magazine (February 17, 1946), 8. All references to this text are taken from M. Fabre, *The Unfinished Quest of Richard Wright* (New York: Morrow, 1973).

22. While this notion of "reality" has, in my view, led many prominent black critics to complain that Wright sacrifices the "literary" to the ideological, that he promotes "protest" over signification, reference over representation, I think this argument perhaps loses sight of some of those insistent repetitions between fantasy and the real that Wright was interested in. For critics such as James Baldwin—who, in his obituary for Wright, "Alas Poor Richard," regrets that Wright "was never, really, the social and polemical writer he took himself to be" (*Nobody Knows My Name: More Notes of a Native Son* [Harmondsworth: Penguin, 1991], 151), or Henry Louis Gates, who, in his pivotal *The Signifying Monkey*, condemns Wright for seeing "fiction not as a model of reality but as a representative bit of it, a literal report of the real"—Wright's notion of the real represents a will to power, a drive to evidence that is already profoundly phantasmatic (*The Signifying Monkey: A Theory of Afro-American Literary Criticism* [New York: Oxford University Press, 1989], 182, 184). This point of view fails to consider Wright's comment, in "Blueprint for Negro writing," on the nonrepresentative links between images and reality: "The relationship between reality and the artistic image is not always simple and direct. . . . Image and emotion possess a logic of their own" (Wright, cited in Paul Gilroy, *The Black Atlantic: Modernity and Double Consciousness* [London: Verso, 1993], 169). It also fails to consider how, for Wright, writing is invariably connected to dreaming: "One cannot escape the intuitive conviction," he declares, in an

unpublished paper, "Roots and Branches," "that stories, like dreams, possess both a latent and manifest content of meaning" ("Roots and Branches," MS, Wright Papers, Beinecke Rare Book and Manuscript Library, Yale University, box 3, folder 138). To push the point, writing, like dreaming, is for Wright an expression of unconscious fantasies which are radically unknowable, even though they may be at work in the text.

CHAPTER 4 — BLACK NARCISSUS: ISAAC JULIEN

1. Essex Hemphill, *"Looking for Langston*: An Interview with Isaac Julien," in *"Brother to Brother*, ed. Essex Hemphill (Boyston: Alyson Publications, 1991), 182.

2. Amanda Cruz, introduction to *The Film Art of Isaac Julien*, ed. David Deitcher and David Frankel (New York: Center for Curatorial Studies, 2000), vi.

3. Manthia Diawara, "The Absent One: The Avant-Garde and the Black Imaginary in *Looking for Langston*," in *Representing Black Men*, ed. Marcellus Blount and George P. Cunningham (New York and London: Routledge, 1996), 208.

4. Henry Louis Gates, "Looking for Modernism," in *Black American Cinema*, ed. Manthia Diawara (New York, London: Routledge, 1993), 207, 205.

5. See J.-P. Vernant, "Figuration de l'invisible et categorie psychologique du double: Le colossos," in *Mythe et pensée chez les Grecs* (Paris: Maspéro, 1965), 251–264; see also his "Image et apparence dans la théorie platonicienne de la Mimêsis," *Journal de Psychologie* 2 (1975); reprinted in J.-P. Vernant, *Mortals and Immortals: Collected Essays*, ed. I. Zeitlin (Princeton N.J.: Princeton University Press, 1991), 164–185.

6. David Deitcher, "A Lovesome Thing: The Film Art of Isaac Julien," in *The Film Art of Isaac Julien*, ed. David Deitcher and David Frankel (New York: Center for Curatorial Studies, 2000), 11.

7. bell hooks, "Seductive Sexualities: Representing Blackness in Poetry and on Screen," in *Yearning: Race, Gender, and Cultural Politics* (Boston: South End Press, 1990), 195.

8. Kobena Mercer, "Dark and Lovely: Black Gay Image-Making," in *Welcome to the Jungle. New Positions in Black Cultural Studies* (New York: Routledge, 1994), 224.

9. Isaac Julien and Kobena Mercer, "True Confessions: A Discourse on Images of Black Male Sexuality," in *Welcome to the Jungle: New Positions in Black Cultural Studies* (New York: Routledge, 1994), 133.

10. Isaac Julien and Kobena Mercer, "De Margin and De Center," in *Black British Cultural Studies*, ed. Houston Baker, Manthia Diawara, and Ruth H. Lindeborg (Chicago and London: University of Chicago Press, 1996), 198.

11. Pierre Bourdieu, "Delegation and Political Fetishism," *Thesis Eleven*, no. 10–11 (1984–1985): 60, 61.

12. Paul Gilroy, "Cruciality and the Frog's Perspective," *Small Acts: Thoughts on the Politics of Black Cultures* (London: Serpent's Tale, 1993), 110.

13. Houston Baker, *Modernism and the Harlem Renaissance* (Chicago and London: University of Chicago Press, 1987), xv, xvii.

14. George Hutchinson, *The Harlem Renaissance in Black and White* (Cambridge, MA: Harvard University Press, 1995), 2.

15. Isaac Julien, "Black Is Black Ain't," in *Black Popular Culture*, ed. Gina Dent (Seattle: Bay Press, 1992), 260, 261.

16. Isaac Julien, "Confessions of a Snow Queen: Notes on the Making of *The Attendant*," in *The Film Art of Isaac Julien*, ed. David Deitcher and David Frankel (New York: Center for Curatorial Studies, 2000), 81.

17. Gary Fisher, *Gary in Your Pocket* (Durham and London: Duke University Press, 1996), 231.

18. My ellipses are in square brackets; question marks denote deleted proper names.

19. At one point in "Confessions of a Snow Queen," Julien refers to "the unspeakable desire for sexual domination" (81). "Unspeakable" is an odd word to use given that *The Attendant* had to exclude, as one of its conditions of entry in the *Time-Codes* "Double Lives" series, all spoken dialogue. In another sense, the attendant cannot speak—represent—his desire to be beaten and punished in his own words, so the tableaux vivants act as representatives of his desire.

CHAPTER 5 — LETTERS TO LANGSTON

1. Alain Locke to Langston Hughes, 17 January 1922, Langston Hughes Papers, James Weldon Johnson Collection in the Yale Collection of American Literature, Beinecke Rare Book and Manuscript Library, box 97.

2. Cullen cited in Arnold Rampersad, *The Life of Langston Hughes*, vol. 1, *1902–1941, I, Too, Sing America* (New York: Oxford University Press, 1986), 67.

3. Alain Locke to Langston Hughes, 13 June 1922, Langston Hughes Papers, James Weldon Johnson Collection in the Yale Collection of American Literature, Beinecke Rare Book and Manuscript Library, box 97.

4. Percy Bysshe Shelley, "Defense of Poetry," *Shelley's Literary and Philosophical Criticism*, ed. John Shawcross (London: H. Froude, 1909): 121.

5. William Hazlitt, "On Poetry in General," *Complete Works* (London: J. M. Dent, 1932), V, I.

6. Alain Locke to Langston Hughes, 10 February 1922, Langston Hughes Papers, James Weldon Johnson Collection in the Yale Collection of American Literature, Beinecke Rare Book and Manuscript Library, box 97.

7. The invocation also manages to conjure midwifery as the product of a spectral or demonic fear. If the midwife severs the umbilicus holding kin to generation, s/he is also the uncanny ghost reconnecting the bonds separating death from life, loss from pleasure.

8. William James, *The Writings of William James: A Comprehensive Edition*, ed. John J. McDermott (Chicago: University of Chicago Press, 1977), 296, emphasis added.

9. William James, cited in Jonathan Levin, "The Esthetics of Pragmatism," *American Literary History* 6, no. 4 (1994): 667.

10. William James, *The Writings of William James: A Comprehensive Edition*, ed. John J. McDermott (Chicago: University of Chicago Press, 1977), 456.

11. Jonathan Levin, "The Esthetics of Pragmatism," *American Literary History* 6, no. 4 (1994): 669.

12. Alain Locke, "To the Young Friend on Reading Jean Christophe," MS, Alain Locke Papers, Moorland-Springarn Research Center, Howard University, box 164, folder 6.

13. Intriguingly, Locke compares Romain Rolland's (1912) novel *Jean Christophe* to a mirror: "*Jean Christophe*, for the modern mind and temperament is a mirror, capable of reflecting one's personality if he will gaze into it fearlessly and straightforwardly. One's reactions to it are one's spiritual features, so beautifully burnished is it for reflecting at myriad points and angles those reactions that subtlety reveal it. I construe it to be the chief usefulness of the book that properly used it can discover us to ourselves. . . . Friendship too, at its best is such a mirror" (Locke, "To the Young Friend").

14. In a lecture on "The Negro and Art," written for a symposium at Mount Holyoke College in 1931, Locke describes the link between spirituality and sterility in interracial terms: "In black America, the white man has either a base or a noble antidote to Puritanism and its emotional sterility depending on whether he contacts with the Negro sprit on the low level of primitive animalism or on the high level of fine artistic expression." TS, Harmon Foundation Papers, box 66, Library of Congress, Manuscript Division.

15. See J. A. Symonds, *A Problem in Greek Ethics: Being an Inquiry into the Phenomenon of Sexual Inversion* (London: privately printed, 1938), chap. 12.

16. Locke cited in Arnold Rampersad, *The Life of Langston Hughes*, vol. 1, *1902–1941, I. Too, Sing America* (New York: Oxford University Press, 1986), 92.

17. Alain Locke to Langston Hughes, 10 February 1922, Langston Hughes Papers, James Weldon Johnson Collection in the Yale Collection of American Literature, Beinecke Rare Book and Manuscript Library, box 97.

18. *Plato's Theaetetus,* trans. M. J. Levett (Indianapolis: Hackett, 1990), 268. See M. F. Burnyeat, "Socratic Midwifery, Platonic Inspiration," *BICS* 24 (1977): 7–16, and Gregory Vlastos, "The Individual as an Object of Love in Plato," in *Platonic Studies* (Princeton, NJ: Princeton University Press, 1973), for commentaries on this trope.

19. According to M. F. Burnyeat, "Socratic Midwifery [Is] Firmly in the Realm of the Imaginary," *BICS* 24 (1977): 7.

20. Locke defines the "New Negro" in terms of an inner struggle to overcome and renounce the literary and social reductiveness of race typology. This is how the "Harlem Renaissance" has been read critically—that is, as the birth of a new consciousness, as the attempt, successful or not, at a transvaluation of the Negro through art. These readings are not necessarily incorrect but a tad simplistic. Henry Louis Gates has pointed out that the term "New Negro" was already circumscribed by complex historical meanings before Locke's definition of the term (see "The Trope of a New Negro and the Reconstruction of the Image of the Black," *Representations* 24 [Fall 1988]: 129–155). That Locke's recourse to the term was part of an already typical image or scene of black rebirth is not controversial. The link between Gates's revisionism and Locke's is clearly the locodescriptive use of a New Negro typology—with this distinction, however, that Locke's reverse typology remains for Gates an apolitical, bourgeois version of the supposedly more radical black typological use of the term. (It's a viewpoint which I respect but disagree with. See my *On Black Men* for a critique of this critique, especially "On Black Types").

21. Locke's writings on art are extensive. See "A Note on African Art," *Opportunity* (May 1924): 134–138; "The American Negro As Artist," *American Magazine of Art* (September 1931): 211–220; "Negro's Contribution in Art to American Culture," *Proceedings of the National Conference of Social Work* (Chicago: University of Chicago Press, 1933), 315–322; and *Negro Art: Past and Present* (Washington, DC: Associates in Negro Folk Education, 1936). For a commentary, see Beryl J. Wright, "The Harmon Foundation in Context," in *Against the Odds: African-American Artists and the Harmon Foundation,* ed. Gary A. Reynolds and Beryl J. Wright (Newark: Newark Museum, 1989), 12–25.

22. Alain Locke, ed., *The New Negro: Voices of the Harlem Renaissance* (New York: Touchstone, 1999): 3, 4, 6.

23. The question of "emulation" is pursued in more detail in part 2, "The Psychograph."

24. Locke cited in Arnold Rampersad, *The Life of Langston Hughes*, vol. 1, *1902–1941, I. Too, Sing America* (New York: Oxford University Press, 1986), 92.

25. Alain Locke to Langston Hughes (1925). Langston Hughes Papers. James Weldon Johnson Collection in the Yale Collection of American Literature, Beinecke Rare Book and Manuscript Library, box 97.

26. On 21 June 1923, Cullen writes to Locke: "Needless to say I am sorry that things have turned out just the way they have; I am more concerned for you and for Langston than for myself." And Cullen writes again on 30 April 1923: "I understood just how matters were and what spiritual and mental anguish you were undergoing at the time." Alain Locke Papers, Moorland Springarn Research Center, Howard University, folder 36.

27. Langston Hughes, *The Big Sea: An Autobiography* (New York: Thunder's Mouth Press, 1986), 218.

28. Hurston cited in Robert E. Hemenway, *Zora Neale Hurston: A Literary Biography* (Urbana: University of Illinois Press, 1977), 40. W.E.B. Du Bois, "Books," *Crisis* 33 (Dec. 1926): 2.

29. Michael L. Cobb, "Insolent Racing, Rough Narrative: The Harlem Renaissance's Impolite Queers," *Callaloo* 23, no. 1 (2000): 330.

30. Locke, cited in Richard Bruce Nugent, *Gay Rebel of the Harlem Renaissance* (Durham: Duke University Press, 2002), 25.

31. Locke's relation to the work of the German-Jewish anthropologist Franz Boas is complex. In general terms, the way in which Boasian anthropology tried to divorce race from culture, race from biology, proves crucial to Locke, as can be seen in "The Problem of Race Classification," *Opportunity* 1 (Sept. 1923): 261–264. In this 1923 review of Roland Dixon's *The Racial History of Man*, Locke sees a confused and contradictory *reductio ad absurdum* in Dixon's "purely anatomical approach to the questions of human classification"; more, Dixon's use of the word "race" is part of the confusion because, claims Locke:

> "there is a flagrant inconsistency involved in treating these abstract race-types as equivalent to actual sub-species or natural and cultural race-groups. No one can possibly be cited to better effect against this procedure than Professor Dixon himself. "If by the term 'race' we mean to describe actually existing groups of people, as I think we should, then our types are certainly not races, since, with few exceptions, there are no groups of men who actually represent them." These types are "but scantily represented among the world's peoples, the vast majority of whom present not the characteristics of pure types, but of blends between them." (Locke, "Problem of Race Classification," 261–262)

What does Dixon's use of biometry and craniology achieve? According to Locke, *The Racial History of Man* bequeaths an error: aside from thinking that peoples' skulls and faces should result in a law of correlation revealing pure racial types, Dixon's criteria, Locke writes, speaks only of a type of make-believe, part of the complex unselfconsciousness which supports racial thinking in the first place. The whole approach, in fact, takes for granted what it is designed to demonstrate: the existence of "pure races"—the existence of which cannot be empirically verified. Further, the word "type" compounds this confusion of the imagined and the real. "Professor Dixon," he writes, "would have us accept as scientific race-types that in one context are abstract nouns of classification, and in another, represent concrete historical stocks or breeds; that on one hand have no determinable physiognomic or structural stability, and exhibit almost limitless variability of their physical components, yet on the other, maintain sufficiently characteristic cultural traits and capacities as to have everywhere in all environments appreciably similar effects upon civilization" (262). "With such types something or someone must be victimized," Locke concludes, "they breed, so to speak, their own characteristic illusions" (262). As an example of that characteristic illusion, compare the following statements made by Felix Luschan, director of the Berlin Ethnological Museum, a young scholar whom Locke described as "the outstanding authority of his generation on primitive African Art." See Alain Locke, *Negro Art: Past and Present* (New York: Arno Press, 1969), 35. In 1902, Luschan wrote: "The more we now learn to know those "savages" [*Naturvölker*], the more we realize there is never a border that sharply and surely differentiates us from [them]" (LuP: lecture "Allg. Phys. Anthrop.," 1902, 169, cited in Benoit Massin, "From Virchow to Fischer: Physical Anthropology and 'Modern Race Theories' in Wilhelmine Germany," in *Volsgeist as Method and Ethic: Essays on Boasian Ethnography and the German Anthropological Tradition*, ed. George W. Stocking [Madison: University of Wisconsin Press, 1996], 102). Compare that sentiment to his address on the "Anthropological View of Race," given to the First Universal Races Congress in London in 1911, a congress which Locke also attended. According to Luschan, "racial barriers will never cease to exist, and if ever they should show a tendency to disappear, it will certainly be better to preserve than to obliterate them. . . . God created the white man and God created the black man, but the devil created the mulatto" (105). Further, Luschan told students in his course on "general physical anthropology" at the University of Berlin that the word *race* was "just a word and a word behind which there is no clear concept" (114). See also Matgorzata Irek, "From Berlin to Harlem: Felix von Luschan, Alain Locke, and the New Negro," in *The Black Columbiad: Defining Moments in African-American Literature and Culture*, ed. Wernor Sollors and Maria Diedrich (Cambridge, MA: Harvard University Press, 1994), 174–184. Irek's article is informative but fails to address Luschan's ambivalent racial attitudes.

Against Luschan's language of natural borders and barriers Locke turns to the opposite concerns of Leo Weiner and G. Elliot Smith, who argue that cultural contacts are "reciprocal in effect" and establish a "composite culture." It is an outlook that would flavor his writings on cultural racialism, a concern he took up a year later in "The Concept of Race as Applied to Social Culture," *Howard Review* 1 (June 1924). In question, once again, is the need to bring to light the "manifestly false and arbitrary linkage" of race and culture; the erroneous but "politically proprietary claims" of an "evolutionary point of view" (291, 297, 298). Locke's attitude is one of skepticism: race and culture are neither immutably fixed nor completely dissociated, but integral: "They [ethnic traits] are in no sense absolutely permanent" (292). So it makes sense to speak of race only in terms of "a vital and significant relation to [ethnic] social culture" (294). Biology doesn't settle the matter, neither does heredity. Aryanism and Nordicism are examples of folktales established by "racial and national bias" (297). Locke cites the "revolutionary" view of Goldenweiser—*"man is one, civilizations are many"*—to define his cultural relativism (295). It is a principle which, once grasped, puts "culture making" at the birth of race in history: "regarding culture as expressive of race, race by this interpretation is regarded as itself a cultural product" (295).

32. Alain Locke, "Value and Imperatives," in *American Philosophy Today and Tomorrow*, ed. Horace M. Kallen and Sidney Hook (New York: Books for Libraries Press, 1935), 312.

33. For Locke's notion of "self-culture" or "self-cultivation," see "The Ethics of Culture," *Howard University Record* 17 (January 1923): 178–185. "Culture likewise is every inch representative of the whole personality when it is truly perfected"; and, "moreover, personal representativeness and group achievement are in this respect identical" (185).

34. See also Alain Locke, "Oxford Contrasts," *Independent* 67 (July 1909): 139–142.

35. Alain Locke, *Harvard College Class of 1908* (Cambridge, MA: Harvard University Press, 1914), 206–207.

36. Ibid., 456.

37. Alain Locke to Mary Locke, 26 June 1905, Alain Locke Papers, Moorland-Springarn Research Center, Howard University, 164-45, box 49, folder 27. Compare the letter Locke wrote to his mother on the publication of "Oxford Contrasts": "I wanted nothing negroid about my first appearance" in print. Cited in Jeffrey C. Stewart, "A Black Aesthete at Oxford," *Massachusetts Review* 34, no. 3 (1993): 422.

38. Alain Locke to Mary Locke, 31 May 1905, Alain Locke Papers, Moorland-Springarn Research Center, Howard University, 164, box 48, folder 5.

39. For a commentary on Locke's experiences in Oxford, see Stewart, "A Black Aesthete," 411–428.

40. Horace M. Kallen, "Alain Locke and Cultural Pluralism," *Journal of Philosophy* (1957–1958): 119–127.

41. Kallen cited in Wernor Sollors, "A Critique of Pure Pluralism," in *Reconstructing American Literary History*, ed. Sacvan Bercovitch (Cambridge, MA: Cambridge University Press, 1986), 269.

42. Alain Badiou, *Ethics: An Essay on the Understanding of Evil* (1993), trans. Peter Hallward (London: Verso, 2001), 24.

43. Compare Sollors, "A Critique of Pure Pluralism," 272: "The birth of cultural pluralism was beset by ironies [paradoxes?]: a non-religious Jewish student was converted to Zionism by a Boston Brahmin professor who suffered from spells of repugnance brought about by race contact during dinners; the student denounces assimilation and endears himself to his professor by claiming the same feelings of repugnance toward a black fellow student whom, with the help of his professor, he yet wants to protect against racism; and he views the young black intellectual, perhaps tongue-in-cheek, not as a fellow-philosophy student, but as an athlete and credit to the university."

44. Horace M. Kallen, "Democracy *versus* the Melting-Pot," in *Culture and Democracy in the United States* (New Brunswick: Transaction Publishers, 1998), 76.

45. In "The Arts under Dictatorship," Kallen also presents the relation of the modern artist to tradition as a mimesis opposed to imitation: "Repeat, not copy. Of copies there are enough; but copies merely reproduce outer contours, not inward character." See Horace M. Kallen, *Indecency and the Seven Arts: And Other Adventures of a Pragmatist in Aesthetics* (New York: Horace Liveright, 1930), 109.

46. I return to this question in "That Within" and "The Love of Neither-Either."

47. Kallen to Locke, [undated] June 1935, Alain Locke Papers, Moorland-Springarn Research Center, Howard University, box 164–128, folder 33. In his own author's note to "Philosophy Today and Tomorrow," in *American Philosophy Today and Tomorrow*, Kallen writes: "Unable to separate my profession from my life, I have always found myself ill at ease with the philosophy and the psychology of the schools. The first has seemed to me for the most part a ceremonial liturgy of professionals as artificial and detached from the realities of the daily life as bridge or chess or any other safe but exciting game of chance, and much of the second has seemed to me the sedulous elaboration of disregard for the living man of flesh and blood." The embrace, here, of the perennial value-opposition between philosophy and real life, seems to be unaware of its tautological use of "daily life" (whose superior reality as reality is taken to define its value) and its dogmatic claim to know and so

embody the real—the philosophic claim par excellence. As such, Kallen's self-presentation is an excellent example of the peremptory authoritarianism of an unprofessed but decidedly professional wish to profess the unity of profession and life.

48. Kallen to Locke, 8 July 1935, Alain Locke Papers, Moorland-Springarn Research Center, Howard University, box 164–128, folder 33.

49. Horace Kallen, "Style and Meaning," in his *Indecency and the Seven Arts*, 141.

50. Alain Locke, "An Essay on the Concept of Value," Alain Locke Papers, Moorland-Springarn Research Center, Howard University, box 164–58, folders 14–24. Locke's relation to the German school of value [Meinong, Simmel, Lipps, Brentano] is complex. However, there are many affinities between Locke's psychological approach to values and Meinong's *Allgemein-Wertheorie* and Simmel's work on values as psychological ultimates or *Denkmodus*. That said, in his 1911 Harvard thesis on "The Problem of Classification in the Theory of Value," Locke is careful to distance himself from what he sees as the main problem of the "Austrian School": namely, the confusion of principles of type relation with principles of relation to type. That is, the fact that values carry the trace of our obsessions does not tell us anything about why we value or how.

51. Alain Locke, "An Essay on the Concept of Value," Alain Locke Papers, Moorland-Springarn Research Center, Howard University, box 164–58, folders 14–24. Locke's rejection of desire as a privileged term for understanding valuation was exemplary for more than one reason. Not only did he reject any biological or behavioristic emphases on satisfaction or satiation, but he also rejected the "anarchic relativism" which, for him, invariably accompanied the fantasy of desire as the sole origin of value. Desire, for Locke, is not reducible to pleasure or drive and requires a more complex notion of affect.

52. Alain Locke, "Value," in *The Philosophy of Alain Locke*, ed. Leonard Harris (Philadelphia: Temple University Press, 1989), 125, emphases added.

53. The cited words are taken from Nicholai Hartmann, *Ethics*, trans. Stanton Coit (London: G. Allen & Unwin, 1932), 2:423.

CHAPTER 6 — THE LOVE OF NEITHER-EITHER: RACIAL INTEGRATION IN *PRESSURE POINT*

1. Donald Spoto, *Stanley Kramer Film Maker* (Hollywood: Samuel French, 1978), 16–17. Sidney Poitier, *This Life* (London: Hodder and Stoughton, 1980), 266.

2. Leslie Fiedler, "Negro and Jew," in *The Collected Essays of Leslie Fiedler* (New York: Stein and Day, 1971), 2:166.

3. Frantz Fanon, *Black Skin, White Masks*, trans. C. L. Markmann (New York: Grove Press, 1967), 140.

4. James Baldwin, *The Devil Finds Work* (London: Michael Joseph, 1976), 29.

5. Albert Johnson, "The Negro in American Films: Some Recent Works," *Film Quarterly* 18, no. 4 (1965): 19.

6. Clifford Mason, *New York Times*, 10 September 1967.

7. Baldwin's reading, here, of a suppressed homosocial element recalls Leslie Fielder's *Love and Death in the American Novel*. In *Love and Death*, first published in 1960, Fiedler argued that America's founding, but disavowed, myth was "the old antifemale dream of a pure love between males, colored and white" (Fiedler, *Love and Death in the American Novel* [New York: Stein and Day, 1966], 170). That mutual love, he argued in *An End to Innocence*, had been "desperately repressed from overt recognition" (Fiedler, *An End to Innocence: Essays on Culture and Politics* [Boston: Beacon Press, 1966], 146). In the 1966 essay "Negro and Jew," he extends the coupling as follows: "I myself can report having heard several times in various forms from young civil rights workers the cry, so authentically American it was hard at first to believe: 'Oh, Christ, things were great when just us buddies Black and White were fighting it out together; but these White chicks are just down here to get laid'" (170). In *The Devil Finds Work*, Baldwin's calculated reworking of Fielder's thesis includes homosexual love as well as homosocial union: "A black man and a white man can come together only in the absence of women: which is, simply, the American legend of masculinity brought to its highest pressure, and revealed, as it were, in black and white"; "A man can fall in love with a man: incarceration, torture, fire, and death, and still more, the threat of these, have not been able to prevent it, and never will" (67, 68).

8. Compare the views of Nathan Douglas, coauthor, with Harold Jacob Smith, of the screenplay: the "thematic resolution of the film occurs with the acts of mutual sacrifice performed by the two men and it could not depend upon the 'triumph' of escape. The real triumph, insofar as an author may be able to state it, lies in the two men overcoming a set of moribund mores learned from an abnormal social superstructure, which had originally made them think they were enemies. . . . We maintain, thematically, the men are liberated—liberated from hate" (Douglas, cited in George Hitchens, "The Defiance in 'The Defiant Ones,'" *Film Culture*, nos. 50–55 [1970]: 64). For Baldwin, that resolution does not, he insists again, bear witness to a liberation from race hate; the unmistakable truth of Poitier's performance, its exquisite ethical discrimination, is achieved in spite of "being placed at the mercy of a lie"—the reassuring lie that white people are not hated but forgiven, that blacks are not angry but prepared to renounce, to flee from, political freedom due to a more passionate worship of interracial male friendship (Baldwin, *Devil*, 62). This political disagreement over the limits and meaning of black forgiveness, I argue, also haunts *Pressure Point*.

9. K.C., "The Defiant Ones, U.S.A., 1958," *Monthly Film Bulletin* 25, no. 297 (October 1958). Those psychological forces, ranging from projection to mimicry, called on blacks and whites to accommodate themselves to certain racial myths or fictions. "The Negro [. . .] is almost always acting," comments Baldwin in his 1948 essay "The Harlem Ghetto," for, like the American Jew, Negroes "try and cover their vulnerability by a frenzied adoption of the customs of the country" (Baldwin, *Notes of a Native Son* [London: Corgi Books, 1964], 56, 57). For Leslie Fiedler, writing on "Race—The Dream and the Nightmare," such transference means that Negroes and Jews must learn to "act out, in addition to their authentic roles, secondary ones corresponding to the inner necessities of quite alien others . . . and like all who lead double lives, they are troubled by anxiety and guilt" (Fiedler, "Race—The Dream and the Nightmare," *Commentary* [October 1963]: 298). Minority identity, then, is defined by an "unendurable doubleness" of being, trapped between the burden of authenticity and obedience to a projected role. For Baldwin this doubleness leads, above all, to an "unendurable frustration of being"; one apparent in the mutual distrust between Negro and Jew: "the Negro hates the Jew as a Jew [. . .] in much the same painful fashion that he hates himself" (Baldwin, *Notes*, 59, 57). Blacks and whites alike use racial projection as a defense, but they are bound unequally by its logic: "Projection," Fiedler suggests, "does not work both ways—only from the more favored group to the less favored one; from, say, white to Negro, but not, in a white-controlled society, from Negro to white" (Fiedler, "Race," 298). But of course, in America, such duplicitous performance is itself caught up in an elaborate and dangerous contest of identification and recognition premised on passing; contempt for the other is itself a performance, one made over by the imaginary force of race. The logic of race, like the "logic" of the dreamwork, ultimately derives from an encoded system of condensation and displacement in the psyche, and racial passing is the expression of that logic, the master key to the encoded projections and wish fulfillments of race relationships. Passing—for Fiedler, "the attempt of the psychically exploited to remake themselves in the image of those who exploit them"—performs the dreams of the oppressed (298). Insofar as cinema performs—projects—those dreams, then it, too, is playing a part in this desire for racial passing and / or denial of black hatred.

10. Poitier, cited in Lester J. Keyser and André H. Ruszkowski, *The Cinema of Sidney Poitier: The Black Man's Changing Role on the American Screen* (San Diego: A. S. Barnes & Co., 1980), 70–71.

11. Sidney Poitier, foreword to Stanley Kramer, *A Mad, Mad, Mad, Mad World: A Life in Hollywood* (London: Aurum Press, 1998), x, ix.

12. Ibid., 154.

13. Robert Lindner, *The Fifty-Minute Hour: A Collection of True Psychoanalytic Tales* (New York and London: Jason Aronson, 1982).

14. James M. Glass, *"Life Unworthy of Life": Racial Phobia and Mass Murder in Hitler's Germany* (New York: BasicBooks, 1997).

15. In the 1940s writings of Theodor Adorno and Ernst Simmel, for example, Nazi anti-Semitism is conceived as the outbreak of mass psychosis that stems from a *"psychology of false accusation"* (Ernst Simmel, "Anti-Semitism and Mass Psychopathology," in *Anti-Semitism: A Social Disease*, ed. Ernst Simmel [New York: International Universities Press, 1946], 50.) On the one hand, racist projection "relieves us of subjective guilt feeling and is a mental defense mechanism against recognizing our own guilt"; on the other, in projecting onto the Jew "the aggressions diverted from his own ego," this regressive response to guilt is inevitably and irresistibly transformed into the delusion of being persecuted by the outside world (51). To be sure, it "is probably the suspicion of this fictitiousness of their own "group psychology" which makes fascist crowds so merciless and unapproachable": fascist crowds—prodigiously and destructively uninhibited—react like psychotics under the spell of aggressive instincts, having regressed to a more primal level of incorporation (Theodor Adorno, "Freudian Theory and the Pattern of Fascist Propaganda," in *The Culture Industry: Selected Essays on Mass Culture*, ed. J. M. Bernstein [London: Routledge, 1991], 131.) For Simmel, paradoxically, one way to avert this mass psychosis is to create a modern "theatre for all"—such as the movies and radio—thereby allowing the masses to discharge their aggressions and augment their superego and conscience "by way of fantasy identification" (Simmel, "Anti-Semitism and Mass Psychopathology," 70).

16. Sigmund Freud and Karl Abraham, *Briefe 1907–1926* (Frankfurt am Main: Fischer Verlag, 1980).

17. For an historical account of the postwar vogue of psychoanalysis in America and the popular emphasis placed on the healing powers of cathartic recall, manifested—in the 1940s—in the new binding covenant between notions of a democratic personality and the institutionalized, therapeutic consensus of psychoanalysis as cure, see Nathan G. Hale Jr., *The Rise and Crisis of Psychoanalysis in the United States: Freud and the Americans, 1917–1985* (New York and Oxford: Oxford University Press, 1995).

18. E. S., "Pressure Point, U.S.A., 1962," *Monthly Film Bulletin* 30, no. 357 (October 1963): 142.

19. Albert Johnson, "The Negro in American Films: Some Recent Works," *Film Quarterly* 18, no. 4 (1965): 19.

20. Compare the following comments by Leslie Fiedler in "Race—The Dream and the Nightmare" on white perceptions of forgiveness and reconciliation: "If only in fantasy we were united, no matter whether in fantasy of reconciliation or revenge, then we could forgive ourselves. But we do not forgive ourselves. And, indeed, it is hard to know which comes first in the logic of the psyche, which on that level is the cause of which: our not forgiving ourselves, or our not being able quite to imagine the dark-skinned people we oppress forgiving us" (298). This fantasy of reconciliation, it should be noted, is quite different from transcending racial injustice. Where the latter implies assimilation—or miscegenation—in the psychic logic of racism forgiveness cannot overcome distrust, nor can the dream of unity ever entirely efface those projections of white Americans' psychic life "with which precisely they find it impossible to live" (298). Indeed, "it is with the projection of our rejected self, which we have called the 'Negro,' that we must be reconciled," (303) he writes, underlining, yet again, what Baldwin calls "the American self-evasion" of black lives and experience (Baldwin, *Devil*, 75).

21. For Fanon's "paralysing" response to *Home of the Brave* (1944), a film directed by Stanley Kramer and, in the transfer from play to screen, also involving the substitution of Negro for Jew, see chapter 5 of Fanon's *Black Skin, White Masks*; and, for a commentary on both film and Fanon's response, see "Frantz Fanon's War," in David Marriott, *On Black Men* (New York: Columbia University Press, 2000), 66–95.

22. For Larry Neal, writing in the *New York Times*, Poitier's onscreen persona was nothing more than an Uncle Tom. "Brother Sidney," he writes, ought to learn that "there is no sense in being a million-dollar shoe shine boy" (3 August 1967). Most of these attacks on "the Sidney Poitier syndrome," as Clifford Mason dubbed it, were attacks mounted in the name of an increasingly radical black dissent from the "artistic NAACPism" of liberal integrationism and Poitier's safe, curiously asexual, image (*New York Times*, 10 September 1967). This dissent by no means amounted to a consistently held black nationalist sensibility; more often than not it amounted to a more general dissatisfaction with the liberal ethics of the civil rights movement and, in particular, Martin Luther King's Southern Christian Leadership. Thus, in a 1966 *Newsweek* article analyzing the moral choices and meanings offered by the new Student Nonviolent Coordinating Committee (SNCC), it was suggested that: "SNCC speaks for a growing bloc of the disaffected when it argues that . . . a black man ought to hit back when a white man hits him, that white liberals are all right only if they know their place and stay in it" (cited in Clayborne Carson, *In Struggle: SNCC and the Black Awakening of the 1960s* [Cambridge, MA: Harvard University Press, 1981], 123).

23. James Baldwin, Sidney Hook, Nathan Glazer et al., "Liberalism and the Negro: A Round-Table Discussion," *Commentary* 37, no. 3 (March 1964): 37.

CHAPTER 7 — BONDING OVER PHOBIA

1. See, for example, W.E.B. Du Bois, *The Souls of Black Folk* (New York: Penguin, 1989), and Toni Morrison, *The Bluest Eye* (New York: Random House, 2000).

2. Erik H. Erikson, "A Memorandum on Identity and Negro Youth," in *A Way of Looking at Things: Selected Papers from 1930–1980*, ed. Stephen Schlein (New York: W. W. Norton, 1989), 648.

3. Frantz Fanon, *Black Skin, White Masks*, trans. C. L. Markmann (New York: Grove Press, 1967), 113–114.

4. Kenneth Clark and Mamie Clark, "Racial Identification and Preference in Negro Children," in *Readings in Social Psychology*, ed. Eleanor E. Macoby, Theodore M. Newcomb, and Eugene L. Hartley (London: Methuen, 1966).

5. Kenneth Clark, cited in Richard Kluger, *Simple Justice: The History of Brown v. Board of Education and Black America's Struggle for Equality* (London: Deutsch, 1977), 318.

6. For an account of Fanon's concept of "real fantasy" [*"phantasmes reels"*], see Vicky Lebeau, "Psycho-Politics: Frantz Fanon's *Black Skin, White Masks*," in *Psychopolitics and Cultural Desires*, ed. Jan Campbell and Janet Harbord (London: UCL Press, 1998), 121.

7. See Jacques Lacan, *Les Complexes Familiaux* (Dijon: Navarin Editeur, 1984).

8. Jacques Lacan, *The Seminar of Jacques Lacan. Book II: The Ego in Freud's Theory and in the Technique of Psychoanalysis 1954–1955*, ed. J.-A. Miller, trans. S. Tomaselli (Cambridge: Cambridge University Press, 1982), 326.

9. Richard Sterba, "Some Psychological Factors in Negro Race Hatred and in Anti-Negro Riots," in *Psychoanalysis and the Social Sciences* 1 (1947): 411–427.

10. In these riots, racial hatred was "directed at male Negroes only." Sterba, "Some Psychological Factors," 412.

11. Compare Fanon: "Over three or four years I questioned some 500 members of the white race—French, German, English, Italian. I took advantage of a certain air of trust, of relaxation; in each instance I waited until my subject no longer hesitated to talk to me quite openly—that is, until he was sure that he would not offend me. Or else, in the midst of associational tests, I inserted the word *Negro* among some twenty others. . . . From this result one must acknowledge the effect of my being a Negro: Unconsciously there was a certain reticence" (Fanon, *Black Skin*, 166–167).

AFTERWORD: ICE COLD

1. See Maurice Blanchot, "Literature and the Right to Death," in *The Work of Fire* (1949), trans. Charlotte Mandell (Stanford, CA: Stanford University Press, 1995). For a reading of a sovereignty that escapes dialectics, see Jacques Derrida, "From Restricted to General Economy: A Hegelianism without Reserve," *Writing and Difference* (1967), trans. Alan Bass (Chicago: University of Chicago Press, 1978). For a fraught but brilliant response to Hegel's phenomenology of death, see Gillian Rose, *Mourning Becomes the Law: Philosophy and Representation* (Cambridge and New York: Cambridge University Press, 1996). This chapter is indebted to all three texts, especially that of Rose.

2. See Frantz Fanon, *L'An V de la révolution algérienne* (Paris: Maspero, 1968).

3. Achille Mbembe, "Necropolitics," trans. Libby Meintjes, *Public Culture* 15 (1): 37, 35.

4. During the Rwandan genocide the Tutsis were repeatedly referred to as "inyenzi" (cockroaches).

5. Walter Benjamin, "Theses on the Philosophy of History," in *Illuminations*, trans. Harry Zohn (London: Fontana/Collins, 1970), 257.

6. Fanon, *Black Skin*, 8.

7. Fanon, cited in Peter Geismar, *Fanon* (New York: Dial Press, 1971), 185.

8. See Hussein Abdilahi Bulhan, *Frantz Fanon and the Psychology of Oppression* (New York: Plenum Press, 1985), 20.

9. My reading of these allusions is indebted to Patrick Taylor, *The Narrative of Liberation: Perspectives on Afro-Caribbean Literature, Popular Culture, and Politics* (Ithaca and London: Cornell University Press, 1989). I depart from Taylor's excellent reading where I believe he remains too Sartrean—that is, too moralistic in his approach to the ethics of authenticity, which misses, in my view, Fanon's insistence on the need to affirm affirmation through negation, which he conceives not as a moral imperative (Taylor presents this as a conscious assumption of ethical "responsibility") but as a psychopolitical necessity.

10. Fanon, *Black Skin*.

11. G.W.F. Hegel, *Philosophy of History* (New York: Collier, 1901), 157–158.

12. Lucien Levy-Bruhl, *Primitive Mentality* (Boston: Beacon, 1923), 123–124.

13. Friedrich Nietzsche, *The Birth of Tragedy; and, The Genealogy of Morals*, trans. Francis Golfing (New York: Anchor Books, 1956), 10.

14. Fanon, *The Wretched of the Earth*, trans. Constance Farrington (New York: Grove Press, 1968), 139.

15. Ibid., 35, 246. Fanon, *Black Skin*, 138, translation modified.

16. See Hannah Arendt, *On Violence* (New York: Harvest-Harcourt Brace Jovanovich, 1969), 65.

17. With reference to the unconscious, Fanon explicitly says, "Since the racial drama is played out in the open, the black man has no time to'make it unconscious'" (Fanon, *Black Skin*, 150). In asking the question, what is it about the racial drama that makes the unconscious untimely, Fanon is asking what is it about the affect of racism which precludes repression and cannot be grasped unconsciously. For Fanon, that affect is always the performance of a hallucinatory "whitening." Which means that the black is already the affect of that hallucination: that is, he is not conscious of it precisely because he is in the grip of it and whose affect, in its instantaneity, is not unconscious even though its symptoms are.

18. Fanon, "West Indians and Africans," in *Towards the African Revolution: Political Essays*, trans. Haakon Chevalier (New York: Grove Press, 1969), 24.

19. Kant, *Critique of Practical Reason* (1788), trans. Mary Gregor (Cambridge and New York: Cambridge University Press, 1997), 106.

20. See, for example, Norman A. Klein, "On Revolutionary Violence," *Studies on the Left* 6 (May–June 1966), 82.

Index

About the Author

David Marriott teaches at the University of California and is the author of *On Black Men* and *Incognegro*.